BEGINNER'S
Luck

James Wrethman

Beginner's Luck

Copyright © 2022 by James Wrethman

PB: ISBN: 978-1-63812-476-4
Ebook ISBN: 978-1-63812-477-1

All rights reserved. No part in this book may be produced and transmitted in any form or by any means, electronic, or mechanical, including photocopying, recording, or by any information storage and retrieval system, without permission in writing from the copyright owner.

The views expressed in this work are solely those of the author and do not necessarily reflect the views of the publisher hereby disclaims any responsibility for them.

Published by Pen Culture Solutions 11/4/2022

Pen Culture Solutions
1-888-727-7204 (USA)
1-800-950-458 (Australia)
support@penculturesolutions.com

CHAPTER 1

It's difficult to know if memories of my very early childhood are my own recollections or simply re-runs of stories related to me, or to others in my presence\, by my parents. Having heard the tales so often, it's logical to assume they've been absorbed and intermixed with my own remembrances to form a conditioned recall of the period.

However, some deep impressions, which I feel are original, now and again re-appear in my mind like brief excerpts from a silent movie.

I see the dimly lit ward and seem to smell the passing food. A remembrance of meal-times in hospital perhaps? In an infancy plagued by respiratory problems I had spent much of my time in those institutions. There is also a journey in some sort of vehicle which roared and struggled to ascend a steep incline. I'm told this could be part of a frantic dash that was made to hospital, this time in a taxi. On the road to Stobhill Hospital in Glasgow where I was treated on one occasion, there is, I've been told, a very steep hill which in winter when there was snow or ice, became almost insurmountable.

I'm sure psychologists would find some significance in these replays but the popularity and growth of psychology has perhaps come about because it's always so easy to find connections between a person's dreams, recollections or imaginings and their actual life: nor will any amateur or professional psychologist be stuck for alternative connections to refute those already made by another. So I'll choose to ignore any possible theories about my recollections.

There's another favourite story of my parents : it seems I was already almost into my third breathless year and once again in a hospital sickbed when I apparently spoke my first full sentence. A nurse had come up to my parents who waited worriedly by the bedside and asked if they would like a cup of tea; they agreed and so it seems did I.

'Me, tea, too!' were the immortal words. Not perhaps particularly grammatical or lyrical but, when one's breath is limited, it's prudent to be economic with words while being concise. My demand, or at least my ability to make one, apparently caused great joy and excitement: I was to continue to be a demanding child for quite some time.

So, I've spent many a boring hour listening to my parents' stories about my brushes with death and their all night vigils at bedsides rigged with oxygen bottles and other respiratory aids. The period of course would leave an indelible mark. For them it must have been a traumatic experience as I had been a long awaited first child and on the doctor's advice, the last my mother could safely have. The origins of my breathing difficulties, in the absence of any hereditary strain, are sometimes put down to the extreme difficulty my mother had gone through at my birth, which in the end had to be done by caesarean section. Another more probable cause, though one which my parents preferred not to accept, was an operation which they had sanctioned - on advice from the doctor it must be said – when I was barely a few weeks old. At my post natal examination it had been observed that I had a slight deformity: On both of my hands the two middle fingers were webbed. As both baby and mother were still interned the doctor suggested that with a simple operation the hands could be put right, adding, that it would be much better to do it before the fingers grew. Like most parents they did not want anything to cause me a disadvantage in later life and so took the doctor's advice. The operation proved to be a more difficult process than they had been led to believe. After an unusually long procedure which involved grafting skin from my inner thigh we all had to be satisfied with only partially webbed fingers. Some time later, a doctor unconnected with that hospital, suggested that the trauma experienced by such a young baby, particularly the effects of the anaesthetic, had probably provoked the respiratory problems which I was to suffer from all my life. As for the partially webbed fingers, there is no doubt that they killed any hopes I may have had about being a world famous concert pianist and on a more mundane level they have somewhat restricted my ability to give the appropriate sign to irritating horn-honking drivers and opposing football supporters.

Anyway, the constant references to my ill-health and the exaggerated but understandable concern of my father, and more particularly, my mother, was to have a profound effect on the way I was to live, and in a way, how I still live today, although for many years I have had no crisis. In fact since my infancy I have had no need to return to hospital except for some structural repairs, after sporting participation, or to be more accurate, un-sporting participation - by my opponents.

    I can now only imagine how cramped it was to live in a single-end (a one room apartment which might be termed a bedsit in the south.) The idea of a family living in one room is to me now, quite terrible although many still do, but as a child I knew of no other life-style, to enable me then, to make the comparison.

    Later a comparison could be made when we moved upstairs to the relative luxury of a two roomed apartment. This was a one living/diningroom/kitchen with one bed and another bedroom, there were no integral toilets in any of these flats, it was outside in the close (passage-way) and was shared with the two other families who lived on the same floor.

    Apparently my ill health had been a factor which had helped my parents justify their request for a move upstairs. A request granted by the local corporation when the doctor reported that the dampness of the ground floor flat was detrimental to my health.

    The age of 5 is the starting age for school in Scotland and I'm sure that the replays are now, for the most part, my own. It always amazes me the way memory works; facts and figures, information, French verbs, mathematical formula, all manner of things which I make great mental effort to retain, slip away and have to be relearned, while the fat girl called Lamb who sat next to me for only a few days remains fresh in my memory. Actually she was far from fresh which is probably why I have retained this experience, for don't they say that smell is one of the most potent triggers of the memory.

    As to why I remember her name, well that's easily explained because the odour which cloggs the nostrils at the mere mention of early school days is definitely farmyard, although not necessarily Lamb, but Lamb it was.

    Perhaps another reason for my recall of those few days next to Miss Lamb was the fact that my nose was receptive, an occasion so infrequent in my early school days, as I seemed to be forever suffering from colds. Even on days when I was not actually nursing some ailment I would be made to suffer for my frailty, by being forced, by my mother, to wear a school cap, scarf and coat. This identified me as a cissy or in todays parlance, a 'wimp'. This is a minority group which has always been well advised to conceal its identity in the streets of Govan, Glasgow; but my own mother had 'outed' me.

Two 'bashings' at the hands of local juvenile toughs, convinced my father that some street education was necessary. One of my assailants was a boy named Ward and my Dad said the only way to stop him bullying me was to give him a bloody good thump. He waited till he saw the boy in the back court of our tenement block then dragged me downstairs to confront him. Reluctance, is a word that doesn't fully describe my feelings at that time, but Dad wasn't in the mood for foot dragging. I've seen the same scene in the movies so many times since, but with a different scriptwriter. I was supposed to give the street bully a lesson he'd never forget instead I gave him a target he couldn't miss. After an interminably long 30 seconds my father intervened to save me from further punishment I'm not sure if it was the lesson I was supposed to learn from the incident but it's one that has served me well ever since- never pick a fight with anyone who is bigger, tougher or fitter than yourself. Actually I believe it did have an effect on my Dad. It seemed to me that I was less mollycoddled by my mother from that point on. Perhaps he persuaded her that I should be allowed to mix more with the street kids, even if I did have asthma and 'needed to be careful.'

As time went by I became stronger and lived a more normal boyhood. Hardly anything from schooldays forces its way through the fog of time but the long summer holidays spent on the streets, and back courts of the tall grimy buildings provide countless memories. Again social historians have covered almost every aspect of life in these industrial areas so I would merely be repeating well worn tales if I described my surroundings and lifestyle in those early days. But, I would not be my mother's son if I didn't repeat some well worn tales.

Rathlin Street where we lived was a relatively short street, the entrance to which started at Govan Road and ended at the 40 ft high, barbed wire topped, fence of Fairfield Shipyard. The buildings were of red sandstone. I can inform you of this now because only in recent years have they discovered that it is easier, cheaper and more asthetically rewarding to convert and renovate the old buildings than to build modern apartment blocks. (for modern, read - ugly). Thus the hideous polution. blackened buildings which we knew as kids suddenly emerged as attractive red sandstone.

Much of Govan was built to house the employees, of the shipyards and other related industries. The apartment blocks were solidly built but lacked the basic amenities which people of all income groups expect today. The most obvious difference was the toilet and washing facilities. The communal toilet on the stairway and the wash-house in the back court have been featured in many novels, plays, folksongs, films and have provided material for local comedians for years.

Perhaps the biggest source of inconvenience in Govan tenements was the lack of space and this led to the 'weans' being put out to play in the street at a very early age and for almost the entire day.

This way the mothers could have space to do their housework and to tend the very young, the old or sick in the family. The long summer days when children were all on holiday from school would have been traumatic for mothers if they had been forced to amuse them in cramped conditions at home, as was some times the case, when the weather was particularly bad.

In a sense we were in a privileged position having only three people in a two roomed apartment where most families in the area were large and only a few had more than three rooms.

Nevertheless I did spend more time on the streets, possibly due to my fathers insistence that I be assimilated more into the street culture if I was to be able to deal with it.

Actually, although tough, the children of those industrial areas did not display the appetite for vandalism or unbridled violence that minors in low income areas seem to have today. A lot of our time was spent climbing or jumping across the gaps between the one story buildings built to accommodate the wash-houses and 'middens' (out-houses where the dustbins were kept).

It was in this activity that my 'cissy' image was to be finally laid to rest.

The most demanding test of jumping prowess and character was the Black Spot. The Black Spot was the name given to a frightening gap between a semi-demolished wash-house and a disused air raid shelter. Even to get into the position to be able to make the leap could be hazardous, as the jumper had to run along the top of the narrow wall, which was all that remained of the wash-house. Having safely negotiated this part then the dare-devil had then to launch himself across the gap to the spot which had been marked years earlier with black paint, probably from a discarded tin found in the midden below.

I'm not sure what made me attempt the feat- a need to establish some identity- over estimation of my ability- a rush of blood to the brain. Whatever the reason, the immediate outcome had a certain predictability. I surprised all onlookers when I suddenly took off on my run across the parapet and became airborne. Unfortunately the trajectory did not quite meet with the requirements and my leg met the edge of the shelter first. I did, I was later told, get part of my anatomy briefly on to the building but I think this was more of a bounce than an actual landing. The landing took place below on the ground between the two structures. I have edited the description of my condition after landing, as the scene may cause distress to some of my more sensitive readers.

The scars I bear to this day; but my gallant attempt and stoic behavior in the face of so much blood lifted the stigma of the cap and coat period: I was now accepted.

Up to the age of 9 it seems I spent my time roller skating on the smooth tarmac of our street, sometimes we would attach a pair of roller skates to a plank of wood, mount an orange box on top with makeshift handlebars. The front would then be painted with Deaths-head insignia. These 'bogeys' would in those days constitute the only traffic seen on the street all day except for the horse drawn coal lorry or the ragman's barrow. In the evenings we might play games such as kick-the-can(a game similar to hide and seek, played between two sides where the captured prisoners can be set free by someone evading the pursuers and kicking the can away from its position in front of the prisoners) or build dens in the back courts from old wood, canvas, carpet or linoleum.

Every now and again I would get a cold and this would put my mother on red alert. To be fair to her the worry was justified as the slightest infection usually carried straight to my chest. My father, who had been brought up in the country by his grandmother, had an unending supply of ancient cures, when the more conventional medicines or doctors instructions, failed to bring relief. Poltices, chest rubs, herbal vapours and sometimes excercises. We have learned in recent years that some of these remedies have more scientific basis than some of the ludicrous suggestions which were put forward by medical practicioners at that time.

When I did have these bouts and was confined to the house I amused myself with toy soldiers and dinky cars. My collection was not really very big as my dad didn't earn much money. His job, a crane driver at the local Fairfields Shipyard, was steady but left no room for promotion or bonuses. Whenever possible he would work overtime; the term - two nights and a Sunday- had great significance for my parents. As a seven year old I wasn't quite sure why there was deep gloom when he was not offered them. Later I would learn that this extra work with a higher hourly rate of pay would be the difference between a subsistence level of income and an income that would allow for little luxuries. One of those little luxuries was a two week holiday on the coast. This for my parents was an essential. We needed to 'get some sea air in our lungs,' particularly me; so all year, economies would be made, if need be, to enable us to go 'doon the water.'

Again, we were in a somewhat better position than most families.

My parents had only one child, neither drank alcohol or smoked (unusual at that time in any community, positively astounding in Govan) ; this meant that even when work was scarce and no overtime was available we were more able to cope with the drop in income. It also meant that the main source of domestic strife, in working class areas such as Govan, was removed; drunkeness.

Most of my friends endured endless battles between their parents and sometimes were caught in the crossfire when dad failed to come straight home on a Friday after receiving his paypacket.

My upbringing was therefore tranquil.

One of the problems of being an only child in a country that has long continuous periods of bad weather, is the amount of time one is incarcerated and with my medical history even a suggestion of cloud would be enough for my mother to bolt the door.

This means a very sizeable part of my childhood was spent playing alone. It can make for an inventive and fertile imagination but it does not do much for communicative skills. My parents being non-drinkers in a society in which alcohol played quite an important role in social entertainment, also lived quietly and only occasionally gave a dinner party for a few close friends, fortunately they would reciprocate. How I loved those nights, but we always seemed to leave earlier than anyone else. I suspect my mother insisted on this because as the night wore on the drinks started to flow more liberally and the party became livelier. I now of course know that my mother with her Presbyterian upbringing could never quite bring herself to condone drunkeness even if her friends only ever reached the stage of being merry. My father, although having no religious conviction, was also uncomfortable in the company of people who were drunk because he himself had never drank. My mother now makes no secret of the fact that my father's sobriety was a major factor in her decision to marry him.

One thing they did enjoy doing, in company with the entire population of Govan it seemed, was to go to the 'pictures.' In those days no one had a television, at least not in Govan; the queues were miles long at the four cinemas in the district. On Sunday after the previous nights visit to the Elder or Lyceum picture halls, 9 and 10 year old Humphrey Boggart and Gary Cooper surrogates stalked the streets of Govan.

The scandalous behavior of our next door neighbours was seen by my parents as a constant threat to my well-being and, when voicing complaints about their late night revelries, my asthmatic condition acerbated by lost sleep was often put forward as the dreadful consequence of their conduct. Actually I don't remember being disturbed by the noise but most certainly my mother and father lost considerable sleep worrying about the probability that I would. Donald and Maisie, as they were known to everyone, were nevertheless public nuisances even if their effect on me was minimal. This infamous couple fortunately had no children, and many said that they were not even married, a scandalous thing in those days and in that society. During their frequent arguments, normally caused by one finding a source of finance for a drunken binge without informing the other, the record of each others infidelities would be broadcast for all to hear. Respite from the bedlam next door could be expected on Monday to Friday. This was determined by economics. By Monday they were both completely broke and were therefore forced to return to work.

If ever my Presbyterian mother needed proof that clean living would not be rewarded on this earth, she was now to have it : Donald and Maisie won the football pools ! Not the jackpot I'm told, but an enormous sum in those years, and particularly in a working class area like Govan. They may have been the original authors of the phrase " it's not going to change my life" for in fact it didn't, it simply intensified it. But it did substantially change my parent's.

The suppression of the nightly singing, swearing, and fighting in the apartment, and on the stairway, either between the couple themselves or among their now greatly enlarged circle of "friends" then became my father's permanent mission. My mother, on the other hand, swung wildly between insisting on him doing something about it and entreating him to stay clear of the drunken thugs who were Donald and Maisie's houseguests. Sometimes the police were called in, but this was not so easy as it would be today. For one thing there were no telephones and therefore this could mean a long walk to the police station. For another the police were often a long time coming, if they came at all, and last but not least there was always a reluctance in working class communities to call in "the Polis". My father probably felt he should handle it himself.

In the end, economics once again saved the day. An effective policy of rapid re-distribution of wealth was initiated by the revellers and all local publicans, bookmakers and dodgy greyhound owners became the main beneficiaries. Incredibly within 6 months Maisie and Donald were broke. Now they really had something to fight about with each other, but the fights were half-hearted without the "golden liquid" to lubricate the tonsils and no inebriated hangers-on to urge them to higher peaks of performance.

While I, was of course aware of the nightly drama enacted during the period of the neighbour's temporary wealth, the most disturbing effect on me was not lack of sleep but lack of T.V. One of the few non-liquid assets acquired by Donald and Maisie when they first received the cheque from Littlewoods was a television : the first on the street, perhaps the first in Govan.

Often in late afternoon " Auntie Maisie" would invite the neighbourhood kids in to see Lash Laroo or the Cisco Kid. Needless to say I was not allowed by my parents to take up this offer, although Maisie and Donald did not seek to discriminate against me.

Even then I was amazed by the difference, between the 'drunken harlot' my parents knew at night and the cheerful, generous auntie I saw in late afternoon as she ushered my friends upstairs. Although I understood my parent's comments I could never quite agree with my mother's view that they were inherently wicked. Looking back I would say now that they were simply uneducated, weak and indisciplined. People around them became victims of their indiscipline and, of course in the end, they themselves became victims of their own weaknesses.

Maisie died at a relatively early age of some incurable disease a few years after the pools win. One year later Donald died when, in a drunken state, he fell asleep with a pot of soup simmering on the gas ring. It boiled over extinguishing the flame and he was gassed.

CHAPTER 2

Years later in 1990 when Glasgow became " The European City of Culture" the marketing men would wax lyrical about the many fine examples of Victorian and Edwardian architecture to be found in the city. But the buildings that most epitomized Glasgow were no longer to be seen. No, not the tenements of Gorbals and Govan that had fallen to the demolition squads but the huge ships which once towered above streets such as ours.

No sight could be more impressive at the end of any street than the enormous bow of a liner, tanker or bulk carrier slumbering on its stocks like some prehistoric monster fussed over and fed by the attendant cranes.

At night the flashes and sparks of the welders torches and the riveter's percussion section would provide a spectacular to match any firework display.

Every day the "horn" (in effect, an air raid siren retained from the war years) would summons the workers to the "Yard" to start work,

It would also mark the start and finish of the lunch break and terminate the day's work for those unlucky enough not to be offered overtime.

Each day it seemed like a loud reminder of how important the shipyard was to the community, as if the people who lived there needed any reminding.

If the weather was dry and I was on the street, when I heard the horn at 5 p.m., I made for the corner of Rathlin Street and Govan Road to look for my dad coming from the Yard. He was usually in animated conversation with his workmates. More often than not the subject was football, occasionally the discussion centred round the marital status of their foreman's parents.

Actually when I first looked up the word my father and his workmates most used, when describing referees and foremen, I was struck by the very high incidence among these groups, of people who descend from parents, with no belief in the sanctity of marriage.

Football and religion of course played a very big part in the life of everyone in Glasgow. To many people, the two words meant one and the same thing. Ibrox the home of Rangers Football Club was within walking distance and my father would go to every home match.

However his pedigree, as a "true blue" as the Ranger's followers were called, could be considered suspect. He had been born to Roman Catholic parents and farmed out to his grandmother (on his mother's side) when still quite young, because of his mother's ill-health and the difficulty in coping with this addition to an already large family. The old woman much to the consternation of the family rejected the faith and chased the priest from her door, changing my father's good Irish surname Curley to her own married name Wrethman.

My father's grandfather had died long before he was born and little seemed to be known about him except that he was a Swedish sailor, which was just about acceptable, and a Protestant, which, most definitely, was not.

It would be ridiculous to speculate on what I might have been had he remained Catholic because I would not "be" I did however thank my grandmother posthumously, many times when I was young, for discarding the name Curley. This name, for a boy with a shock of unruly hair, would have been, to schoolmates and schoolmasters, a temptation to great to resist.

On the other hand there is no telling what I might have achieved with the all additional time saved by not having to spell, re-spell, repeat, and correct the name Wrethman. Rethman does at least have some logic as does Wrethmann but Redman, Retham, Wetham, Rothman, Wetman, Wreathman, Rehman. It is one of the world's phenomena ; a name with limitless permutations.

Every other day I spend at least a minute on repetition or corrections, be it on paper, on the telephone, in bureaucratic institutions or in normal discourse.

This makes 182 minutes per year for more than 50 years (since I could talk).

That's at least 6 days I've lost ! God, it is said, made the world in 6 days !

It's probably no coincidence that he picked such a short manageable name, otherwise he would not have got it finished on time.

I am also thankful I did not inherit my father's first name which was Farick, can you imagine the additional time explaining and spelling that one.

I have digressed from the story.

My father, in spite of my grandmother's teachings, was never a convinced Protestant but he was a devout follower of Glasgow Rangers Football Club. To most people in Glasgow this is one and the same thing.

My mother on the other hand was brought up in a strict Presbyterian family but has had a barely concealed loathing for 'The Gers' all her life. This is natural, as she viewed them as other women might view their husband's mistress. The team had, on many occasions, vied with her for his attention and won.

My official baptism at the shrine at Ibrox took place when I was very young. It must have been a minor fixture as I can remember there being enough space for me to sit and build little castles with the earth and dirt (in those days the terracing was not concreted) while the second half was still in progress. To my father, having spent the entire first half, identifying the players and explaining the intricacies of the contest so that I might fully enjoy the experience, this was an early indication of learning difficulties. To other fanatics around him it may have appeared as a denial of faith.

I was returned home in disgrace, but my mother took the news of my conduct like a mother who'd just been told her son was unfit to go to the trenches at the Western Front.

But unknown to both of them the seed had been planted. To this day I believe that my interest in football was ignited by a name, or to be exact, the sound of a name. Although a favourite with the fans at that time, he was certainly not one of the greatest players or the most charismatic I had heard his name mentioned no more than several other players: Tory Gillick It became a mnemonic trigger. At the mere sound of his name my interest could be aroused. I would then go to the match with my dad to see Tory Gillick. Later I would go to matches he was not playing in; to see how they team would fare without him. The conditioned response to Tory Gillick would eventually be replaced by the name "Rangers" to be replaced finally with the word "football".

As I grew a little older the street where we played became a territory to be defended at certain times against the empirical ambitions of those from the next street. Battle-axes were fashioned by flattening a tin can on the end of a stick and sharpening it on the wall or pavement stone. A coal dump at the back of the cinema across from my house provided us with head seeking missiles, so our armaments were complete. I had managed to come through unscathed after several campaigns and the latest was proving, once again, the superiority of our firepower. Howie Street boys, having made an unprovoked attack on us, were now being routed and I pursued them in their flight towards the small public park at the bottom of their street with dashing bravado. Military strategists will tell you not to advance beyond the limits of your communications with base. My adversaries with the option of further retreat denied them by the River Clyde, at the bottom of the park, turned to find themselves being chased by one individual. I sensed in mid-stride a fresh resolve, perhaps even optimism in the behavior of my enemies and sought the same resolute determination in the faces my colleagues behind me. Alas.

I will not try to conceal the true depth of my emotions at that time by calling my action a strategic withdrawal or even a prudent retreat ; it was a panic driven, shit streaming race for safety and it took me across the kiddies playpark, through the sandpit round the roundabout and bang into an empty fast rising swing which caught me at eyebrow height. I woke up some time later in my bed at home surrounded by voices. I recognized immediately my mothers worried tones the others were not so clear but one of them was asking me if I could tell him how many fingers he was holding up in front of my face. I could not, in fact I could not see anything and the terror I felt must have evident for he immediately identified himself as my doctor and offered assurances that the condition would be temporary.

I did not lose my sight; nor have I lost the memory of those few fearful hours of darkness before my eyes started functioning again.

When the pictures started to roll I could then concentrate on my other physical injuries. Apart from the enormous lump on my head just above my nose, in line with my eyebrows, there was also a wound on the back of my head, which could have been when I fell back having been struck by the swing (incidentally having been propelled not by one of my pursuers, but by some petulant kid who had been called away from his place of enjoyment by his mother. She being the one who would eventually rescue my prostrate body from the vindictive mob who had chased me) and several other bruises in delicate places.

My recovery was prolonged by the sure knowledge that when my suffering was over, the debriefing would start; to be followed up by correctional nagging on a grand scale.

As with my previous beating at the hands of the street tough, I had learned another lesson - never let momentary success go to your head. Life is full of swings and roundabouts.

The term 'street-wise' has more meaning for me now that I can compare the attitude and approach of my own son to everyday life, with that of my own views at his age. The kid brought up to roam freely on the street without any restraint (even when his home life is stable and respectable, as my own was) is an altogether tougher and more cynical person. The playtime of the middle class child (in these ranks, I suppose I must number my own son) is shorter and tends to be organized by school or parents.

The free-range type is not only, not under control of responsible adults, but also has less means to amuse and distract themselves. They therefore come under continuous peer pressure to perform increasingly more adventurous and daring deeds. Inevitably these activities will not only become dangerous but even more often, illegal.

If this was the case in working class communities 40 years ago, it is not difficult to see why criminal activity in children has increased enormously in recent years. Whereas before, the street child would always have the anchor of a close family unit at home. And watchful neighbours with common values would support, reprimand or report back to parents at any hint of trouble : today the neighbours are either a different ethnic group ; uncommunicative, suspicious or even antagonistic. They may be too far from the scene, possibly on the fourteenth floor of a high rise apartment block, too frightened to intervene or completely disinterested. The family unit is also likely to be one tired and dispirited woman or a couch potato in a shell suit who has long ago given up looking for work and exists on handouts.

Whereas in the past the children were encouraged to go out because of lack of space, the street child of today will be sent out because of a lack of patience or even worse a lack of interest. In the search for status, at least within his own friends, he will therefore be drawn into crime.

What is the answer ? The complex solutions put forward by politicians, sociologists and journalists are all too ambitious.

Even if the political will and the resources were there, it would not be possible to resolve the major problems in today's society. The massive investment required to create work for everyone and destroy and rebuild inner city slums including the high rise disasters, would be impossible to find and take generations to complete. Even then there are the racial tensions in many areas which make the re-creation of close knit communities a pipe dream.

What must be done, is to get children off the streets: less holidays, more after school organisations.

Create entertainment centres in every problem area. These should be marketed to give them street cred, using pop music video and computer games as attractions. Even hiring personalities from the entertainment or sports world, who have credibility with the youth, to appear or even work there, as a further draw.

Churches or other organisations which might be viewed disparagingly by the very problem child that needs to be attracted should under no circumstances, front these centres.

If run successfully by marketing professionals these places will cater for children from across different income and racial groups and by exposure to each other remove some of the prejudices.

Expensive as this programme may be it will still be cheaper than any alternative, including doing nothing. It will have the immediate advantage of taking large numbers of children off the street where they are at most risk.

CHAPTER 3

When I reached the summer of my eleventh year I was hit by a bombshell : we were moving out of Govan.

The new apartment was in Penilee a housing scheme originally built to accommodate the workers in the nearby Industrial estate of Hillington.

In Glasgow with my parents, 1952

In making this move, my parents might be classified today in the ever so slightly upwardly mobile group. It was seen by them as a great improvement in their fortunes for although it was still a council property, we had a living room, kitchen, two bedrooms and wonder of wonders, a bathroom and toilet, inside the apartment, to ourselves.

However, at that time no amount of salesmanship by my parents could convince me that this was a good move. Likewise no amount of tears and tantrums could convince them that I would be better staying in the back courts of Rathlin street where I could catch giant beetles and throw slates at the rats which populated the middens.

The trauma lasted until the removal van pulled up, with me inside, at the new home. The novelty and excitement of the "Flittin" (house-moving in Glaswegian) overcame my sadness at leaving, and fear of the unknown.

The neighbours (there were only two other families " up our close") came to lend a hand. This included their sons and their friends who were eager to see if the new boy had any interesting toys.

It was a Saturday so the boys in the ground floor apartment invited me to the matinee at the local cinema. Being more conversant with the workings of parent's minds nowadays I am sure that the whole afternoon was pre-arranged.

If so, it was a masterful plan: I was, after only a few hours, fully integrated into the new community.

Penilee was a suburb in southwest Glasgow and between it, and the next town Paisley, was a stretch of dairy farmland. This area, only five minutes walk from our house, to a boy used to the dark, if familiar, surroundings of tenement blocks, smokestacks, cranes and the massive hulks of unfinished ships, was a new fresh and exhilarating experience. It was summer when we moved so I did not have a school schedule to interfere with my programme of exploration.

The building we lived in was in those days considered to be of a new and better class of council residence. All the tenants on the ground level had gardens. The block had 18 apartments in total, three at either end of the block which could be entered by a common passageway or close. The first apartment being on the ground floor and one on each of the other two floors accessible by the open stairway. Between the end closes, there were two more, which gave access to six apartments, two on each floor, three on either side of the close; their doors could be seen from the street as they were located on the open porch on the ground floor and balcony on the other two levels.

Four such blocks were built in a square formation to leave a large backcourt, which had been fenced off, in sections. The dustbins were located in low buildings that could not really be worthy of the name 'midden' as they were structurally intact, emptied and cleaned regularly and as a result had no resident vermin. Some of the wooden fences dividing the courts were broken thereby giving free access but otherwise everything else was maintained to a much higher standard than was Govan. Our backcourt actually had a grass lawn. We were now surely among the gentile working class.

A few minutes walk, across the rail bridge and we were on the farm road. Here you could walk with fields on either side for about 1 mile to the dairy farm. If the direction of the wind was eastwards the farm would reach you before you reached it, because the farmer kept pigs as well as free-range chickens, cows and some sheep.

If I accompanied my father on his Sunday walk we would go by the road while he reminisced about his early years spent in the Vale of Leven and fishing in the nearby Loch Lomond. The subject would inevitably turn to football, replays of matches with the many juvenile and junior teams he had played for; the arthritic leg which brought a premature end to the soccer dream just when a trial for Liverpool F.C. had been offered.

If on the other hand I went with my mates we cut diagonally across the fields through a clump of trees, across a small burn, taking care to avoid the farmer as we skirted round his house, to cross the road into another stretch of shrubland, whose inhabitants seemed to alternate from sheep to cows. This ground was high and it fell away sharply into a valley below, part of which was fenced off to protect the local reservoir.

This slope we called 'the Froggie.' A title which showed divine inspiration as literally the "joint was jumpin" with frogs.

From this high point we could also look into the valley below where the Abbotsinch Airport was located. Today this is Glasgow's International airport but then it was a small military base and take-offs were infrequent, so we would often have to wait for some time to enjoy the sight. Perhaps in this sense nothing has changed as sometimes I still seem to have to wait for ages for my flight take off.

I now turned to crime.

By turning left at the top of our road and walking through, what was for us, a posh area of small and some large private houses, we came upon another farm which was adjacent to a large public park.

This farm had an apple orchard that had branches dangling tantalisingly near the road. As we had all been told 'an apple a day keeps the doctor away' we decided to cut down on the doctor's necessity to see us for some time.

My accomplices were a mixture of green novices and hardcore apple snatchers. At the age of twelve Billy, a redhead, who was known (in winter only) to reveal small patches of pink skin between his freckles, was an old hand. He warned us against going for the reddest one, which always seemed to be just a branch higher. Andy, all belligerence and bravado scoffed at this advice. Running his fingers through his sparse hair, incredibly he seemed to be going bald even then at thirteen, he pushed Billy's younger brother Brian (a lesser freckle) aside and proceeded to climb the fence which the tree overhung. George, the least convinced that this enterprise was a winner, suddenly found my head between his legs and my shoulders push him upwards and on to the top of the fence, where he remained, perched and petrified while we all clambered up.

Farmers are supposed to be crotchety old codgers with scruffy mangy old sheepdogs. They are not supposed to be thirty year old ex-olympic atheletes with a brace of lean and mean alsation dogs because this throws doubt on the viability of apple-snatching.

Farmer Daley Thompson, or whatever his name was, suddenly emerged from a shed covered the fifty yards in 4 seconds, vaulted his own fence and cut off our escape from the road side while his two sneering and slobbering canine companions dared us to "make their day" on the farmside. This development called for a re-evaluation of our position. George had already made a lighting assessment of his situation and was blubbering uncontrollably on the fence alongside of me. Andy higher up on the tree suggested we all drop down on the roadside together as the farmer couldn't hold all of us.

Before I had properly calculated the odds on who he might hold, the dogs suddenly took off across the field, hot in pursuit of a bright red apple. Billy having caused the decoy, dropped to the ground on the farmside closely followed by Andy, Brian and myself. We raced through the fields in the opposite direction of the dogs. The farmer for a moment unaware of what had happened was now attempting to retrieve the situation and was scaling the fence, being this time too near to vault it as he had done before.

Fully aware that our advantage could be momentary, we now careered at full speed through ditches, hedges and under a barbed wire fence. The chastised dogs were by now in hot pursuit with the farmer not all that far behind. Anxiety and excessive exertion can bring on an athsmatic attack. My chest was now heaving and wheezing; I was dripping with sweat, covered in mud and sharp branches and barbed wire tore my clothes and flesh. I was now about to become dog meat. I made a last despairing dive over a fence and began to tumble downward landing eventually under a clump of bushes at the bottom of a hill.

I lay there for a long time with my lungs wheezing loudly, expecting at any moment for my slobbering pursuers to find me. Not least because I was conveniently, if uncontrollably, whistling their attention.

Just when the passage of time was beginning to alleviate my fear and my chest was becoming slightly less vocal, the bushes parted. I closed my eyes and waited to be savaged.

" What are you doing there?" said the authoritative voice in the unmistakable blue uniform.

There I lay under the bushes, torn, sweating, mudspattered with whistling sounds still being omitted from my lungs, what could I say ?

"I'm……. bi-bi- birdwatching "

There seemed a long interlude while he absorbed this information perhaps measuring it against visibly observed evidence, probably feeding it through his mental database for inconsistencies before arriving at a probability factor.

" Get up, and get to hell up the road before I book you "

I stumbled my way along the road hastily but thankful that there was no sign of the farmer and that I had been able to think of a credible story for the policeman.

On arrival, in a somewhat distressed state, at my apartment block George who had been able to calmly descend from the fence and stroll home untroubled, met me. Fortunately for him he didn't choose to comment much on the incident. He was happily munching a big red apple and another he selflessly proffered to me. I ignored him and dragged my damaged body and torn clothes up the stairs to the interrogation that awaited me.

CHAPTER 4

School was a place I went to, between bouts of cold and flu. Those viruses posed a much greater threat to me because they could provoke the return of my respiratory problems and I seemed to be particularly susceptible to attacks at certain times. A few rasping coughs, a gasp for air and a tedious double period of maths or science could so easily be avoided.

This cynical manipulation of an over protective parent I could rationalise as compensation for all the other inconveniences brought on me by my early illhealth.

The school time lost on suspected, threatened, imagined and simulated illness left little time for real illness, though I still managed to squeeze in a few genuine bouts of cold and flu.

The first school I attended in Penilee was Linburn Primary. At this time a new Primary school was under construction so my stay here was to be relatively short though at this point I was probably unaware of the impending move. The building was a one-story construction which formed a quadrangle on a large open field in the centre of the housing scheme. Curiously, as most of it was pre-fabricated, the solid brick toilets were the only permanent-looking structure in the compound. They took pride of place slap-bang in the middle of the large square which constituted the playground.

Two events in particular stand out from my period there. One was an International match between Scotland and the Magical Maygars. This was the great Hungarian side of the 50's, which included the magnificent Ferenc Puskas, and was reckoned to be the greatest team in the world at that time. The matches, in those days played in daylight and on weekdays, was broadcast live on the radio and the teachers had re-arranged and extended play-time to permit them to listen to the match on the staff-room wireless. As I remember the janitor's radio could be heard from the playground and when Scotland scored first the entire school screamed in triumphant celebration. However, in spite of a gallant performance, Hungary finally won 4-2. So here, at primary school, we passed the initiation ceremony for the nascent Tartan Army.

Thus initiated, we could continually re-enact the same passion play at Scotland matches for the rest of our lives. Unrealistic expectation-momentary elation-hubris-devastation-resignation-consolation (in another gallant attempt).

Another memory of Linburn is similar, in that it also involves football and a descent from a momentary high. The School was encompassed by a six-foot high iron fence or railing. In those days it was probably there to keep pupils in; today such a barrier's main purpose might well be to keep maniacs out. The height was no doubt deemed sufficient to deter 10 year-olds or younger pupils from absconding during playtime. It was unfortunately not high enough to stop my left-foot(a foot meant only for standing on) shot. So instead of rebounding gloriously from the railing between the two hanging jackets which marked the goal, it ballooned enfuriatingly over the perimeter and into the waste ground behind. Missing a golden opportunity in front of goal is enough to make you unpopular with your own side. Losing the ball over the fence attracted unanimous displeasure. There was only one way to retrieve the situation and here my dyke-climbing experiences could be put to good advantage. I hauled myself up on to the perpendicular bar which joined the rails about one foot from the top and perched there with my feet lodged between the spiked-tops. I paused to select a place on which a short-trousered schoolboy could safely land, as the waste ground was almost entirely covered by tall nettles. I also lingered for effect. I was sure not many of the guys and certainly none of the girls, who I hoped were now watching, would have been able to perform such a feat. Satisfied that I was now the centre of attention I sprang forward and downwards from my perch. There seemed to be a momentary resistance but the gravitational pull carried me through it and I landed safely if a little clumsily. But the momentary resistance I had overcome, drooped on the fence like a flag at half-mast : my shorts.

Much later I would reflect that the situation could have been worse. The trouser leg which had snared on the spike could have held, instead of giving way at the seams. In which case I would have been left dangling ridiculously from the fence and would have required assistance to get down. But, at that moment I could find no immediate consolation amid the laughter emanating from the other side of the fence. Neither would I quickly retrieve the situation. Boys being boys, my trousers were gleefully seized and were now being paraded around the playground to maximise my embarrassment. I was now obliged to re-scale the fence as the only other alternative was to walk round to the street entrance, in my underpants, and ask for admittance from the Janitor. This option I did not find immediately appealing. Apart from the fact that once again I would look ridiculous I would have to admit to breaking the rule against leaving the school grounds which would put me in deep trouble with the Head.

Before starting the ascent I did try unsuccessfully to barter the ball for my trousers, in the vain hope that when I did get over I could somehow salvage some pride by wrapping them round me. The sound of the assembly bell to mark the end of playtime made my return to the other side all the more urgent. Unfortunately, a dip in the ground on the waste-land side, and clumps of barbed weeds and nettles, made the climb from the outside a much more formidable task. Haste does not aid precision. Several shin bruises and nettle-stings later I was finally able to land on the other side. Just in time to arrive red-faced and trouser-less to the centre of the playground, where the now massed ranks of sniggering and guffawing pupils were only just being kept under control by several teachers who awaited my explanation with interest.

I was punished, and sent home with borrowed pants and a note about my disgraceful conduct.

My parents said the event only served to reinforce the points they had been making for some time. Dad: that I should practice with both feet. Mum: that I must always wear clean underwear.

A happier consequence of my brief period with Linburn was two weeks spent at a residential school in Wigtown, Galloway. This was a scheme to take entire classes of children from Glasgow state schools to spend an activity based holiday in a large estate called Galloway House. The massive stately home had sports fields, forrested land and its own private beach.

The trip was an exciting event for most of the children, many whose parents could never afford to take them on a normal holiday and some whose parents could have afforded to, had they changed their priorities from alcohol and tabacco to family holidays. In this sense I had been fortunate, as I had gone almost every year to the seaside with my mother and father. Nevertheless even for me the idea of being away with classmates for a whole two weeks without parental supervision sounded too good to be true. However to get permission to go the old spectres of asthma and bronchitis had to be overcome first. Much agonizing took place before Dad to my delight, finally convinced Mum that I should not be set aside from my classmates and the experience would be good for me. There were still weeks of medical instructions to endure before we finally took of by bus from the school gates.

The feeling of freedom was immense. We were accompanied by teachers but unlike school the atmosphere was relaxed. Although I had seen some of the colours of Autumn in the local parks and in the green belt between Penilee and Paisley I had never really been aware of the spellbinding variations of colour that this season brings. Our long rambles took us crunching and kicking leaves through the forrested estate and down to the bracing wind-swept deserted shore to fill our nostrils with the smell of salt and seaweed and our ears with squawking seabirds. This play on our senses seemed to be having a tranquilizing effect on the normally rumbustious street-kids. Perhaps wishing to capitalise on this new awareness of nature's wonders one of the teachers suggested we collect leaves and shells that we might later discuss the species and origins of the collected items. Even this apparently quiet pastoral activity awoke a competitive drive. Before long the obsessive urge to have the most, the best and the biggest leaves and shells was causing unseemly disputes over property rights, monopolistic cartels and petulant destruction of rival's collections. The project was abandoned.

The next day we were taken to the sport's fields where we might utilize our competitive instincts in a less destructive and more organised way.

It was here that I played football for the first time in full kit, on a proper pitch with goalposts and a referee. Up until then I had only played in the street or school forecourt.

Another lifelong interest was to be implanted there. In the assembly hall after tea we would sit on the floor and listen to a teacher read from a chosen literary work. I think it was not the book itself, good though Coral Island is, that fired my imagination. It was the dramatic skills of the reader. Nevertheless, from that moment I feel I took a new interest in the written word.

As I write this I'm not sure if these trips still take place for state school children, if they do not, it is a great pity. I, and I'm sure many others, in the end returned from the trip with a more mature outlook and new perspectives. A very small part of the child had gone.

For parents waiting for children to return from their first trip away from home this small change is often evident, a little sad, but inevitable, and although at that moment they might not want to admit it, ultimately desirable.

CHAPTER 5

Inevitably, extra-curricular activity dominated my thoughts in and out of school but the move from the old Linburn school to the newly built Sandwood Road Primary did see two teachers achieve some sort of breakthrough because at least I remember their names ; Mr. Petrie and Mr. Dunne. Both taught English and no doubt the life-long interest in reading and writing which I have said was already taking root was cultivated by their patience and teaching skills.

However, I did not excel at anything and in the Qualifying Exam for secondary school placement I got the lowest possible pass-mark. It was later discovered that there had been a bureaucratic error and I had been too young to take the exam and would therefore have to sit it again. One month before the retake of the examination I suffered a genuine attack of bronchitis and missed the crucial build up to the big day. My parents managed to obtain revision and test papers which when added to the evil tasting medicine I had already been prescribed would make this the most unpleasant illness I have had to date.

"There is no gain without pain" I achieved two grades higher than my previous attempt. Still no indication of genius but my parents were delighted.

It may be unfair but I have always felt that my parents, only too happy to have seen me survive an unhealthy infancy, were satisfied with the smallest achievement. They had a very low level of expectancy, not only where I was concerned, but in all matters.

Low aspirations are easily conveyed to a young person causing indolence. This is my excuse anyway.

Schools in Scotland and in particular Glasgow perpetuate the religious divide because they are either Catholic or Protestant. In fact, a polite way of determining the religion of a stranger or newcomer to the area, is to ask the name of the school he or she goes to, will go to, or did go to. Almost all catholic schools start with Saint.

In spite of my mother's constant pleading, I, like my father, took no interest in religion. Being a Protestant simply meant not being a Catholic or more importantly being a Rangers supporter. Nevertheless I was categorised as a Protestant and having passed the qualifying exam would now be enrolled in Penilee Senior Secondary School. The main obstacle to this was a lack of a Penilee Senior Secondary School. The school, which was being built, was behind schedule, a fact that I could confirm because I could see the project from my bedroom window. I had also attended various site meetings. Not to discuss the progress of the building with the architect and construction manager, but on one occasion to expropriate materials which might be useful for the construction of Billy Wilson's back-court hut, on another to obtain some paint to decorate a home-made buggy. In actual fact the visits were simply to amuse ourselves. A large unfinished building site is a sort of theme park in the evenings and weekends when no workers are present. One can ride on wheelbarrows, climb ladders slide down rubbish shutes. Today a company with dogs and mobile guards with walkie-talkies would protect a site such as this. Then, it was one old retired policeman who could be aroused, when all our other entertainments had been exhausted, to provide the final chase to the high fence which we would vault to make our escape, when he was within yards of catching us.

The delay meant that all children in that area who had just recently passed the exam would go to one of two schools. The bottom half, in terms of passmarks, would go to Govan High School in my old hunting ground. The top half would go to Bellahouston Academy a old school with traditional values and a reputation for higher academic standards (i.e. a posh school) To my horror I scraped through into the top half and was forced to wear the dreaded blazer with yellow braid.

The year spent at the Academy was for the most part tiring because I had to travel by bus a considerable distance which necessitated an early rise. I also found the school tiresome with its petty disciplines and constant speeches from teachers about its traditions.

I really have only two memories of my time spent there. The first centered on the location of the school, which was in the district of Ibrox.

A name synonymous with Glasgow Rangers as their Stadium was named after the area it was built on. In fact the school was only a few hundred yards from the gates of the football ground.

In those days the grounds had no floodlights so cup matches which had ended as a drawn game on the Saturday were replayed on a Wednesday in early afternoon. This particular game had generated intense interest as the opponents of the 'Gers" was Glasgow Celtic Their age-old catholic adversaries. Some factories and shipyards almost closed down when such a fixture took place; but unfortunately not the schools. In fact teachers were doubly vigilant and had handed out warnings of dire consequences if anyone was suspected of playing truant. The teachers ignored a sudden bout of athsmatic wheezing which I suffered around lunchtime although my distress was genuine. As I have said before athsma can be brought on by anxiety and I was certainly worried that I was going to miss the biggest match of the season.

By 2 p.m. the teachers were now being confronted by an altogether more serious problem than the anxiety of one pupil - the beginnings of mass hysteria. The roar from the 90,000 crowd as the teams took the field rattled the windows of the classroom and at once the importance of knowing how to conjugate a French verb diminished for 22 boys in my class and for hundreds throughout the school the Theory of Relativity, the date of the Magna Carta and other facts became complete irrelevancies alongside the more serious gap in their knowledge: had Jimmy Miller the Rangers centre forward passed his late fitness test?

The agony of hearing the crowd's response to events on the field was causing serious disorder in my classroom. Goals could be determined by the volume of noise, but with equally fervent and voluble supporters on both sides, who was scoring ? Four roars, was it 3-1 for Rangers or maybe 4-0. We hated to consider it could it be 3-1 for Celtic or horror of horrors 4-0 for the 'Tims' We had changed classes and in the corridors during the periods rumours were rife - orderings off, disputed penalties, disputed goals, crushing defeat and glorious victory in prospect. The first chime of the bell triggered an end to the school day and a riotous dash to the main street. I'm sure my feet did not touch the ground on my way out of the main doors. The match should by now, have been finished; but we could hear the oohs! and aahs! of the crowd. This meant only one thing a draw 2-2 and extra time was being played. I raced to the gates. They were being opened to permit the exit of those few spectators who wished to leave. What could be their reason for leaving with the score at 2-2 the game finely balanced and only minutes left to play ? Their house was on fire, they had a sudden attack of gastro enteritis! There seemed to be many Rangers fans leaving. I didn't ask anybody the score, people often leave early when their team was convincingly winning the match. But it seemed strangely quiet. Perhaps our people were restraining themselves before the thunderous celebration at the final whistle.

I raced through the gates and sprinted up the steep stair to the top of the terracing. Now the sound was reverberating in my ears as my heart pounded with excitement and the exertion. At last I plucked up the courage to ask, "What's the score?"

"Wan nuthin fur the huns" came the reluctant reply from a man suffering the agonies of seeing an attack break down which had promised an equalizer.

A green and white hooped shirt was now on the ball as I caught the first clear view of the action. It was Fernie of Celtic he was weaving his way through the Rangers' defence.

There is always that split second as you see the ball hit the net and you see the sea of opposition colours rise, before the sickening explosion of sound from the other end reaches you. You dare hope that its not true, especially when its the last minute of the game, that the referee will have seen some infringement and disallow the goal, but really you know, it's all over it's 2-0.

Drenched in sweat, chest heaving, bitter, angry and devastated I slouch home.

I've always enjoyed my football.

The second most abiding memory of Bellahouston Academy was the end of term concert and the days immediately before it, when the preparations were being made. For the first time I felt a unity of purpose between teachers and boys, the relationship had been changed there was no need for conflict the objectives were the same. Neither was being judged. Everything went like clockwork Even the science teacher showed a human side by assisting the skiffle group.

The concert was a tremendous success and permitted me to leave the Academy having learnt something thoroughly - the words of 'Heartbreak Hotel' which the group practiced constantly while I worked on the scenery on the stage.

Those wishing to stay on at the 'prestigeous' Bellahouston Academy instead of going on to the new school were given the possibility of a reprieve. By specialising in Gaelic one could remain at the Academy, the only school in Glasgow offering this course. My parents did not take up this option thereby denying me a once in a lifetime opportunity to have a common language with a few hundred crofters.

CHAPTER 6

Penilee Senior Secondary School when finished was not nearly so interesting as it had been when it was a building site. Whereas in my previous school they had prided themselves on the fact that everything was so old, now the headmaster was proud that everything was so new; this included many of the teachers.

I did not know it then, but I was probably witnessing at first hand the beginnings of the new philosophy that educationalists would adopt throughout Britain. Our classes consisted of a wide range of subjects to suit the abilities of the slow-witted right through to the bright. Sometimes it seemed that the school or the teachers had given up and passed the time doing projects that had only a tenuous connection with the subject.

The P.E. teacher was one of the few who could maintain order probably because he had the respect of most of the boys being an ex-footballer and ex-army. I say most of the boys because there were a few who were habitually excused from games and never was so much abuse heaped on so few by so many and usually this was initiated by the teacher himself. I didn't come in for any of the taunting that note-carriers suffered because although my mother would have been quite prepared to protect me from the rigours of P.E., it was the one subject at which I performed well and enjoyed doing. It was also in the gymnasium that I experienced the first sexual awakening. She had the preposterously apt name of Miss Blue. She was the girl's gym mistress and the human equivalent of "crack" : dangerously addictive. One look and you were hooked, you couldn't break the habit. Her short gymslip was a lethal additive to a mind-blowing concoction of curves and curls.

Now that Miss Blue had established that females were not just people who had the irritating habit of getting the right answer to teachers questions or the infuriating tendency to ask for lengthy explanations just when the bell to end the class was about to ring, I should have been re-appraising their value but still on the whole they seemed more trouble than they were worth.

Activities that helped to give a rounded education were enthusiastically promoted 'by the teachers and while ballroom dancing and dramatic art perhaps don't quite give the image a Glasgow council house boy would normally like to portray, a little bit of fancy footwork and a few well chosen words have been known to come in handy. Especially when they permit you to miss a maths or science period because of rehearsals for the end- of-term artistic presentations for parents.

'The Man Who Came to Dinner' was to be my first triumph on the boards. The part of John the butler while perhaps not the lead, or even main supporting role, it was nevertheless a meaty little part which required me to make a dramatic entry onto the stage, and deliver the immortal line " they want pillows" with the full range of emotion implicit in the authors' choice of words. I would then exit by the stairway on the centre of the stage having captivated the audience for a full 10 seconds.

We opened to a packed house on the first night of a run of 2 nights. I had been in costume for hours to enable myself to get inside the part. I had even contemplated serving tea at home for my parents, to live inside John the Butler, but had feared I might set a precedent and have to serve it every night. My parents waited expectantly in the audience.

I stood on the wings going through breathing exercises and rehearsing my line. The breathing exercises had a dual purpose the first of which was to prepare my vocal cords to ensure that I could fully project my voice across at least the first three rows to the fourth where my parents were sitting. The second was because of the mini-crisis the producer had caused when he suddenly decided that the 'pillows' they wanted should be carried by me. Being an athsmatic I am allergic to feathers which the newly produced props contained. Another re-write was hastily ordered when my sneezing, coughing and wheezing threatened to disrupt the entire performance.

I was now to enter hurriedly on stage, minus the offending props, straighten my black bow tie, don my white linen jacket, pausing by the stairway to deliver my telling contribution and bound up the stairs and off-stage. My part was being fleshed out and as the great moment came, the enormity of the challenge began to hit me. Cue ! I was in the action ! I was immediately faced with problem number one, the stair was not a tie straightening and jacket donning distance from side stage. It would have been, if I had been going at a casual stroll but I, as the script demanded, was hurrying. I reached centre stage still wrestling with the linen jacket. " They want. [at that moment the metal button of my jacket popped off and hit the floor with what seemed like a resounding clunk].pillows" As I turned to bound up the stairs, the pocket of the now free flowing jacket caught on the end of the staircase rail. My momentum carried me forward in spite of the resistance and the linen jacket gave way, right up the centre seam on the back.

Those who had been privileged to be there, recalled the splendour of the performance, as I took myself through an incredible range of emotions from shock to embarrassment, irritation to anger, tired resignation and finally to a quiet dignity as I retrieved my jacket and left the stage with head held defiantly high.

Unfortunately I was unable to reach the same peak of performance the following evening. So I could not rescue the play as I had done the night before when in the opinion of my Dad I had been the only laugh of the night.

CHAPTER 7

Across from our house(even if they are strictly speaking apartments or flats, Glaswegians always refer to the place they live as their 'house') was a one storey building which served as a community centre and behind that was a spare piece of ground not quite football pitch size on which Scotland beat Brazil in the World Cup Final of 19.ty something. Rangers also won the European Cup countless times as unfortunately did Celtic. Even I personally scored in several cup finals.

These matches were spontaneous daily events and mostly played in the long summer days and nights or at weekends in winter when weather permitted.

To initiate the game one had only to appear on the grassless well trodden square with a football and within minutes boys were appearing from every close and every doorway. As soon as there were enough boys to pick two sides the match got under way.

Others were permitted to join as they appeared as long as the two sides were maintained on a more or less equal basis.

As a latecomer to the Penilee area I had not played football as much as the others. Strangely, although Govan was almost on the doorstep of one of the two most famous football clubs in the country the kids did not play as often, because there were no spare tracts of land. Our back court was pitted with spikes and broken glass and the streets were too near the tenement windows. The boys therefore played all their football at school or later when they started work.

Another reason for not playing as much had been my medical condition. Now with my attacks becoming less frequent and being in an area with perhaps less industrial pollution I could begin to play sport more often. My father had long maintained that exercise would be good for my condition, an undisputed fact in the medical profession today but still a heresy then.

I was now starting to play ten years later than some of the kids in the area and my lack of experience showed only too clearly. Sometimes when I arrived on the scene with another football veteran, of 12 years of age, the teams would argue about the unfairness of having to take me onto their side. My father would watch some of the games from our bedroom window and offer some sympathetic advice, when I eventually trudged home after yet another ineffective display.

I wanted so much to be good but lacked, not only the ability which came to them from playing since they were toddlers, but also stamina. The more criticism I got the more I avoided doing anything new. I needed to get confidence from somewhere, my Dad did try to encourage me but to some extent he was only too pleased I was fit enough to play. The inspiration when it did come arrived in typical abrasive style from McNeil the P.E. teacher during a practice game at school. " You want to put a little bit more into the game Wrethman, you're a lazy sod, it's a pity because you've probably got more positional sense and football brain than most"

I don't know if he was a motivational genius but he transformed me, not immediately, but from then on I stopped trying to emulate unsuccessfully the attributes of others. Some displayed individual ball skills, others a tireless combative style.

I concentrated on something that McNeil had been referring to, finding space, knowing where teammates were, playing the simple ball and ghosting into dangerous positions. I would never become a football star but almost four decades later, at 55 years of age, I would still be playing and still feel as excited as a teenager on the day of the match.

During winter when it became dark as we were leaving school and the weekends were often wet, no football could be played, so I would spend most of the time indoors. Often my parents would be watching something on T.V. which didn't interest me so I would retire to my bedroom after tea and devise ways of amusing myself while listening to Radio Luxembourg. Most of the games centred around football, either selecting teams from players featured on the cards issued by cigarette companies and those given by boys comic papers or playing an imaginary game with a ball made of rolled up socks.

When the 17 years old Pele of Brazil scored one of his three goals in the World Cup Final in Stockholm against Sweden in 1958 he probably didn't know it but his score was almost a carbon copy of an goal registered in the bedroom of 105 Craigmuir Road when an almost unknown Scottish International took a crossed ball(sock) on his chest past a defender as if he wasn't there, then on to his knee past a bedroom chair before flicking it deftly between the posts (legs of cabinet) to take the Cup to Scotland for the first time.

When not playing for Scotland or Rangers I was performing at the same venue as the latest rock sensation; Scotland's answer to Elvis Presley. In those early days, rock singers did not yet appear at soccer stadiums so I suppose I was a forerunner. In fact I sang at the very site where the World Cup Final had taken place and only the night before.

One thing the players and rock performers don't have to put up with, is the whole event being suspended when their Dad decides to look in on them. At times my father became quite concerned when he looked in to find me sweating from my exertions. Being an extremely practical and probably less imaginative person than myself, perhaps because he had come from a large family, he at first could not fathom out why I had such an agitated and guilty look. The truth of course was that I wanted to keep my little games to myself and was embarrassed about being caught in such childish pursuits. In my youth I always thought of him as more serious person than myself who would perhaps scoff at my behavior and think me too old to be playing make-believe. I was therefore embarrassed to admit what I had been doing. I of course was under-estimating him. He had no doubt played his own fantasy games.

Nevertheless I am sure that this type of secret role-playing is more common in children with no brothers or sisters. In larger working class families there is seldom time when one is alone with one's thoughts and fantasies.

Parents with one child are of course aware of their child's need to play with other children, and recently with my own son, my wife, in particular, has gone to great lengths to ensure that he had company during weekends and the long summer holidays when he does not have the daily contact with his friends through school.

His background is of course entirely different to mine. Today, because of traffic and the dangers of society, children are not as safe playing on the streets and middle class children, the group wherein

I suppose he must be categorized, have their leisure time organized for them.

In one way, my mother did make an attempt to do this by enrolling me for the Sunday school, the Cubs and later the Boy's Brigade. I was a misfit in all these institutions.

The Scottish Presbyterian Minister often talked about saving our souls. Perhaps he deposited them away in some vaults off the premises for safe keeping because as far as I could see the church was a completely soulless place as were many of the parishioners.

I remember being chastised by the Reverend Balfour for laughing in the church hall " this is not a place for hilarity" He did not detect the irony in my voice when I agreed with him.

I am not sure how it works with other religions, although I am sure the catholic church has similarities, but there is always a hierarchy of unpaid church officers and helpers(usually women) who although have no official mandate to determine philosophy or theology feel compelled to influence policy. If given leave as they were done at St Andrews they will evolve into a Praetorian Guard. They and the members of their family 'run' the church, set the tone, determine what events should be organised, who should be permitted into their inner circle.

Presbyterianism being a religion that is censorious and strict in its basic tenets gives enormous scope for zealots who wish to protect their prized position within the parish. Every small deviance from what they see as appropriate behavior is noted. Very soon they will let it be known that you are beyond redemption. To those wishing to become respected members of the community this is a fearful outcome. To someone such as myself this was a terrible temptation.

In spite of continuous brushes with the Boys Brigade captain and his senior officers all sons of people in the "Guard" I remained in the Brigade for a year, mainly for the P.E. and the football. On one of my last missions for the B.B. I collected sacks of money for a new extension to the church. Having previously been criticised for the small amount of money I had collected. This time I needed help to carry my collection in to the counting room. The value of my input may still have been inferior to most other boys but the sheer volume could not be surpassed. I had changed it into halfpennies and pennies.

This did not amuse the "inner circle" I was advised to leave.

I gleefully did, collecting my soul on the way out.

CHAPTER 8

A few times in the year my father would take me on a trip down to Balloch to see his family. I don't know why he always said he was going 'down' to Balloch because it is higher above sea level as well as being north of Glasgow. But it was always 'down'.

Dr Freud might say that this was a subconscious categorization because everything seemed to be 'down' at my father's home; morale above all.

My mother never went with us, there seemed to be (at least in my presence) an unspoken agreement that she would not be going and he would not ask her. My mother had apparently been on good terms with his Protestant grandmother and had visited the area often when she was alive, but had never quite fitted with the rough and ready ways of the Curley household.

The Renton in my father's boyhood would have been only a small town perhaps even a village and being only a few miles from Loch Lomond was surrounded by some of the most picturesque scenery to be found in Britain. Therefore although being a child from a financially disadvantaged family it could be said that he was environmentally privileged. His days were spent playing sports in the open spaces, swimming and fishing in the beautiful loch and the nearby river Leven and rambling in the hills and mountains.

His enjoyment at being in the open country was apparent but the visit to the family house, now run by his sister Mary, always seemed to be more of an obligation than a pleasure. As I grew older I became more aware of the barrier between my father and the rest of his family. The foundations of the barrier may have been put in place by his grandmother. Her Protestant work ethic and frugal lifestyle and code of behavior may well have contrasted with the more laisser-faire attitude of the Curleys. Mary, my Dad's sister was not so much head of the family now that both parents were dead, more a beleaguered caretaker. She seemed to have long ago given up any efforts to keep order in the house. Hardly surprising since she, I've been told, had the responsibility for their brother Alec who was a chronic epileptic and spent a large proportion of his time in bed. This in addition to the duties of a wife, and mother to numerous children, including many who had been left by other members of the family.

Her husband, brothers and several other male members of the family, it was said, suffered from continuous bouts of unemployment and prescribed for each other large doses of alcohol to help relieve the condition. A proportion of the time and money spent on this activity could well have improved the living conditions, but perhaps when hope of appreciable improvement is gone, one easily succumbs to the temptations of momentary pleasures.

The passage of time and my experience of life lead me to a more charitable view today than the uncomplicated opinion I had then as a child. The house had a smell and seemed to me to be very untidy. I did not want to eat there. These opinions I of course kept to myself, but my father who perhaps understood the reason for my reluctance to eat there, always made excuses for my abstinence.

Up to this point in my life I had not really encountered people who were substantially better off than ourselves. One or two families had a husband who commanded a higher salary than my father but this was usually offset by them having more children.. There were however many who lived a more impoverished lifestyle. This might be because of unemployment but in fact was often the consequence of their chosen lifestyle rather than the other way around. The condition of many poor families, even today, is often put down totally to external circumstances. In effect a lack of discipline and effort are often the real causes of abject poverty in a welfare society. My parents even through early periods of unemployment were able to maintain an acceptable quality of life by abstaining from the inessentials in favour of the necessary.

Where the streets of Govan were our playground, in Penilee there were more open spaces and this encouraged more sport, particularly football. There was no great need to hang about the closes as we had done in the Clydeside area. Nevertheless our meeting place prior to taking to the fields was often on the small thigh-high wall which surrounded the gardens of the ground floor flats. I can well imagine the middle class tenants of gardened houses in the area where I now live, looking on with horror at the sight of an ever-increasing group of boys on the wall of their garden. But this was a working class area of Glasgow and people were well used to the young being on the street. There were as yet no cars to damage, graffiti had not yet been imported from U.S.A. and the mindless destruction of a garden even to these rough kids would have seemed.eh.well.mindless, I suppose.

Nevertheless there's always a "behind the curtain watcher" One such person was Mr Herron, a one man vigilante group and forerunner of "community-watch". But, whereas today, these groups concern themselves almost exclusively with criminal activity Herron had a more extensive list of proscribed behavior: youthful exuberance, excessive levity, bouncing a football noisily, whistling, greeting mates too audibly, the list was endless and subject to continuous update. Nor did he fall into the usual category of cantankerous, childless old busybodies; for he was robust youthful man in his late thirties with a young child.

He did not like anyone sitting on his wall although the flat-top brick perimeter around all the houses in the area was considered by almost everyone as an amenity, including women with shopping, pensioners, people waiting for buses and parents whose tiresome and tireless tots wanted to imitate tight-rope walkers. Nor was his garden worthy of any special protection being mainly populated by weeds.

This day however Andy Nixon was to perpetrate a capital offence which was to unleash the full force of Herron upon us, and me in particular. We were sitting on the wall on other side of the passageway from the dreaded 'H's' garden when Andy, ever impatient, decided he would juggle with the football he was holding. His skill did not match his aspirations; the ball bounced off the edge of the wall we were sitting on, took one other bounce across the passage and over the wall into the ogre's terrain.

Foolishly optimistic that I could thwart the surveillance system I quickly stretched over the wall to retrieve the football. But no! Just as I grasped the ball the 'all seeing eyes' locked on me from the window. His immediate disappearance from the window meant only one thing : he was coming after us. We scattered in all directions.

I raced through the close and upstairs to our flat, bolting past Dad as he opened the door. Naturally an explanation was demanded and given. The truth this time.

Apart from the fact I had no time to make up something else I didn't feel guilty.

"I told you not to do anything to annoy that idiot" shouted Mum who had overheard the brief exchange. Dad was about to say something when the doorbell rang several times. I stood in the hallway as my father opened the door to the dreaded Herron.

" I've come about your bloody boy who's been jumping in and out of my garden and creating a disturbance" shouted the fearsome neighbour, his jaw jutting out aggressively towards my father.

"It's time he was taught a lesson" he added threateningly and looking as if he might brush past and go for me.

" Really" said Dad taking at the same time a step sideways and forward to simultaneously block his path and to crowd him " and who is it, that's going to teach him a lesson" he added taking a menacing tone that I had heard before, but not directed at another adult.

"Well if you're not, I'll."

"You'll nothing, you'll get your arse down the stair before I kick it down" Dad cut in, adding " you're a bloody idiot who thinks he can intimidate kids who are not doing anything except act like kids, GO ON.GET T' HELL! "

Herron blanched and shrunk away, the fearsome ogre made some face-saving comment halfway down the stair about people's failure to control their children; but the myth was dead.

I'm not sure if I then expected a stern warning or I now consider that I should have.

As expected, I received the mandatory warning against provoking Herron or giving him any justifiable cause for complaint. I was sent to convey the same message to my friends. Timely: because Robert the boy who lived downstairs had heard the exchange between the two adults and was already relating the tale to the others, with embellishments, as the lads congregated again on the opposite side of the street. It took all my powers of persuasion to dissuade them from taunting him.

From that day I had no further direct conflict with him but the police were to bear the brunt of his campaign from then on. No longer confident to take matters into his own hands he, his wife and his mother, who also lived there, directed a continuous barrage of complaints to the local police station. At first the "Polis" would respond. Usually the complaint was that we were playing football on an unauthorised area and causing damage and disturbing the peace.

There was no sign to say we could not play football on the ground behind the community centre. But in theory, because there were, on either side of the touchline and across the road, gardens and windows that could just be reached with a very strong and wayward clearance; it could be said that we presented a threat of damage.

None of the tenants of those particular houses complained and indeed many had children who played on this ground, nor could Herron's garden be reached even by a professional player, but complaints had sometimes to be answered.

The entire operation became an exercise in futility. The "law" arrived, sometimes we scattered more for the fun of it than any genuine concern. At other times we remained to present a surly and defiant front. This would prompt the officers to "book us" This in turn would provoke an angry reaction from those parents who had watched the arrival of the forces of law and order. Never the most popular people in working class areas, these visits only served to cause further animosity between the police and the community.

Herron continued to wage his petty vendetta using the police as his tool. But it wasn't long before they grew tired of him and he became a public nuisance in their eyes too.

CHAPTER 9

I have read recently that the long term memory is the last to suffer the ravages of old age and attendant diseases such as Alzheimer's. If it were the other way around I would be more reassured. Because, although I may strive to remember the name of a useful contact I've just met, or the sequence of important events recently past, the details escape me. While the names, physiology and idiosyncrasies of people I have not seen or heard of for more than 35 years can so easily be recalled.

There are no doubt people who can tell me why this is so and no doubt I could find many references to this phenomenon in the library under an –ology. I may well look it up later, if I remember.

Leaving aside academic theory I would say that it might be logical to assume that people who have played a pivotal role in your formative years or who have been a major influence in your chosen career or lifestyle would be the people to be remembered. If this is the case, why Derek Ormiston or James Higgins?

Derek Ormiston was an unlikely mate for me. He was what now would be called 'nerdish' and if he's still alive and I most fervently hope he is, he will be surfing the Net at this very moment. If he's not doing that he'll be editor of the Twitcher's Monthly.

Why I should have befriended him for a brief period of time I do not know. On the surface we were completely incompatible. I can see his bespectacled face, which incidentally had a small scar by his mouth, turn pale at the mere thought of a P.E. period or sports day. Why do I remember him, what did he give to my life? Was it simply variation, a view of alternative lifestyles?

I know what James Higgins gave me: cricket. Not that I have been an avid fan. But at least I would not have the opinion of most Scottish working-class boys that it was just a poofy English game. The red-haired Higgins was also an unlikely pal being somewhat older and being the only Catholic so far to have entered into our little group. I first got to know him playing football on the aforementioned spare ground across the street. He was a formidable footballer with a fierce shot. But one hot summer's day when we were sitting on the wall(not Herron's) discussing what to do next, he mentioned his interest in cricket.

At first his suggestion of playing at the local public park was as enthusiastically received as an invitation to a double period of algebra, but he persisted.

I'm not sure what convinced a group of died-in-the-wool football freaks to take up this game but had a non-footballer, or one who played that game badly, been the proposer I'm sure he would have been seen off in a chorus of derision. As it was his credibility, perhaps his seniority and most certainly his knowledge and enthusiasm won us over.

Cricket did not replace football, not even in the summer, but it did offer another interest.

Higgins not surprisingly was a venomous fast bowler and a free scoring opener. Billy Wilson became a tantalising spinner and several other of our group developed individual skills. I became the keeper, not a wicket-keeper, the equipment keeper. This way I could be assured of a game. The category of tail-ender was beyond my wildest aspirations. I suppose I could be described as a slow to medium paced fielder.

The matches were played in Barshaw Park which was the nearest space with a maintained grass surface. All the other spare ground, of which there was plenty in Penilee, was rough or had been worn down with football. The area we played on was not ideal either because there was a very steep incline. The wicket was set across the incline so that when batting you either looked downhill on your onside or uphill on the offside depending on what end you were at. Higgins who had the ability to choose his shots could therefore sky shots uphill presenting you with a continuous bloody run up the gradient or play them forcibly off the front foot along the ground and downhill, and in the words of the cricket commentators, 'hurrying along to the boundry'. By the end of the day I was knackered.

James Higgins also introduced me to Test Match Special. There was no immediate conversion; I first became aware of it because Higgins would use terms and language unknown to me. To be able to speak a good game is the next best thing to being able to play, so I eventually twiddled the knobs on my antiquated wireless in the right direction and Arlott's 'English summer's day voice', hooked me. Much has already been written about the influence of the programme and the protagonists but I don't know if an appreciation of the 'Special' has ever been penned from the point of view of a working class Glasgow boy.

One thing is clear the game itself is not what makes T.M.S. interesting; although it must be said that no other game could have a programme built around it in this way. The pace of the game allows for detailed description and the medium of radio necessitates it. Add to this the wealth of statistics the game throws up and the endless technical terms and idiom, much of which is used in analogous form in everyday language.

The game's language has grown and changed but it in still intrinsically English in tone and it was even more so in those years. The languid effortless delivery and understatement used by the commentators to describe the activity is pure public school upper-class, even if sometimes the speaker is not himself from that background. This is because the game's origins stem from those 'playing fields'.

So what in all this appealed to me, a Glasgow street kid? It's difficult to define but it may be 'the exotic'. It was a world away from the Glasgow tenements. Perhaps it was the language itself, strange yet understandable, a kind of poetry. Then of course there is always the intimacy of radio; the feeling that they are talking to you or for you like the difference between theatre and cinema.

Then of course in common with many people from all different backgrounds I enjoyed the Dream Team: John Arlott and Brian Johnson. One to emphasize the beauty of the game the other the fun.

It's a great pity they both 'got themselves out' still I suppose one could say they had a reasonable innings.

CHAPTER 10

I have spoken of the visits to my father's relatives and the strains within that family;
on the surface my mother's side seemed to be more unified. My Grandmother, Jane Hamilton, was already a widow when I was born. Her home was quite the most impressive I had seen; at least up to that point in my life as I reached my early teens.

It had a back and front garden, four bedrooms, living-room and kitchen. All other people I knew lived in tenement blocks; this was a house. It seemed to me like luxury, but in fact the house, then home to my grandmother and two of my uncles (one of them intermittently), had at one time served two adults and 11 children. My grandfather had been a foreman docker and this conjures up the image of a rough talking, hard drinking muscleman; it seems nothing could be further from the truth. He was a non-drinking Presbyterian lay preacher who brought up his children (nine plus two adopted), in fear of God. After his death the fear in each one diminished by different degrees.

The visits to Gran Hamilton were always intriguing, her house was a museum. Two of her 'boys', my uncles, had served in the Merchant Navy and four in the Army. Another had worked in Africa while a daughter was in Canada. In addition, all the daughters had married and their husbands had also travelled, mostly during the war. All had brought home souvenirs from their foreign adventures.

By far the most interesting was a collection of books brought to the house by my Uncle Robert called 'Battles of the Nineteenth Century'. There were originally 7 volumes and I now have five. As they were specially published for subscription only, and were not generally available, I would think anyone having the complete set would be in possession of a valuable collection. I was unable to find out what happened to the other two volumes.

Those books, as the name suggests, describe the major battles which took place during the last century. I'm not sure how objective the authors are in their assessment of the causes of the conflicts, or how accurate they are in their descriptions of the battles. But the engraved leather cover, showing a sword-wielding officer commanding a troop of colonial soldiers in their defence against a horde of dervishes, is enough to fire the imagination of any boy. Inside there are illustrations and plates showing artists impressions of the battle scenes and little sketches of the protagonists with captions such as 'Moorish types'.

Apart from the books there were also numerous exotic vases, brass ornaments, cushion covers and photographs. I was also entertained by the sea-tales of Uncle Peter, who lived with Grandma. Peter had been invalided out of the merchant navy with a nervous disorder; attributed to the trauma he suffered when his ship was torpedoed during the war. He of all the children, apart from my mother, had inherited his father's fear, or was it love, of God; in the Presbyterian Church the two are often confused. Although he walked to the Alter many times he was never to arrive there with a woman. He remained devoted to his mother all his life. Both my Mother and Gran made much of the fact that he had once been engaged to be married; it seems to me now, this may have been a form of anticipatory disclaimer.

Jack was the other Uncle who lived in Gran's house. He was also to remain unmarried and after the war had spent time in the merchant navy. There the similarities in the two brothers ended. Jack was the degenerate of the family who spent most of his time in pubs and dance-halls with whatever female company he could find.

Gran was a kind old woman who seemed to have a perpetual supply of thick hot vegetable soup. In my recollection she never once uttered an angry word nor showed favouritism to any one of her many children and grandchildren.

However it seems the continuance of normal relations between all the members of the large family depends on the longevity of at least one of the parents. As Gran's health began to falter and her benign but powerful influence over her children waned, the differences started to come to the surface. By the time she became bedridden the relations between her children had reached such a low point that no concerted plan could be put together to share the burden of her care or even coordinate visits. My mother took it upon herself to shoulder most of the responsibility. Her regular visits became frequent and progressed to daily. Her duties during these visits also increased. She started by doing some light cleaning and buying-in some basic groceries as well as comforting my Gran. Before long she was doing all the housework and shopping, had taken on the laundry including the washing and ironing of her two brother's underwear and shirts. All this she performed for a long time with the stoicism of a martyr. Was her sacrifice appreciated? Far from it.

The three married brothers and her sister Maisie, perhaps inspired by a little guilt, looked upon her as a self righteous meddler. Jack, who's lifestyle she had always frowned upon, now resented having to rise after a hard night's carousing to a barrage of 'advice'.

Peter, ever possessive of his mother and guardian of her home and its treasures, objected to another having the run of the house. In the face of such opposition my mother became more and more nervous and irritable. It started to affect our home life and my father who had tried to support her, also began to lose patience with the situation. His complaints put further pressure on her. As my grandmother moved nearer to death and the realisation hit Peter that he would soon be alone he became more and more dependent on my mother's services but paranoid, and protective of his place as keeper of the house.

His accusations that Mum was systematically removing stuff from the house to a cynic's ears might have had some credibility; except that the items registered as being missing included his much used underwear. My mother's obvious distress at accusations of theft enraged my father and he challenged Peter. As I have already documented my Dad could be a intimidating presence when angered but I think after forcing a partial climbdown he realised he was facing-down a deeply disturbed man.

Mercifully, my Gran who was suffering, as was her family without her gentle admonishments, passed away quite soon afterwards. Her death did not bring the family together in grief, there were to be some reconciliations at a later date but the immediate effect was to provide further fuel to the war. No estate, to speak of, existed to be contested, but the many small treasures were guarded over by a Gorgon-like Peter. Some members of the family notably those who had visited Gran less, and as such had not incurred the suspicion of the obsessive Peter, managed to ingratiate themselves into his trust. They obtained for themselves little items of jewellery, ornaments and other household goods. Needless to say my mother ended up with practically nothing, unless we can count the incomplete volumes of the 'Battles': appropriate perhaps.

CHAPTER 11

I have spoken previously of the influence individual teachers had on my love of football and literature But it might be argued that I was already pre-disposed to those activities, and they simply re-inforced my interest. It is undoubtedly true that nothing I have achieved in my professional life can be attributed to school in Glasgow.

It would be interested to know just how many of my classmates benefited professionally from their schooling at Penilee Senior Secondary. My guess is few. School was not looked upon as the first step on a career ladder. The ambition of most parents in that area was to get their sons into a good trade as soon as they were eligible to leave school. And while good results at school were to be welcomed, they sometimes also caused a dilemma. Most families were poor and had fairly low expectations of their sons and even less of their daughters. There was always the fear that allowing their children to stay on at school would incur only expenses, achieve little and perhaps lose them the opportunity to serve an apprenticeship. Even of those few who were considered to be 'brain boxes' that I know of, none of them ultimately found academic or professional success through early schooling. One became an actor another returned to study later in life.

Perhaps because of the low academic aspirations in that area the teachers in turn became demoralised, or perhaps the good ones went to other institutions and only the poor remained. On the other hand my estimation of their worth from my childhood recollections might well be flawed and unfair. Nevertheless we did seem to have a disproportionate share of uninspired and uninspiring individuals. They didn't even have the excuses of today's state educators that they were poorly paid and unsupported. Their conditions in relation to other professions in Scotland was, at that time, fairly attractive. Neither did they have to face the problems of ethnic diversity and excessive classroom violence. The pupils were almost one hundred percent Scottish and all of the same religion. Although we did have some disruptive pupils and I'm sure, unresponsive parents, the term 'underclass' had not yet been applied; on the whole the 'working class' still had a respect for authority and normally classroom discipline could be maintained. Except, it must be said, in Miss Freeman's class.

This was a diminutive female teacher of French. I am unsure of her origins she gave the impression of being French although the name Freeman implies an altogether different background. Perhaps she was also unsure of her ancestry. She was certainly unsure of everything else.

To be fair, the teaching of the French language to boys who are convinced they are destined to work in Shipyards or Factories and Girls similarly programmed to be housewives, laudable as it may have been, was a difficult and thankless task. Neither the pupils, the parents nor in many cases the teachers could see any point to it.

Pointless as an activity may be there are some teachers who can create interest by the skill of their presentation, there are others whose main objective is to maintain discipline, cover the curriculum. and if you learn something that's a bonus.

Miss Freeman could neither create interest nor maintain any kind of discipline. Serious defects in any teacher, even more so, if you are in front of a class of street-kids.

Mayhem, is not too strong a word to describe French classes. Pupils treated her with insolence and contempt, refused to follow any instructions, and taunted her mercilessly.

In those days corporal punishment was permitted and often used. The thick leather tawse known as 'the strap' would be brought down with force on the outstreched and upward turned palms of your hand. It could be a fearsome deterrent but not when wielded by Mademoiselle Freeman. On a few occasions she plucked up the courage to use it, but this only became a battle of wills with the offending pupil always coming out on top. Boys, including myself made a point of demonstrating how feeble her punishment had been.

I am not now proud to say that I probably removed forever this punishment from her feeble armoury by asking, to the great delight of my cohorts, for more. This, after she had dealt out what she considered to be a particularly draconian - three lashes.

The ultimate and effective deterrent would have been to send us to a more senior colleague. We quickly learnt she would not resort to this policy. Probably because she would have been admitting she was incapable of handling the classes. Most definitely because she would have been terrified of her head of department Miss MacNiven a Margaret Thatcher-like figure but without the heart.

Other teachers come to mind, 'Eggy' because of the shape of his bald head, Wishart who if he saw you distracted from his lecture would throw any small object at you he could find; a method not perhaps included in today's teacher's training manuals. Mr Gillespe, a stern science teacher with rimless glasses who never smiled and we suspected might have carried out experiments on humans for the Nazis. Mr Redpath who inadvisedly brought in his guitar at the end of term, to serenade avid Elvis Presley, Jerry Lee and Bill Haley fans to a rendition of 'Owl and the Pussycat'.

Little of what they taught comes to mind only their appearance and idiosyncrasies which in some cases include the teaching methods they employed. One geography teacher, did nothing else but write endless notes in chalk on the blackboard which we were to copy and learn at home. About the only thing that could be said was that it was an impressive display of stamina on his part. Each period after about half-an-hour most of us began to tire and missed whole passages some pupils stopped completely. He never tested us throughout the term nor did he ever explain anything he had written. I'm not sure what he hoped to achieve but I suppose it removed the tediousness of actually communicating with us. I don't remember his proper name but as he was permanently covered in a thin layer of white dust, not surprisingly he was known as 'Chalky'.

A recurring thought as I make my way through this story will be 'I wonder what happened to……' Sadly, in the case of the people who were mature adults when I was a child, the answer is likely to be that they are no longer in this world. Even the passing of people you did not particularly like, brings a tinge of sadness, if only for the selfish reason that it draws a line, finally, under a period of your life and emphasizes once again, as if you needed reminding, there will be no return. In the case of people who are probably still alive there is always the hope that you will meet up once again. But here I must wonder, would I be quite so willing to meet up with them if I had not had a happy and successful life since our last meeting. In my defence, I can say that I do not want to meet them to gloat over my good fortune especially if things have not gone so well for them, on the contrary I would be delighted to hear of their success and well-being. But I suspect when things have not gone well for people they might feel a little less inclined to swap life's tales with long lost friends and acquaintances.

Nevertheless, whatever the circumstances, I cannot deny that my curiosity awakens when old names come to mind.

In the space of a few years I had attended five different schools and even my brief stay at some of them had been punctuated by absences for illness; real, imagined or feigned. Child psychologists will tell you today that this disruption can be traumatic, and detrimental to a child's development. Well, it's a bit late telling me that now! It would have been a handy excuse at the time, when my form teacher Miss MacLean was berating me for lack of effort.

However, although academic achievements may not have been forthcoming there had been an improvement in my quality of life.

The long overdue improvement in my bronchial condition now seemed to be coming about. Doctors had predicted that I would improve as I got older and the underlying medical condition probably had. But if the mental condition does play a part in fighting illnesses, as many people believe, perhaps my extended stay at this school had also helped.

I now had an established group of school-mates; I was contending for a place in one of the football teams; I was in the school drama section. Motivation can often overcome a sniffle and a wheeze. I'm not so sure it can not overcome even greater afflictions but I'll be happy not to have to put it to the test.

One of the school-mates was a boy called Charlie Dickerson. He was a thick set boy with a hair style that could only be described as a rolling wave. He mouth seemed to be full of teeth. His house seemed to be full of sisters. There was never a time when there wasn't at least one around. The youngest Muriel was pretty and at her age would probably have taken an interest in any boy her brother brought home even if they had not been dashingly long and boney, sexily pale-faced and red-nosed like me. I should really have been flattered, it was after all my first real triumph with a member of the opposite sex, but to be honest she was a pest. However, had I known what would transpire with her brother I would probably shown more interest in her.

The gay rights movement will tell you that young men can not be lured into performing sexual acts they do not themselves feel comfortable with. Well, I can't believe I was the first and last of the naive thirteen year-olds. It was during the school summer holidays. Charlie and I were passing the time on a rainy afternoon at my apartment. Both my parents were at work. It started with generalities about sex and then verbal boasting about the size of our 'pricks and balls' A competition that could only be decided ultimately by physical demonstration: we removed our trousers and underpants.

There was no doubt that the discussion itself excited me and whether he took my physical manifestation of this frission as an interest in him, or whether he just took advantage while he could, I am still not sure.

Refusing to be convinced by my dimensional superiority he suggested closer physical inspection; the first alarm bells rang, closely followed, fortunately, by the door-bell. My father had come home a little earlier than usual. I had fortunately left a key in the lock on the inside so he had been unable to use his own key. We scurried to re-dress. I relieved, he disappointed. It was effectively the end of our friendship. I did not completely stop talking to him but I always felt awkward and embarrassed in his company. Needless to say I did not tell anyone about the experience with him.

At that age you can be embarrassed by many things. I'm not sure to what extent I was embarrassed by the fact I had almost been caught doing something 'dirty', as my mother might have put it, or because it was a homosexual act. I did know that I was unhappy with myself and with Charlie's final reaction. Perhaps it was my first realisation of what homosexual actually meant. The shortened form 'homo' and it's synonym 'poof' were freely used in the playground and street as a form of insult, but if asked to define exactly what they meant I would probably have said it meant a 'pansy'. If pressed further to define this, I would have described it broadly as someone who was timid, invariably excused from sport, probably good at music and wore a school cap. Using this criteria Dickerson would have immediately been discarded as likely candidate.

Anyway, I now knew what a homosexual was and also knew, if I wasn't aware of it before, that I wasn't one.

But I was beginning to feel certain sexual ambiguities.

I could not reconcile the irresistible attraction I was now feeling towards some girls with my other view that they were tiresomely silly, and an undoubted nuisance on the sports field.

However, their silliness was never allowed to tire me for long. They just didn't hang around me. It may have been the skinny frame, the round shoulders and the enormous flat feet. I even changed my hairstyle to the new American crew cut. But now with so little hair my large ears protruded even more. My father gave me the final confidence booster –'You've got a heid like the Scottish Cup'.

So, in a misguided effort to establish my male heterosexual credentials, for a brief period I aligned myself with several of the tough macho types in the school. But this didn't last long, I think the truth was, I found them boring. Before long I was looking for new friends again.

Sandy, couldn't ever be described as boring; enigmatic yes, humorous often, sensitive, provocative, all those and more, but never boring. He was, at the ripe old age of 14 years, like me, a non practicing heterosexual, and having heard and believed the dubious testimonies* of sexual conquest by our other mates was already beginning to despair of ever sampling the same delights. My continued celibacy was his only consolation.

His continued celibacy seemed guaranteed for some time. Of the guys we knew in those days I felt he was probably the only one that might be less attractive to girls and less comfortable in their company than me. Someone cruelly but rather accurately observed that he looked like a albino negro. Glasgow youths are not famous for their sensitivity but although this type of comment, often made in his presence, did nothing, in those days, to increase his confidence with girls, it didn't in any way diminish his enthusiasm to go on to an acting career. I now see Alexander Morton, to give him his full stage name, in plays, the occasional film and on T.V.as Golly in Monarch of the Glen He's not a star nor even the lead but I suppose he's following the career he always wanted and perhaps he's still expecting a bigger breakthrough. I'm not sure, of the two of us, who made the big sexual breakthrough first, but that's another story.

I owe him some sort of debt. His intense interest in films, theatre, music and politics did ignite a spark in me. I would never become an expert or take up a career in any of those subjects but in those early years they offered another dimension to life, something else to think about. Important for a young working-class lad soon to be caught up in the unholy Trinity of football, booze, and girls. All three of them leading inexorably each weekend to a punch-up and sometimes to a brush with the 'Polis'.

The other two guys who made up our group were both called Alan. One of them had to change. He became Rick. It was a pop/film star name and a logical next step for a boy about to make the career leap from State school to factory worker; an image make-over. He didn't of course change it to help him with his career he changed it to help him with his hobby – collecting women. A cool matinee-idol, film-mag type name helped to distinguish him from the Jimmys and the Sandys. And of course a tall dark, well proportioned good looking guy like him certainly needed something to help him compete with the likes of the Albino and the Scottish Cup.

The other Alan, who retained his name, was almost aristocracy. I remember asking my Mum and Dad for some money for a trip and mistakenly using him to indicate that other boys were being financed by their parents. 'Oh yes and well might they afford such an expense, his father's a foreman!' Hob nobbin' it with the upper classes has it's cost.

Fame is relative, it's funny looking back at the things which conferred status on a person in our community. (Translation provided)

'Ian's faither was a Powderhall runner'.– His father ran for an amateur athletics club 'His brother's a big yin in the Bens'. – He's an official in a local junior football club 'Her mother's a heid bummer at the Rolls Royce club'.– an unpaid committee member of a social club.

I'm not going to scoff at other people's vicarious claim to fame but it's not as if their father, like mine, was offered a trial for Liverpool F.C. But come-on, be honest, what would you prefer to discreetly slip into the conversation?

Actually, to get back to Ian of Powderhall fame. He was to be another name change. Ian was a bit parochial for a handsome blond athlete who was the star of the school sports teams. But not for him a blatant change to some unrelated alias, no, his conversion was as smooth as his relay baton hand-over or as deft as his body swerve – Ian to John to Johnny. No change at all really, just an upgrade to a much more marketable title.

I resisted the temptation to call myself something else as I did not think it would increase my possibilities with girls. Rick and Johnny's catch didn't seem to rise appreciably either, but that may have been because there are only so many hours in the day.

A more traditional measure of status in society, other than being an official in a club, was the area where you lived. This applies not only to the three main categories of upper, middle and working class but also sub-categories within those groups.

So we had moved ever so slightly upwards when we moved from Govan to Penilee.

However my new mates lived in Hillington another rung up the social ladder. To Govan-ites, in those days, this area was decidedly posh. Most of the semi-detached houses were designed for two families. The tennants downstairs usually had the front garden and the upstair's tennant the back garden. Sandy, Rick and Alan lived in these palatial residences.

On holidays and after school I often walked over to Sandy's house. It had absolutely nothing to do with the fact that on the way there I had to pass the house of Doreen Forrest who I considered the best looking girl in the school. Although sometimes I did happen to see her hanging around with her mates or in her garden. She always just managed to resist the temptation to chat me up and had obviously instructed her good looking mates to do the same. I strode by, oblivious to their feigned indifference.

When pocket money permitted, and that wasn't often, I would walk over to Hillington and muster whoever I could of Sandy, Alan and Rick before making my way to the Westway Café. I don't know why this café became the 'in' spot. This is one of those anthropological mysteries. Why young humans herd together in one particular spot especially when that spot is indistinguishable from others or as was the case with the Westway, inferior in some ways. The custom apparently continues I recently asked some young people why a certain coffee shop was always full of people of their age group; none of them knew.

If we could not afford to go to the café I often remained at Sandy's house. Wherever we were he held court. He was the authoritative voice on all matters related to popular culture, the arbiter of good taste in films, theatre, T.V. and music.

Marlon Brando, Paul Newman, Elvis Presley and Bob Dylan could never really be said to have made it until they received the Sandy endorsement. But lest you think he played safe with big names, no, he could pluck people from relative obscurity and bestow the Sandy seal of approval. Thus people we had never heard of such as Francoise Hardy, Lee J Cobb, and Bert Jansch suddenly came into our lives.

To get the nod, all actors, singers, authors, even sportsmen had to be perceived by Sandy to be rebellious or in some way anti-establishment. If not, he would find it hard to justify his support for them, because they would fit in with his beliefs: he was a Marxist.

Most boys of our age didn't even know what a Marxist was, and certainly no girls I knew. Some had a vague idea about the basic differences between a capitalist and a communist. Many had heard their fathers mention socialism and trade unions. But no one conducted a passionate discussion on anything except football. Sandy did not of course encourage passionate discussion. He already displayed what, I only came to realise many years later, were the characteristics of a Socialist, and most particularly a Marxist, total certainty and a disdain for any opinion which might cast doubt on any part of the philosophy. Of course he was on safe ground in those early years. Firstly, no other person in his immediate circle knew anything about politics and, unlike him, read nothing on the subject. Secondly, he was in any case sowing on fertile ground. His listeners, who actually were few and with a short attention span, were all working class boys whose futures seemed destined to follow the same path as their fathers; into the factories and shipyards. The basic proposition that communism would deliver us from this capitalist exploitation to a better world of equal share for all, was seductive, if simplistic. Unlike religion which also promises delivery to a better place the solutions seemed to be in our own hands, the changes could be made in our lifetime. Also, it's easier to blame and fight the enemy without; it's more difficult to fight the enemy within.

As I have said before, his introduction to the subject led me to the world of books. I wanted to be able to understand and contribute to the discussion. I did not become studious over-night, but whereas before, I had read only comics I now found myself picking up the occasional book from the library. The seeds were sown.

It's a strange irony that a whole succession of professional teachers had failed to inspire in me any love of study yet a misguided amateur philosopher invoked a submerged spirit of curiosity. Too late however to make any difference to my immediate academic future.

My form teacher advised me before the final exams of that year that I should prepare to leave school and find myself a job. I would still be only 14 years old by the end of term and officially too young to leave, but as my 15th birthday fell in late September just as the schools reconvened after the summer break I could be permitted to leave. No, let's get it right – encouraged to leave. My results and my attitude to the principal subjects would not justify continuing, she said.

My parents seemed neither disappointed nor surprised. They had never had any great expectations of academic achievement and my father had already sounded out someone at Fairfield Shipyard. A job as store-boy was available and I could start almost immediately. But before that came the end of term results. Though perhaps not good enough to warrant a re-think they did surprise several people. A low pass mark in all subjects save one, in French where I failed by one mark, pointed to a general consistency. Probably a fair indicator of the abilities I would always show; a capacity to manage most things without excelling at anything. The form Mistress Miss McLean, herself a French teacher had the French mark upgraded to show a pass(I'm not sure if this was within the rules). This was not any last ditch attempt to qualify me for another year but more of a going away present. So my leaving certificate showed a pass in all subjects. Not that it mattered, It meant nothing except perhaps as a bureaucratic record in the school that they had fulfilled their statutory duty.

CHAPTER 12

One of my mother's favourite sayings when she heard or read about some rich person's extravagance was 'they have more money than sense'. As most of those people in question seemed to be enjoying their condition, I resolved to one day attain this distinction. Therefore on my first day at The Receiver's office at Fairfield Shipyard when my boss Willie Hutcheson asked me what my ambition was, a little lost for something to else to say, I replied 'to have more money than sense'. He promptly gave me sixpence and said he was happy to see me realise my dream so soon. Within a very short time I would have more money than he could have imagined.

The Receiver's Office was the sorting department for incoming deliveries of all kinds. My job was basically to take parcels and letters around to the various departments. In joining Fairfield Shipyard I was back in Govan in familiar territory and, of course, in the same work-place as my father. However, I didn't see much of him as his crane was on the West side of the basin and, as such, quite far from the places to which I usually made deliveries. Even on the few occasions when I was on that side I could not attract his attention. His cabin was 100ft off the ground.

Since moving to Penilee his lunch-time routine had come more into line with that of the other crane drivers. Our close in Rathlin Street had been only a few hundred yards from the main gate so he could come home for lunch. Now, like his work-mates, he actually made his tea and ate his piece(sandwich) before the horn sounded for lunch. He could then go for 'a bit of a walk' before hanging around the corner by the main gate with his cronies until the horn summonsed them back.

I soon found my own mates and lunch time pursuits, but sometimes I would go to see him at the 'forum'.

The discussions, as always, centred around football or unpopular gaffers; very occasionally, about politics. No matter how much exposure I had to the lingua franca of the street and sports field, I myself using it no less than any other Glasgow boy, I still felt a strange embarrassment when I came up to their group and heard my Dad, like all the others, swearing.

The custom has probably died, along with the term – working-class – but in those days no matter how rough the man or his manners, he usually tried to restrain his use of bad language when in the company of his wife and/or kids or anyone else's wife or kids. There were slips of course, during bouts of drinking or very heated discussion, but the un-written code was maintained by most men.

Therefore the passion and fluency of my father, or his work-mate's, advocacy for a certain policy, be it the castration of their gaffer, or the dropping of the Ranger's full-back, was greatly diminished while I was present. I didn't hang around for too long.

I also had to get accustomed to hearing my father being called Peter. Many years before when he first started work, he was asked by the foreman for his name. When he said it was Farick, and that it was Irish Gaelic for Patrick, someone said it was Scottish Gaelic for Peter.

He was therefore given an instant re-Christening for the foreman's convenience. Peter it had been ever since; but only at work.

Another curiosity where names were concerned was my Dad's habit of always referring to work-mates by their surnames. Hence, at home, we only ever heard of King and McGurn, although he was friends with those two men for more than 40 years. It was not like the practiced form of address of the public school type nor, as one might expect from robust working men of this generation, did it indicate a lack of affection. In fact years later when both passed on, much in advance of Dad, he was profoundly affected.

So what is this thing with names? Have I uncovered the secret? Did Glasgow man's dissatisfaction in the 1950's with their own and other people's first name lead eventually to everyone being called Jimmy. As in - 'Hey Jimmy huv ye goat the time?' or 'Heh, wait a wee minute Jimmy'. Perhaps my parents anticipated this and saved me from the necessity to change.

Anyway, I quickly settled into the job and got to know just about everyone in every department. There was a lot of ground to cover each day because Fairfield stretched across an enormous tract by the Clydeside. On either side of the big main gate stood the main offices. One section of those being the Admiralty offices. The shipyard had for a long time built and repaired ships for the Royal Navy and orders from them as well as for cargo and passenger ship for the merchant fleets, were essential to the survival of the company. So much so, that one ship the H.M.S Blake which was on the stocks for years because of design modifications, budgetary disputes and other delays, came to be known by the workforce, ever-fearful of redundancy due to low orders, as the 'rent-book': because the continuing work on this ship enabled them to meet what was one of their major living costs.

Going west from the main gates one would pass by the various sheds where component parts for every stage of shipbuilding were made and repaired. All were called 'shops' so we had the light machine, heavy machine, boiler, copper, and brass finishing shops. Within these shops worked the turners, fitters, boilermakers, millwrights, electricians, plumbers, and many more. Further down on the dockside the cranes driven by people like my father would lift large pieces on to uncompleted hulls assisted by riggers. While stagers, platers, riveters, and welders bashed and banged her together.

There were of course many categories of worker but the two main categories were 'bunnets' and 'hats'. The bunnet being the flat cap which was commonly worn by members of the work-force and the bowler being the 'hat' worn by the managers, and foremen, or as everyone called them, the 'gaffers'. The bowlers, though a hard-hat, was worn as a badge of rank and not as one would expect today as some kind of safety precaution. Another aspect of the Industrial landscape in those days was the absence of women, especially in the shipyards. While women had been taken on for assembly-line work in factories during the war, Shipyard trades were still considered too physical and demanding for them and many who had been taken on left as soon as the men came home from the forces. Therefore apart from secretaries in the offices, the cleaning department was the only other section to employ women in numbers. When a ship was near completion or had come in for repairs an army of them stomped on board to clean up. Army, is an appropriate collective noun, for they were indeed a warrior breed.

Seldom did I get the opportunity to actually get on board one of the near completed vessels but one day when I was delivering an urgent package to the dock manager's office his secretary, knowing her boss was waiting for the contents, sent me aboard to seek him out. I was told

I would find him in the purser's office. It seemed so simple, but on board chaos reigned. There were no signs on the doors. The noise was deafening. Even when I asked for directions, and the worker thought he could help, the directions he bawled out to me, I invariably could not take, because the passageway was temporarily blocked by cables, equipment and workmen. I eventually found myself several levels below the deck from which I had entered. There seemed to be some relative quiet in one of the larger cabins and a number of cleaning women appeared to be having a tea-break.

'Excuse me ladies, anybody know where the purser's office is?

'Oh ladies is it, sweetheart?' called out one, loudly.

'Come oan in, an' we'll tell ye!' said another laughing and winking to her mates.

I was already realising that I was going to be some fun for them but it was a small price to pay to get proper directions. I moved into the centre of the room.

'Come ower here, Mary'll sort ye oot,' said this hard looking woman in a filthy blue boilersuit and oil-soaked headscarf. She put her arm round my waist.

'Noo, whit wis it ye ask'd again? Oh yeah, wher' ma purse wis…. it's doon here,' she said, grabbing my hand quickly and sticking it down inside her overalls. I recoiled rapidly and backed off towards the door. Another harridan, by now covering the door, groped at my arse causing me to jump. Their hysterical laughter, mingled with obscene shouting, carried right down the corridor as I made my escape.

This initiation apart, my transition from school to work was going smoothly. I was beginning to get to know everyone. I now found that my position offered several advantages. Being a messenger boy, I had authorisation, and reason, to move anywhere within the entire complex. More importantly, there were no restrictions on me leaving and entering Fairfield Shipyard. It very soon became apparent that most of my work could be completed by noon and that save for an occasional item the rest of the day was free.

In actual fact I had two bosses. Hutcheson the number one, who had helped me realise my early ambition, and Willie Patterson his assistant. Of the two Willies he was my favourite probably because he was a soft spoken, less demanding and because he unconsciously set me on the way up to the next financial level. Paterson like everyone else was happy when he could get some overtime. When he did he would ask me to get him something to eat from the local bakery. He also suggested one evening, that there were quite a number of people in the store-rooms who might also want something brought in.

As I went around I started to ask everyone if they needed anything brought in for their tea. There were other message boys in the complex but they either faced more restrictions or had never shown any great willingness to go out of their way. I not only preferred to be on the move than be sitting around the office waiting for work but also started to investigate other possibilities. Further down the Govan Road there was a fish and chip shop. If I placed an order earlier in the day I could pick up the hot food just on time to deliver it to the various departments dotted round the yard. I not only made myself good tips for delivering these working-class delicacies but also received free bags of chips as a form of incentive and reward for bringing this business. The free chips could easily be sold in any one of the departments once the aroma reached the worker's nostrils.

I then discovered another service I could provide. One of the sparks (electricians), convinced that he had a sure thing, asked me if I could put a line on, in 'the bookies'. I had visited bookmaker's shops before but not those nearest to the Shipyard. My only doubt was that the bookie might refuse the bet because of my age. 'Sparks'convinced me that with my size and heavy facial shadow no one would question me.

My new activity provided a temporary profit for 'Sparks' a temporary loss for the bookie and for me a continuous income. Word spread that I could not only be trusted to place bets but also collect winnings before the bookmaker closed. Something, the punters were sometimes unable to do, particularly if they were working overtime.

To place the bet I got a small tip. If the punter backed a winner I often got a generous gratuity. As the volume of betting increased I also received an incentive from the bookie, worried that I would walk two blocks to the next shop.

My private workload had now increased considerably and occasionally Willie Hutcheson became a little annoyed when I was absent from the office for long spells and an official errand was left undone. I had therefore to race back to the office every so often to make sure there was no letter or package to deliver. Although he knew I was making quite a lot of tips I'm sure he was unaware just how much I was making. At that time probably more than his salary, definitely, as a young single man with no commitments, my disposable income would have been far superior to his; a married man with children.

As yet I had no mates at work, I was still knocking about with Sandy, Rick and Alan. They were still at school. On the spare pieces of ground around Penilee we would often get up a challenge football match against other groups. One such group we played seemed to all come from the one area, a row of houses bordering the nearby Industrial Estate. Their self appointed spokesman was a small pugnacious good-looking guy called, you've guessed it ; Jimmy. I had come into contact with him before at the small shop across from where he lived which being the only one for miles must have catered at one time or another for just about everyone who either worked in the Industrial Estate or lived in either the two housing schemes Hillington and Penilee.

Jimmy McCarvill was part of a large family of proud Catholic Irish stock and he and his brother Eddie were unsurprisingly vocal in their support for Glasgow Celtic. Even without this as a potential point of conflict the probability of us becoming friends seemed remote. His smirk, swagger and challenging demeanour were sufficient provocation without his compelling need to make smart-ass comments. I'm unsure when and how the friendship developed although football was the catalyst. Before long I was part of a group of a dozen guys, ten of whom, including the McCarvill brothers, lived with 100 metres of each other. Apart from me, the only other who did not live within that confined area was Tam Tunicliffe (Tunny) whose family, coincidentally soon moved across the street from me. Tunny's father did not work as his health was bad due to his imprisonment and mistreatment in the hands of the Japanese during the war. Though I had already heard many stories about the war he was the first one I had met who had been in this theatre.

I was intrigued, but in the few occasions I had to talk to him Tunny ushered me away lest he 'start up with all that again'. I'm not sure if this was to prevent him from becoming maudlin or simply because he was personally bored with it ; I suspected the latter.

Tunny, a bespectacled lad with an in-built cynicism that fueled a dry humour was also a Celtic supporter. Along with the McCarvill brothers and another pair of brothers called Rab and Gus Findlay, Tunny made up the 'Tims' group while myself, Johnny MacIntosh, Vic Turnbull, Ronnie and Kenny Drysdale and Eddie Farrish we made up the Blue-nose brigade. Apart from the ribbing that both sides had to endure when results went against their team it was a surprisingly united group. From time to time other people joined our ranks for football and other social events. The Devine brothers Vince and 'Nank' were two who appeared from time to time. They were particularly interesting for different reasons. Vince was an Elvis devotee with haircut to match, the early style, not the much copied dyed-black bouffant much loved by latter-day impersonators. His other devotion was to whichever woman he happened to be going out with. So much so, that for long periods he would disappear out of circulation while his latest obsession lasted. Reports of his continued existence came from his brother Nank. I have yet to find out why and when his name Frank became Nank. Had he been nicknamed Wank there would, according to some of the lads, have been ample justification, as he was said to be determined to make himself blind before he reached his 20th year. There is no body of opinion which holds that the first stage of this is going colour blind, so this does not explain the Roman Catholic Nank's other perversity, his support for Glasgow Rangers. I think it was Tunny who said that, because of this, when he finally went to confession he would have to admit to self-abuse as well as to the wanking.

    The original intention of my father when he first secured the job for me in the Receiver's Office, was that I would work as an office boy for a minimum of one year and thereafter, be on hand to apply for any position that arose for a trade apprentice. I was more than happy with this plan at the time but when the first opportunity presented itself I was already earning more, as a "service provider", than any other apprentice. Furthermore, the position offered, that of Apprentice Miller, was for me one of the least attractive of the trades; being an operator of a small metal cutting machine. But once again, my father was fearful that if I refused a chance of learning a trade, any trade, the opportunity might not present itself again before I was obliged to leave the message-boy job. Both Willies in the office supported his argument. So at the tender age of sixteen I gave up a thriving cash-healthy business to don a blue boiler-suit and be assistant to "Yorkie" in the Light Machine Shop (LMS).
    George Geotens, was peculiar in many ways, not least because he was – in a Celtic dominated workforce – the only Englishman I had come across in Fairfield. He was, in fact, from Yorkshire, hence the inspired nickname Yorkie. He made no great secret of the fact that he wasn't entirely enamoured with the idea of having an apprentice. I didn't think

of it then, but on reflection, I believe he viewed me as an extra responsibility with little or no compensation. His basic salary could only be made attractive by piece-work and overtime so I suppose anyone who might take up his work-time or who could conceivably, in the future, take some or all of his work would have been viewed as a threat. However, after the first few days he did his best to conceal his displeasure and looked for ways in which I might be utilised to best serve his interests. So, the first lessons in my apprenticeship was how to fill his tea-can, clean down the machine, lift the heavy raw materials on to it and secure them ready for work. These new skills I managed to acquire without too much difficulty so within a few weeks he was extending me even further; I was now being allowed to stand by the machine as it performed its pre-set task and switch it off when the work cycle was complete; all this, while Yorkie ate his sandwich and drank his tea. Gradually I took over the other tedious parts of the work, leaving him free to wander off to chat with work-mates or read his morning paper. If a job was not carried out satisfactorily there was always the possibility that you could 'get yer bum felt' This was a "joke" of Yorkie's where, to keep a young apprentice on his toes, he assimilated a "poofter" and playfully groped his arse.

Because he did it so openly, and in such an exaggerated way, this didn't seem to arouse suspicion about his sexual proclivity, though it had to be said he picked his victims carefully – it was always a young boy and usually the least aggressive. I'm still unsure to this day if it was simply a crude, unfunny and overplayed joke or an indication of some suppressed tendency. In any case I began to indicate my dissatisfaction, not only with this but with my lack of instruction on the skills of the Miller.

It must have been around this time I started smoking in earnest. I had of course tried it before, but now it seemed to be almost obligatory; if one was to be taken seriously. Though cost was a factor, now that I had dropped down the income scale, a man had to be seen to be smoking something substantial; so I graduated to roll-ups along with a majority of the machine-shop work-force. With oil and grease covered hands hastily cleaned on a rag I would perform the delicate art of preparing a ciggie without dropping the tobacco tin or the fag itself on to the oily ground. I had also to take care not to saturate the paper, with any oil still on my hands, or it would flare up like a beacon when I lit it; destroying my new 'cool' image.

This was not the only new skill I was to pick up: I now became a contender for the crown of shove-halfpenny King. Archie Faulds, a senior apprentice, had for some time held the title. He had also been the founder of the Shove-Half-penny Cup and designer of the site where the daily competition took place. He discovered that the waist-high metal cupboard provided to store the machine operator's tools - not to mention tea-can, sugar, sandwiches and dirty magazines etc. – had an area and surface that, when buffed and polished, was ideal to house the LMS Open. Through his tireless efforts the Championship Arena had been completed within a few days. All this, without the lottery money that sports associations can call on today and with very little investment: except the work time and materials that he would normally have employed to make Fairfield's ship components.

Anyway, in this 'Theatre of Dreams' in my very first competition I went all the way to the final only to lose narrowly to Faulds in an extra time battle which took us past the lunch break, obliging us to post a look-out for a Hat's unwelcome arrival. The LMS had two "Hats": Archie Campbell and "Yogi". Campbell was the senior of the two but Yogi named, I'm still not sure why, after the cartoon character of that period Yogi Bear, was certainly the more active, and as such, the greater nuisance to those wishing to skive off or bend the rules in some way. Fortunately, being exceptionally tall, he, or at least the top of his bowler, could be seen from some distance. After my first Final there was no time for after match interviews Yogi was seen to be on his way: I scurried across to the Milling machine. Yogi approached.

'You're going t'get yer bum felt now,' sniggered Yorkie.

'I think yeh don't have enough tae take up yer time, Jimmy,' boomed Yogi, 'so we've goat somethin new that might interest you. If yeh want tae follow me?'

I had heard about the new machine which was being installed at the other end of the Shop. It was, to use today's terminology a cloning machine. A model of a large valve or bolt would be attached to the machine's cylinder and the raw material to be cut to the exact same shape and measurements would be secured alongside. After the set-up and tool adjustments had been made the machine would then, at high speed, cut an exact replica. Therefore multiple copies could be made within a short period. I was being offered the opportunity to learn and operate this new 'Profile Machine'. There was no need to give it much thought; not only would I have autonomy but in the bosses eagerness to get maximum rentability from their new toy – hence the offer to a low paid apprentice rather than a journeyman - I would be offered special piece-work rates to encourage production. Yorkie, who had come to value the flexibility an assistant afforded him, now found himself complaining that the apprentice he didn't want was being taken away from him. His dissatisfaction was also perhaps tinged with a little envy; the new machine looked like a money earner.

The Light Machine Shop was a Protestant department, had it been otherwise my father would not have suggested my entry and I'm sure others would have advised against it.

Not everyone who worked there was a Rangers' supporter, that was not a necessary qualification. The only qualification one needed, was not to be a Catholic. Nevertheless, many were Blue-noses, and my being one, certainly helped with my assimilation into the new group at the top end of the shop-floor. Here, the unofficial but generally accepted leader of the Gers' community was one, Maurice Nelson, who worked alongside me in the same machine-bay.

Nelson was in his mid 30's, of medium height and muscular build with fair hair in a cropped crew-cut style; he had an aggressive swagger and was ever-ready with a joke for his friends and a challenging comment for those who were not. Lunch and tea breaks were now usually spent, in his group, analysing the Blues' previous game, predicting the outcome of the next, celebrating Celtic's lost points, or denigrating their latest 'lucky' victory. Push half-penny competitions were now considered tame; in the space between the machines and the back wall we started keepy-uppy practice. Someone then marked out a goal and this became a daily cross and shoot in session in which Maurice and a few apprentices such as myself participated while older hands shouted advice. Disputing Maurice's decisions on whether a ball had crossed the line or not implied a willingness to engage him in another of his interests; wrestling. I spent many periods of my lunch break with my nose pressed to the oily floor. To him this was all good, if not exactly clean, fun. I along with the tall lean Joe Shepherd became his favourite boys; he convinced us that it was not enough to watch Rangers at home we must join the 'Brake Club' as the travelling supporter's club was called.

But it was not all fun, I was beginning to do some work at last. The set-up was the only technical part of the Profile-machine operator's job. Once this was done, the rest was simply vigilance: make sure the coolant was directed on to the tool ; make sure the cuttings didn't clog up the cutting area; check the cycle had been completed; measure the finished article; download it and prepare the next. The first two of those duties were particularly important because the machine tool cut through metal at great speed, creating intense heat, so much so, that the metal cuttings coming off would be glowing red then turn to a burnt blue. Sometimes the cuttings would come off like a continuous razor-edged streamer and this could wrap round the tool or the cylinder causing a jam-up, broken tool or damaged product. To remove or break this streamer I was equiped with a long metal prod with a hooked end.

Maurice Nelson had said when I first started on the machine that I would learn 'The Blue Chip Dance' one day, and though then I didn't know what he was talking about, I was soon to find out.

The customary blue boiler-suit I wore was open at the neck as was the shirt below. Crouching down behind the face-guard I was hacking the cuttings away from the tool-point; they then began to fragment and fly off as small super-heated metal fragments. One or two of those chips arced through the air and dropped down, inside the collar of my boiler-suit and shirt, on to my unprotected back. I now performed movements and gyrations - while kicking off my boots, to shed my boiler suit; then shirt – that a circus acrobat would have found difficult. Finally; topless, breathless, sweating, with my skin still stinging I looked down to the small blue fragments on the floor that I had dislodged from my back, then looked up to meet the smile of Nelson.

'Noo ye know whit the Blue Chip Dance is.' he said laughing.

But I was learning, and my productivity was increasing. Even Yogi, not the easiest man to please, seemed satisfied with my progress. I was surprised some months later when he asked my if I would like to be a Turner. My mate Rick was now serving his time as a Fitter in a factory. It seemed a good trade to have and I rather hoped I might get an opportunity to transfer just across to the other side of the LMS to the Fitter's Bay; but Turner also sounded good ; it was a step up from being an Apprentice Millar or Profile Machine Operator. My Dad was delighted.

Entrance to Fairfield Shipyard

The Crane in Fairfield Shipyard driven by my father

CHAPTER 13

Though he didn't say much then, save for a few general comments about the damage it could cause, my father would have been less than pleased with my integration into the Glasgow drink culture. Being unusually abstemious, for a working-class Glasgow man, one would have thought he would have taken a harder line with his only son but in most things he took the view that he should set the example, offer advice, but resist making futile prohibitions or ultimatums that might fracture relations. He was of course right; though he had chosen to abstain from alcohol and the social activity that goes with it, he knew that it was one thing for a country boy who spent most of his early years fishing, playing football and looking for work to take this path but quite another for a Glasgow youth to ostracise himself in such a way. Almost all social life centred round the pubs.

At least I did manage to make it home with my pay-packet after work on a Friday night, which is more than can be said for many of my older work colleagues, but this was only because I was anxious to get home, get cleaned up and get down the pub for a few 'bevvys' with the mates before we sloped off to the 'Flam'; the local Flamingo dance hall.

Those were the days when the pubs closed at 10 o'clock so customers 'raced the bell'. Though it was plain to everyone who frequented public houses that this limitation was the cause of much of the binge drinking, it was to take many many years before the message got to politicians and the licensing laws were liberalised. Actually, they probably got the message same time as everyone else but legislative change at that time might have proved politically troublesome with no immediate electoral or fiscal pay-back so they ignored the problem.

Anyway, by the time the bell was ringing for last orders, like most other regulars, we had built a reserve of two or three rounds and they stood on the bar waiting to be consumed. Though we would now try to stretch the drinking time out to the maximum, in effect, pressed by the barmen, to comply with the law, we usually gulped them down rapidly, then boldly and biliously made our way to "the dancin". Here we would meet with the next obstacle to a fulfilling night out – the door control. Dance hall owners, wary of being charged with keeping a disorderly house tried to limit the potent combination of – sex, in the shape of teenage girls, Glasgow street youth(often gang-affiliated), and alcohol. This they did by ejecting those obviously under the influence of the hard stuff. So while we shuffled along in a queue, bouncers would parade up and down the line looking for tell-tale signs. Obviously those staggering, singing, arguing, jostling or vomiting were first to receive marching orders and Police were nearby when, as was often the case, the decision of the judges was disputed.

But an even more stringent criteria was applied as you neared the door. Drooping eyelids, beatific smiles or pavement gazing could find you challenged and sniffed by the human bloodhounds. The - 'you've been drinkin' huvn't ye? - was a pointless question to a Glasgow youth on a Friday night but it was used more as a provocation than a genuine enquiry. It's still difficult to say if any particular response to this question was more successful than another; it was literally a lottery. However I must have been fairly successful at concealment for I was rarely ejected.

Once inside there was still the danger of ejection but even more humiliatingly there was, for me, the ever likely risk of rejection.

The primary reason, in fact the only reason, for a guy to go to "the dancin" was to pick up a bird. Some blokes liked dancing, though not many, and even those who did, would still admit their first priority in going, was to get themselves 'a lumber'. A lumber, was a agreement with a girl to let you take her home; that is - escort her to her street, maybe her close, possibly her door. Anything more was a major triumph. A modest objective it will probably sound to the autonomous youth of today but in the still naive early 60's when most teenagers in provincial cities lived with their parents this was a necessary if sometimes tedious procedure in the mating game. But before that, the other rituals had to be performed.

Usually your group of guys would take up a position on the perimeter of the floor from where they would "eye up the talent".

In effect, this meant we would watch the girls, some of whom would dance in pairs or groups on the dance floor, bunch together at certain points around the room or go for a sorties round the dancehall; all of them waiting to be approached by the right guy. Who invariably was not me.

The customary approach when you saw a girl you fancied was to sidle up and ask her if she would dance. To people such as my mates Jim McCarvill, Johnny Carmichael or Rick a smile, wink or slight inclination of the head would normally be enough when they caught the girl's eye.

For me, though emboldened by the alcohol, even the sidling-up required a test of nerve while articulating the request involved a few silent rehearsals. I may even have been the first to inspire the now cliché-ed put-down to the question " are ye dancin?"

" Naw, it's just the way I walk" said the little smart-arse as she walked on by.

As the night wore on, if the early refusals, had not completely sapped the confidence, your selection criteria became progressively less demanding. One had to measure the damage to the image of walking out with a bird, who had not quite made the list of most desirables, against the ignominy of going home oneself or in the company of other no-hoppers. But even in a last desperate attempt to salvage the night the ultimate humiliation could befall you. To get the knock back from the fat wall-flower who hadn't been on the dance floor all night.

But when you did get one, and had persuaded yourself that she wasn't too bad looking, the sniggering from mates as you took her out through the reception and cloakroom area, served as a preliminary to what you would suffer next day at the post mortum.

'Well, where did she live…Crookston cat and dog home?' *explosion of laughter.!!*

'So, did ye get a snog…or the haun in, maybe?' Whatever your answer the response would display the level of hypocrisy inherent in the young Glasgow male. If you announced any success with your sexual advances – 'yeh, she looked like a slag'. If you said she discouraged any such advance – 'Yeh, we could've telt ye she wiz a waste o time!'

It must be admitted that I often had to use the excuse that I didn't take a lumber because I left early to go up the 'chippie' because I wiz starvin'.

After one Wednesday night at Hampden Park in May 1960 the lunch-time kick-about at Fairfield Shipyard took on a new flavour. Instead of crosses into our makeshift goal-mouth coming from an Alex Scott impersonator and the conversion from a pretend Jimmy Millar or other Rangers' favourites, those being imitated were Fransisco Gento, Alfredo Di Stefano and Ferenc Puskas. Although Brazilians and Hungarians, in previous years, had already made an impression on the insular minds of Scottish football fans, the Real Madrid European Cup Final victory over Eintracht Frankfurt in our own national stadium was to have the greatest impact. Gers' supporters, such as my father and myself, had already endured the humiliation of losing heavily to the German Champions and we fully expected them to shock the already famous Real Madrid.

At first, though I loved all football, I wasn't sure if I really would enjoy watching two foreign teams playing for the title I had hoped so much that Rangers would be there, especially with the final being in Glasgow, but Dad had bought the tickets and said it would be a match worth watching. That must go top of the list of sporting understatements of all time. For the quality of its football the game still must be the greatest club match ever. The final score was Real Madrid 7 Eintracht Frankfurt 3, Di Stefano scored three and Puskas three for the Spanish club after Frankfurt had taken the lead, but the statistics can never accurately reflect the magical performance we witnessed that night.

Things were going relatively smoothly, I was learning the Turner's trade and had enrolled in Stow College of Engineering on a one day work release course with a view to giving myself even better qualifications. At nights I would meet the guys from the Penilee group or ex-school mates in the pub or in one of the cafes. Though I don't remember the period as being particularly violent there were of course skirmishes between the various gangs, particularly after they spilled out from the pubs or the dancing. Drink-fuelled macho posturing or disputes over girls rather than any territorial battle seemed to be the catalysts. At this time I had befriended a boy at the day release class who turned out to be a younger brother of one of the leaders of a notorious gang of that time; the Govan Team. This put me on nodding terms with people who normally I would have tried to avoid and gave me a kind of vicarious street-cred that I have to admit I did not at first discourage.

I made no attempt to join their ranks on any official basis but occasionally at the dancehall, if my young friend John was bunched with other members of his brother's group, I would wander over to chat with him. This pathetic attempt to re-brand myself had nothing to do with wanting to be an actual hardman, with all the dangerous activity that this entailed, and everything to do with the fact that those guys always seemed to have birds hanging around them. I saw no immediate effect but one night as we were leaving the Flamingo a girl chose to recognise my new found identity. Encouraged by her smile I launched into my infallible chat-up line but her response was not as quick as a bloke who stood nearby.

'Hey Marie, never mind that skinny bastard, come o'er here!'

Before I - the skinny bastard - could retaliate, she answered him.

'You better watch yersel, he's wan o the Govan Team!'

'Oh zat right?' he said swaggering up to me, backed by two others. 'Well we're the Pollock Team. Whit ye gonny dae aboot it?'

Having no immediate plan to do anything about it, but street-sharp enough to know that while I did not want to provoke action, it was also never wise to show vulnerability. I stood my ground, eyeballed my protagonist while smirking confidently, and tried to stay alert to any sudden moves on their part. Silent prayer also played an unseen part in the strategy. After a few endless seconds they began to melt away in retreat. But as hubris was about to take over and provoke in me a taunting response to their back-down both my arms became locked in tight physical restraint. Other blue clad figures now brushed by to also apprehend my Pollock opponents.

We were hustled to the nearby Police station.

It was not, of course my, nor the Pollock boys, first brush with 'the Polis'; no Glasgow street kid could escape their attention. But it seemed in the light of increased gang activity they had decided to be more pro-active. I'm not sure what rights of detention or what interview procedures were in place back then, but I'm sure the tactics employed had not come from any textbook. We were lined up army style, and one by one a sergeant put himself in our face in what seemed to be an attempt to provoke us into a hasty comment or arrest-able offence.

'So you think you're a fuckin hardman, Eh? Ye look like a poof tae me!'

No response.

'So whit team is it, the Govan Team? A bunch a big Lassies if yeh ask me!'

No response.

He threatened charges of unlawful assembly and loitering but it was clear they had no real justification. They proceeded to take our names and addresses and I heard one of the Policeman saying he had heard the girl saying I was one of the Govan Team. I was warned before they let me go that they would be looking out for me. I decided then that there was no great advantage from gang affiliation and to the great disappointment of my many female admirers I also decided that a period of absence from the Flamingo would also be advisable.

Another of Glasgow's institutions was next to receive a visit from me; the Southern General Hospital. I was of course no stranger to hospitals but this time it was not to be about a respiratory problem although the accident did cause some heavy breathing for a while.

Though not quite so fast as the profile machine, jobs on the centre lathe could present similar problems. It was necessary to regulate the temperature not only of the tool but also the metal being cut, with coolant liquid while keeping the point of contact free from cuttings. I was having difficulty removing some debris from the bore of a flange and inserted a small brush to sweep it away when a large cutting wrapped round my finger dragging my hand onto the cutting point. Fortunately, though shocked and in extreme pain, I had the presence of mind and luckily a free hand within reach of the button, to stop the machine. My colleagues on either side, no doubt hearing my scream of pain, were quick to the scene and helped me extricate my mangled digits. I was now sitting on my tool-box in shock. Somebody was holding my wrist in the air, while another wrapped a towel round it to stem a fountain of blood. Yogi was now on the scene, putting a cigarette in my mouth which my trembling mouth promptly chewed before it dropped in the pool of blood at my feet. This he attempted several times and I'm told that the notoriously mean Gaffer was now becoming even more distressed than I was.

The shipyard ambulance took me to the emergency ward at the Southern which was only ½ mile down the Govan Road. The scars I still bear today although the surgeon stitched it well, but according to the LMS wags, Yogi never fully recovered from the loss of an almost entire packet of Senior Service.

Although Apprentice Turner was still not as lucrative as my earlier position of Bookie's Runner I was managing to pay for the essentials of life such as beer, cigarettes and match tickets while putting a little aside for a summer break. But once again my kitty was to be enlarged by income from a bookmaker. A Saturday in March 1961 and after a couple of pints we left the pub to be on our way to the match at Ibrox making a brief stop at the 'bookies' as the lads wanted to have a bet on the big one – the Grand National. Because of my previous experiences with betting at Fairfield I got the usual jokes about me being an expert and therefore should decide what horse to put the money on. I gave my traditional response that I myself didn't gamble, and had only made money before from the mugs who did. Nevertheless, while I waited and perused the list of runners I decided to have a flutter, in the end employing the dumbest system possible to make my selection; it was an outsider, the horse's name for some reason caught my attention and was unusual, it being grey. I actually placed the bet while they were still studying form and didn't tell them.

When the announcement was made at Ibrox over the loudspeaker that the winner at 28-1 had been Nicholas Silver, I think my roar of surprise may have been the loudest ever heard at the Stadium.

The Glasgow 'Fair Fortnight' was by tradition two weeks in July when local industry more or less closed down to enable the workforce to take off for a holiday to Largs, Rothsay or - for those with more exotic taste and a little nest-egg - Blackpool.

Sandy, Rick, Alan, Bally and yours truly hit the sea and sand on July 1964 for fourteen days of activities we normally reserved for only Fridays and Saturdays, boozing and bird chasing. We also hoped to catch a little sun, if there was any, and if we managed to get up before it set. One major event was planned, a live performance at the Empress Ballroom by the Rolling Stones. It was to be historic gig, not only for us but also for the Stones.

As I write this it has just been announced that after a prohibition lasting 44 years the Stones will finally be permitted to return to Blackpool. Although the Group, or to be accurate Keith Richards, was the main catalyst for what eventually became a riot, the naivety of the organisers was a major contributory factor.

During the Glasgow holiday Blackpool overflowed with drunken Glaswegian youths many of them affiliated to street gangs. Most of them would have great difficulty entering a Glasgow ballroom in the inebriated state they were in that night. Even when permitted to enter sober, in such numbers, there would have been a large Police presence.

It must also be said that although the Glesga' guys had embraced the new swinging sixties, Beatles and all that, the prancing effeminate antics of Mick Jagger was still too much of a target for the bevied macho members of a Gorbals or Govan team.

From where we stood half-way down the hall and to the side we could see quite clearly that some of our rowdiest compatriots were right at the front of the stage and there were no steward/minders to restrain them. I was personally enjoying what was then a revolutionary treatment of what was really traditional rhythm and blues; but it was evident from the gestures at the front that trouble was brewing. Suddenly we saw Richards aim his boot at the face of one of the guys at the stage-front and effectively the show was over. The Stones fled backstage as the horde mounted the stage and those officials and police who were there had to throw themselves into the fray while reinforcements were called. Fortunately we were able to make a fairly untroubled exit through one of the side doors as 'rock n roll' history was being made.

Almost all of my mates talked continuously of making a break from Glasgow. Most of them had no definite plan, just a vague idea that things would be better for them elsewhere. This was to some extent the restlessness of youth but also a response to the very obvious decline in Glasgow's main industries. Jim McCarvill was already discussing a career in the Army, Sandy and Alan had decided to go to London, others had even more ambitious ideas. Those with no immediate plans to wander, had a serious relationship going on with a girl. So I, who was not 'winchin', and therefore footloose and girlfriend free, could see myself spending all my time with other sad, single, stay-at-homes waiting for the eventual redundancy notice.

Though he would have hated to think he had contributed in any way to my decision to leave home, my father's oft-expressed fears that the Shipyard's sparse order books might mean lay-offs also had an effect; though he was worrying about his own job security and not mine. So, during the period of inactivity, while I recovered from my industrial injury, I considered for the first time one of the traditional paths open to shipyard apprentices - the Merchant Navy.

Each time I was about to act on this idea of going off to sea, a new and exciting prospect appeared on the horizon. The first prospect was a

I contrived to bump into her several times in the following weeks. My surprising and unusual persistence must have worn her down because she eventually agreed to go out with me. We were already into the decade which was to be called 'the swinging 60's' and the 'the years of sexual liberation' but she hadn't yet made the adjustment. She preferred plodding to swinging and hibernation to liberation. It soon blossomed into a fully fledged platonic relationship and after one tempestuous night when I twice managed to kiss her on the cheek she suggested a cooling off period. I then took solace in my music and football.

A couple of guys I had recently got to know at the engineer collage were forming a band and were looking for a singer. Was this to be the start of a decadent life of sex, drugs and rock-and-roll? If it was, it had a rather tame start. After several months of practice we finally got a gig. The occasion was a birthday party for the son of our base guitarist's Scout leader and the venue was no less than the biggest Scout Hall, at that time, in Springburn. The booking did not go without hitches. First our drummer arrived home without a key to find his mum had gone out. So we were short of a drum-kit and could only borrow a side drum from one of the scouts. Then someone blew the electric circuit and we had to begin the first part un-plugged, many years before such sessions became fashionable.

Nevertheless, with fame now beckoning, the seafaring idea was put on hold.

Almost in tandem with potential pop stardom my football career was taking a massive lurch forward, from the back end of the Light Machine Shop and the spare bit of ground in Penilee, to the dizzy heights of juvenile pitches. Shuggy Fernie was a modest forerunner of today's soccer agent. He assured me that by signing for the newly formed Clyde Rovers I would be taking the first step to a professional career and I might conceivably be the new 'Slim Jim', a reference to Jim Baxter of Rangers the current idol of Ibrox. He assured me, that this new team would probably become the nursery for their namesakes in the First Division and in any case he was already working on getting me trials for other top teams including Queen's Park Strollers (the reserve squad of the famous amateur team). Though ever willing to embrace any idea that rescued me from being a shipyard or factory worker or even worse a redundant factory or shipyard worker, I took his claims with a pinch of salt. Nevertheless, I did pay his introductory fee of two pints of heavy.

I couldn't say it wasn't fun, but the scouts present at the first performance were to be the only type I would see either at my matches or the gigs. After nearly two years of muddy pitches, postponed matches, depleted teams and dodgy referees on one side and half empty halls, drunken accompany-ists, bad acoustics and late paying publicans on the other I decided fame could wait until I had made some money at sea.

CHAPTER 14

It's probably as well that young people can not fully comprehend the effect their decision to leave home can have on some parents; it might unreasonably inhibit them. Only now, as a father myself, having experienced the departure of my own son, do I realise the mixture of sadness and concern my parents must have felt when I suddenly announced that I had signed up to join the Merchant Navy. The decision must have appeared impetuous, although unbeknown to them I had been thinking about it for a long time and anticipating their opposition had avoided discussing it at home.

Probably for the first and last time my mother prayed I would fail a medical but I was given the all clear and the rest of the process moved with indecent speed. Within two weeks I was given notification that I would be Junior Engineer on board the S.S. City of Birmingham. Perhaps the recruitment team feared that young men given too much time to contemplate their decision might change their mind, or have it changed for them by their mother.

Dad had resigned himself to the inevitable and perhaps in a way felt some pride that I had taken such a bold step, but Mum could not reconcile herself to the fact that within a few weeks her sickly waif would be on his way to the other side of the world without someone in attendance to advise him when to wear his coat and scarf.

To this day I remember that only a few nights before my departure when we were sitting round the television, the BBC with perfect timing chose to offer the film "the Cruel Sea".

'You see whit happens at sea?' said mother as the crew took to the lifeboats after their ship had been torpedoed by the German U-Boat.

'Good God Woman! Have ye no noticed, the war's bin o'er fur nearly twenty years!' intervened my father in irritation, before I could respond. But she made no attempt to qualify her statement.

With the benefit of experience and hindsight I can now look back on their reactions with more understanding. The example my mother chose may have been illogical but the concern for her only son's welfare was not. My father's frustration with her, was probably a lot to do with her re-awakening his own concerns at a time when he was trying to come to terms with them.

Today the world is a smaller place, when my own son is going abroad alone he carries a mobile phone with an international roaming connection, so we have the comfort, and he perhaps some irritation, of knowing we can contact him at any time. This was not so, in those days. As I waved goodbye at the station on my way down south to join the ship my parents knew that apart from a quick long distance call from some phone booth in England, once I had set sail the best they could expect was to receive a letter every now and again that had been written weeks before.

The agent met me and took me on board the S.S. City of Birmingham, a 7599 ton Ellerman Line cargo and passenger ship which had been built on the Clyde. Entry qualifications in those days being more relaxed than today I was given the post of 6th Engineer Officer; not as exalted a position as it sounds, being that there were only six engineers on board.

The information on my duties, the constitution of the crew and the ship's itinerary had, and continued to be, sketchy to say the least; I was not really to find out everything until my first meeting with Scouse George. But before that, the first person I was to meet on board was the small bespectacled 2nd Engineer, who on a day to day basis for those first few months of my Merchant Naval career was to be my direct boss. The mind's filing system seems to reject certain people as unmemorable because at this moment I cannot even recall his name. No such problem exists with (Scouse)George Barton the 4rd Engineer who for this trip was to be my mentor in all activities both professional and personal. The six feet plus, muscular ex-SAS man had an opinion on everything and a name for everyone. He looked indestructible and was certainly indefatigable. It was he who first warned me that Chief Engineer Greenacre was 'an unpleasant bastard' but probably wouldn't be too visible or active during the trip.

The Birmingham was a passenger ship only in a very limited sense in that it had 12 cabins allocated for passengers who fancied a longer and more adventurous type of voyage than those offered by companies with sleek ocean going liners. As I remember there were only a few passengers on board and I was rarely to see them. The real commercial viability of the ship rested principally on the transportation of cargo.

It wasn't long before I became aware not only of the importance of professional ranking on board these ships but also the underlying social divisions. For some reason a Deck Officer invariably considered himself superior to an Engineer even though the latter was sometimes senior in rank and salary. This was, not only, because as deck officers they were directly subordinate the highest ranked Officer on board, the Captain, and aspired to hold that rank one day, but also because they were recruited from a supposed higher social section of the population. This snobbery was even more clearly exemplified by the Purser, who being an administrator, also exuded an air of social superiority. Like myself, most Engineers, the Chippy (carpenter) and Sparks (electrician) were from working-class stock. But not to worry, there were plenty of people on board that we could feel superior to. Under a long standing arrangement, ships of the British merchant fleet employed Indian and Pakistan crew. So all crew on the City of Birmingham below my own particular rank were Lascars. A term which today seems to be considered pejorative though it was in common usage then and described seamen of Asian or Far Eastern origin.

There are many tasks, especially on a cargo steamship, which are labour-intensive and do not require a great amount of education or skill so Lascars from impoverished backgrounds were a cheap and readily available means of crewing the merchant vessels. Among their ranks there also existed clear professional, social, ethnic and religious divisions which often had to be taken into consideration when addressing them or assigning them duties.

In my newly acquired working uniform of white boiler-suit I reported to the 2nd on my first day to be informed of my duties. We met in the locker room and from there a door led to the engine room. Surprisingly for one employed to be the ship's junior engineer officer I had never actually been in a fully operational engine room, only having seen, in Fairfield Shipyard, part finished ships and engine constructions in the main shed. The frightening maze of tubes, valves, casings, pumps, shafts and gauges stretched below us for three levels connected by the metal stairway which we now descended to 'the plates' on the bottom level. Once down there, with the gauges of the control panel in front of us and the boilers behind, the 2nd started by explaining the work schedule. I already knew the 24 hours of each day was traditionally broken up into six four-hour working shifts called 'watches'. Each Officer and crew member was scheduled to cover two watches per day with eight hour breaks between: So there were two 12 to 4 watches, two 4 to 8 watches, and the two 8 to 12 watches. The 2nd Engineer covered the 4 to 8's, and I was earmarked to take watch with him until we were on open sea, then I would cover some day duties. At my request he seemed to grudgingly go through the main responsibilities the watch-keeper had, drawing attention to the gauges and what potential problems they might indicate, and how those were to be avoided or rectified. He also covered the more serious alarms and how we should react to them if they went off.

I had already been warned by my new mentor, Scouse George, over some beers the night before, that during the watch, as junior, I would have one particularly onerous duty – the blowing of the tubes. This was a procedure involving the opening up of valves which in this particular vessel were at the back of the boilers. This sent a burst of steam up the tubes to dislodge, and expel accumulated impurities via the smoke stack, that if left could cause problems to the efficiency of the steam generation process. According to George - behind the boilers, when the ship was at full steam, opening by hand these large stiff valves was hard work. It was stiflingly hot, dirt particles and dust stuck to your sweat soaked hair and skin and clogged up your lungs if you remained too long in there.

Though I would not be obliged to carry this out until we were in open sea the 2nd did confirm I would have this little responsibility. In doing so, he didn't use his 4th Engineer's dramatic and colourful language to describe the task. He was also more diplomatic when talking about the abilities of the native crew, pointing out that, occasionally they could be less than efficient, and I should always make sure they had carried out essential maintenance duties. At this point I was introduced, without ceremony, to the two crew members hovering in the background; the Serang who was chief of the native crew and the Kassab who was the store-keeper. Both men gave a little bow of the head and greeted their new Chay-Sahib, which means Sixth Sir, with all due deference. Only right, it wasn't their business to know that Chay-Sahib was totally ignorant of his duties as 6th Engineer Officer and was becoming more daunted by the minute.

By the time I turned-to for my first watch we were already underway. Entering the Engine-room when at full steam was quite a different experience than when the engines were at rest. The deep throb could be felt on the upper deck but the incredible noise, which later I would become accustomed to, assaulted the ears when I climbed through the upper door. The temperature had also risen considerably.

I was down on the plates before the 2nd arrived and happy to hear from Scouse George, before he took off, that it had been a quiet watch with no irregularities. We watched as a short pale figure made his way slowly down using the handrails as crutches. Never particularly animated at any time my superior looked as if he might still be asleep but he did nod recognition of our presence and seemed to listen as George went through the hand-over procedure. I was to learn as the trip progressed that at least one hour had to pass of the morning watch before the 2nd recovered the power of speech. Not that this presented any great hardship to me as even when his vocal chords were functioning, he rarely said anything of any great interest. We were not yet in open sea so the pleasure of blowing the tubes would wait till the following morning; I busied myself with the few tasks I had been allocated the day before, and slowly acclimatised myself to the new surroundings.

The next morning was to be more eventful to say the least. I had started with the tube-blowing having, as instructed, first called to inform the bridge officer. This was done to permit a temporary change of course if he assessed that they wind direction might cause the expelled materials to end up on the decks. I was quickly learning that Scouse George never understated the difficulty or unpleasantness of anything. Breathing heavily, covered in grime and with my sweat-soaked boiler suit stuck to my body I returned to the desk in front of the control panel after my first experience of this daily task. I was about to call the bridge again to inform them the tube blowing was over when the 2nd Engineer propped upon a stool, sipping tea but not yet through his waking period, annoyingly mimicked a phone call with an economy of effort to remind me of the procedure.

Having communicated with the bridge I was then offered, by another silent gesture, some tea and was about to pour when suddenly all hell broke out. A repetitive bleeping and then a sound like an air raid siren had my superior tumble from his stool, before gathering himself to move off with uncommon haste towards the pumps on the starboard side. The Indian crewmembers were shouting – 'Lube, Lube!' I followed him uncertainly and looked up to see Harry the 3rd Engineer still in flip-flops come slaloming down the metal gangway closely followed by Scouse George. To prove how unsuitable, but aptly named, this footwear is for fast nimble descent Harry caught his toe on the last flight and flipped over, flopping on the plates of the lower level with a metallic thud. Scouse George with no room for manoeuvre joined him painfully and noisily. I say noisily, because as they collided the overriding sound of the alarm ceased, permitting us to hear their exclamation, grunts and expletives. They hadn't yet recovered or raised themselves from the floor when the 2nd appeared.

'Everything's in order, you can, get yourselves back up top when you've, er,' he looked at them with mild curiosity then turned to me, 'Sixer, come let me explain about this pump.'

The importance of lubrication to the rapid moving parts of a steam turbine engine hardly needs emphasising. The malfunction of lubricating machinery did not inspire the term – *all hands to the pump* – but it could have. This alarm was one of several that would rouse those off-duty as well as on. It was an early lesson for me though fortunately this time one with no serious consequences, except of course the bumps and bruises suffered by the 3rd and 4th Engineers.

One of the eight hour periods off-duty each day was usually spent in my cabin, sleeping. My notion of a sailor's life had been taken from films where only the Captain and First Mate had their own quarters, but before signing up I was informed that I would have my own cabin. It wasn't de-luxe but for a boy who'd lived his earlier years with his parents in a single-end it was more than adequate, measuring around 18sq mts and furnished with a bunk, day-bed, chest of drawers, desk and hard chair. Compared with the other officers' cabins I'd seen it was still somewhat Spartan, but several of them had been with this ship for some time and the others all had put in sea-time on other ships. They had therefore brought the little extras that make a cabin more homely such as family photos, alarm clocks, record players and radios etc., while I had brought only the basic necessities of life, as advised by the agent. Scouse George had already promised to show me where to get the best deals in radios when we reached Aden, one of our ports of call.

But in these early days these refinements didn't matter that much, my mind was fully occupied learning the technical necessities of the job and absorbing the experience of life on board a ship at sea.

The galley and Officers' Mess provided me with insight into the general workings of the ship outside of the engine room; the tensions within and between the various departments; and more scarily, the news of political and military developments in countries where our ship would dock. It was 1965 and increasing instability in the Middle East promised an interesting trip, our initial stops being Port Said on through the canal to Suez and then Aden.

As we sailed down to the Mediterranean I was scheduled on day-work, so apart from the dubious pleasure of tube-blowing a lot of my time, weather permitting, was spent on open deck, repairing and maintaining winches. These fixed steam-driven machines would be used extensively for stowing and discharging cargo in ports unequipped with cranes or dockside winching equipment so they had to be in good condition.

I was assisted by an Indian crewman whose tasks included carrying, and providing tools on demand, assisting to lift heavy equipment, oiling and cleaning. He performed another function unbeknown to him. When the ever-changing natural light played with mesmeric effect on the similarly ever-changing vast open sea, his clattering and chattering often broke the hypnotic trance into which I'd fallen, as I sat on the cargo hatches gazing outwards. By inadvertently breaking the spell, he no doubt rescued the new Chay Sahib from a bollocking for falling behind on the work schedule.

I was scheduled back on watch as we approached land on my first trip; not with any specific duties more to observe the engine-room procedures as we received orders from the Bridge. The urgent ring of the bridge telegraph, used dramatically in so many early naval films, caused my pulse to race. I could imagine all sorts of things going wrong. Two teams, separated by five decks and communicating with each other via a mechanical device were regulating the speed of thousands of tons of steam-driven metal to bring it to rest at a specific berth. Of course I knew it had been done many times before by the same crew and, on the bridge, the staff would be guided by the expert knowledge of the local Pilot. But in the whole procedure the engineer's part, played blind, was something I found just a little disconcerting. Naturally, I tried to conceal any sign of nervousness and give the impression that the next docking could safely be left to me.

Port Said is at the Mediterranean entrance to the Suez Canal which was first constructed in 1869 and had been nationalised by Egypt in 1956, an action that led directly to what was called the Suez Crisis. Now the region, which had never really settled at any time, was in turmoil again and though so far our passage through the canal did not seemed threatened in any way, news was coming through that at our next Port of call Aden we would receive special instructions to cover emergency orders now imposed because of insurgency from neighbouring regions.

I'd been told that the ship's agent at each port delivered any mail addressed to us and despatched letters we wished to send. I dashed off a letter to my parents to assure them of my well-being and the intriguing aspects of my new profession. I didn't bother to give details of my next port of call, because by the time the letter arrived we would've already moved on to the Far East, but more importantly I omitted reference to Aden as I knew it would currently be in the news for all the wrong reasons.

Ships travelled through the canal in convoys entering by Lake Manzala on to Al Ballah, Lake Timsah and Al Kabrit on the Great Bitter Lake, all points where Northbound convoys could be seen passing. The journey through to Suez took about 15 hours some of it I was able to watch from deckside.

A feature of Middle and Far Eastern ports which I would come to recognise would be the 'traders' who'd come by the dockside or near to the ship in their small craft referred to as 'Bum-boats'. These days some of these people will undoubtedly be offering more dangerous products such hard drugs but then, although customs officers disagreed, the goods on offer were harmless if not legitimate. I'd already been advised by Scouse George that I could equip my cabin with necessities such as transistor radio and record player and alarm clock when we got ashore in Aden. There was also a possibility, he said, that I could make some extra money by buying cheap goods in one country and sell them for profit in another, but for now I should resist the sales pitches.

'How's it gon' Jimmy?' A Glaswegian voice greeted me as I passed the gangway. I turned to see a dark skinned person in Arab clothes. He sidled up closer.

'D'ye want tae buy a great wee tranny? He said opening the zip in his bag to display a transistor radio. Our Chippy, standing nearby, could see the look of surprise on my face; he smiled and shoo-ed the salesman away.

'How'd he know ...'

'He came on board with our agent,' Chippy laughed, 'A lot of them picked up accents from the British soldiers out here –they're good at it. He takes advantage of his work with the agent to peddle things while he's on board.'

'But how'd he know my name and that I was Glaswegian?'

'Oh, he'll know Glasgow lads use Jimmy as a name for anybody they don't know and maybe he's heard you speak to a deck wallah or asked one of them who the new officers are.'

I was told to expect even more commercial activity round the ship in Aden but when we got there security measures had drastically changed all that. Terrorist outrages in and around Aden had forced the Government to declare a State of Emergency so military personnel were everywhere in evidence and access to the docks for those with no good reason to be there was prohibited. There was also a rumour that British crew members might be confined to ship which would've been a great disappointment because this was to be my first opportunity to get ashore in a foreign port , or to put it in seamen's parlance- get *up the road*. As it turned out I was to get ashore with Alistair the 5th Engineer and Brian one of the junior deck officers; it was to be a short visit. We had been advised to keep within a certain area and as both my companions had been here before, I left the orienteering to them.

There had been a number of bombs thrown into bars and restaurants by terrorists so they had been declared out-of-bounds for British Military personnel and we were advised, if we were to venture ashore, to comply with this policy. Under my colleagues guidance we set out to explore a nearby commercial area, our main objective being to have a look around and pick up a few bargains. Ominously, on our way through the streets, we passed several British Army foot patrols and armoured cars.

Shopkeepers were to say the least forceful, and once again we heard their full repertoire of British dialects, but with some I felt an underlying current of animosity. The custom of bartering each price, being in essence confrontational, didn't help.

But I was quite happy. I'd managed to get a transistor, alarm clock and a few souvenirs all within my budget and Scouse George's price guidelines. Alistair and I were by the entrance to an arcade of small shops and stalls, waiting for Brian, who had returned inside to re-engage in bartering for a record-player that had earlier caught his eye. Suddenly, an explosion of shouting broke the relative calm and a few moments later a disturbed Brian came hurrying out followed by a group of Arabs.

'Move, let's move!' he called to us. 'They're getting really nasty!'

We followed him quickly to the nearest corner and though the rabble had pursued us for a few yards they'd now stopped and contented themselves with verbal threats and insults, most of it incomprehensible, except – *Kill British Pigs*.

We were about to turn the corner when two fully equipped Squaddies appeared from nowhere. 'Whit's up here boys, a wee bit o' trouble?' said one of them as they cast their watchful eyes down the street to the now dispersing Arabs.

'Yeah, I was trying to buy a record player,' Brian sighed, 'I agreed the price and gave them some money, then first they refused to give me the change and then claimed it was for another player which wasn't as good. When I told them to forget the whole thing and give me back my money, they got nasty, started threatening me and then some others joined in.'

'Okay, sounds like one of their stunts,' said the other soldier, 'Let's go and have a word.'

By the time we reached the arcade they had all gone back to their sales points. We marched in, an armed soldier on either side, with a mixture of bravado and apprehension.

Brian pointed them to the vendor he had been dealing with who was pretending not to notice our approach. He then looked up with feigned surprise.

'Yes, can I help, ees there some problem?'

'Yeah, this man gave ye some money but the sale didnae go ahead, so you should return his money,' said the soldier as his colleague kept a wary eye on the other sellers.

'Ah I theenk maybe meesunderstand, but okay no problem I geeve money,' the Arab shrugged and began rummaging about his drawer for the pounds.

When Brian had received the money we edged our way out but not before soldiers had given them a warning about their threatening behaviour.

Thanking the soldiers profusely, we made our way back to the dockside to take their advice and stay aboard ship until sailing time. We had invited them back for a drink but they couldn't take up the offer as they were on duty patrolling the streets until after we sailed. The 'Dizzies' had to be kept at bay, they said. A Dizzie, we had learnt, was the Squaddies' abbreviation of their official categorisation -Dissident. A somewhat benign term for a violent terrorist; my bet is that they were originally designated thus by a Politician or Bureaucrat, far removed from their bombs and guns.

CHAPTER 15

Only now, when writing about this period of my life, have I come to realise just how self absorbed I was as a young man. Political events of historical importance were going on all around me in the countries we visited and with the exception of incidents that affected me personally, such as in Aden, I was for the most part oblivious of their importance.

Today I would study each country and each city before I got there. I would know, what I was not aware of then, that Singapore, the first of four ports we would visit in Malaysia, was in the midst of a period of turmoil and transition and would become an independent City State within months. But I was wrapped up in my own world of blowing tubes, maintaining steam winches and oiling pumps while anticipating only, when I finally got ashore, a cultural study of the activities on the famous Bugis (Boogie) Street; a visit essential in the educational programme of a young mariner, according to Scouse George.

Another example of this self absorption is the fact that to this day I can't say what cargoes the ship was carrying either to or from our ports-of call. Amazing when one considers that the only purpose of all our work was to enable the transportation of materials from one place to another.

'Up the road' was the term used for going ashore. I was to learn yet another term when I got to Boogie Street. My shipmates had, for their own amusement, discretely communicated to the 'katies' the beautiful prostitutes who patrolled the area, that the young *inexperienced* fresh faced officer, who accompanied them, was on his first trip. I therefore became 'Cherry Boy' and as such the focus of much attention. As my alcohol consumption increased, any resistance I might have mounted diminished, and I began to consider which of the beauties would win my cherry. Fortunately, at this point I was forced to answer another call of nature and broke off for a quick visit to the toilet. There, I started a brief conversation with an Aussie about the Bar's poor wash-up facilities but moved on to an appraisal of the place's other attractions.

'…yeah, bloody amazing place, and those *katies*…they're gorgeous. If you didn't know they were all guys you could get yourself in a lot of trouble.'

My look of amazement alerted him. 'Aw bloody Hell! I've ruined it! Hey don't tell your buddies I blew it, will you…?'

I didn't tell them, as I preferred to pretend that I had always known and I was playing them along and, to further substantiate my sexual preferences, I insisted they show me where I'd get a real woman. They did, and that night I officially lost my Cherry-Boy epithet.

Labuan, Jessleton, Sandaken and Tawau, from there on to Manila and Masinloc both in the Phillipines. The names of the places changed as our trip progressed but for some the backdrop was largely irrelevant. The plan was more or less the same wherever they were – knock off watch; scrub up; get 'up the road'; maybe, buy a few items including a souvenir for someone at home; and then, in spite of earlier resolutions- get pissed and 'bag-off' with one of the local bar-girls. I could see myself being caught up in this cycle and made an effort to limit my activities ashore to some sightseeing and shopping. Not until we reached Hong Kong was I to come under any real temptation and even there with all that the former colony had to offer the former Cherry Boy stood firm.

Bangkok was to be a different story.

I'd gone ashore with one of the deck officers and a cadet but as the night wore on had drifted to the company of engineers from another ship who were unfortunately downing drinks like there was to be no tomorrow; my session with them was almost to make that the case.

Inevitably as I became more and more drunk I attracted attention from the nightgirls and a few drinks later reached an agreement with one of them. To this day I'm not sure where we went or how we got there but she must have taken me by taxi to a shack almost in the jungle. At some point before, after, or maybe even during the sex act, I must have fallen asleep to be wakened abruptly by screaming and shouting. I propped myself up and found several dark skinned youths with knives had formed an arc around my bed, another was holding the distressed girl against the wall. A drink and sleep-induced stupor mixed with paralyzing fear prevented me from moving or uttering a sound. One of them rifled through the pockets of my discarded clothes, removing what little money I had left before throwing the garments to the bed where I now crouched, un-moving, in wide-eyed silence. The apparent leader pointed to the clothes with his machete-like weapon and commanded me to dress. My failure to do this as quickly and efficiently as I would have liked was obviously amusing them and though I couldn't understand the language I could imagine the ribald comments. More signals with the blade indicated I should accompany them out through the hallway to the main door. Once outside I quickly took stock of my surroundings. The shack seemed to have been built on a clearing in the jungle the only real access being a track which the taxi had presumably negotiated to get me there. But my more immediate surroundings consisted of a group of armed thugs who at that moment seemed to be in animated discussion, the subject of which, if I was reading the gestures correctly, was what to do with me. I considered the options. Run? Beg for my life? Wait for their decision? A dismissive wave of the machete and a parting of their ranks seemed to indicate they'd resolved their differences and had decided that I should leave them in one piece. I accepted this decision without protest and walked briskly up the track only occasionally glancing back and hoping no one had appealed the verdict.

My journey back to the ship was uneventful only by comparison with the rest of my night. In actual fact it involved a frantic nerve racking walk in several directions, negotiation with three so-called taxi drivers and an eventual agreement with one driver that, for an outrageously inflated price, he would take me to the ship and wait while I borrowed money from a shipmate. That shipmate was inevitably Scouse George.

Later, though I had resolved to keep it to myself, I began to relate the experience to him but there was no need, he was able to complete the tale. The girl, the driver who took us there and the gang was one organisation. They simply looked for a I, stupid or drunk foreigner to take the bait. In me they had found someone who ticked all the boxes.

A new sober and celibate 6th Engineer Officer stayed on board when we docked in again at Singapore and returned to Aden. But mess room stories of a rampant and deadly venereal disease called 'The Bangkok Drip' kept my earlier indiscretions firmly on my mind. I couldn't in all honesty say that I'd used protection during my sexual adventure. Actually, I'd been so drunk I couldn't in all honesty say that I'd even performed a sex act. But to be safe I obtained a disease kit from the company medical officer in Aden. It consisted of two tubes of ointment, one to be applied on the exterior of one's privates the other to be squeezed down the urinary tract. Worried as I was by the possibility of having contracted this scourge I was not nearly as nervous as Mike, the cadet who had been with us in the earlier part of the Bangkok evening. Obviously, he had also succumbed to sexual temptation though presumably without my dramatic finale. Being embarrassed to admit this to his deck officer superiors or the medical officer he had asked me to get him the kit. The next day while several of us chatted in the mess he looked decidedly uncomfortable and when I rose to go to the toilet he followed closely behind.

'Jim, I think I've definitely caught VD,' he was almost in tears.

'Why d'you think that, have you used the kit?'

'Yes, but I'm in pain down there, and I'm havin' a problem to piss.'

'Well, you better report it and at the next port you can see a doctor,' I said, as we entered the toilet. Harry the 3rd Engineer was at the urinal, I let the distressed Mike take the cubicle and waited for Harry to finish. Groans emanated from the cubicle and then a terrified yelp. Harry and I moved quickly to see what had happened.

'What's up!' we asked in unison.

'I knew I'd caught omething! Mike backed out holding his penis, 'blood.a blob of blood came out, what's that mean?'

I patted him on the shoulder, not knowing what to do or say to him.

Harry, who had entered the cubicle, came out laughing, 'This is your problem,' he said, holding up the small red object, 'you're only supposed to squeeze the ointment down, not the cap as well!'

During the entire trip I had only come into contact with the Chief Engineer two or three times. Apart from his perfunctory greeting when I first joined the ship the other meetings consisted of a gruff command to remove some equipment from the deck and a surly enquiry in the engine-room as to the whereabouts of the 2nd Engineer. That didn't exactly endear me to him but neither did it reinforce Scouse George's opinion that he was an unpleasant bastard. However, my next encounter was to set the tone for our relationship.

We had concluded the major part of our voyage having passed through the Suez, the Mediterranean and now entered the Atlantic via the Straits of Gibraltar. I was scheduled on day duty but when we hit an unexpectedly rough patch of weather which caused the ship to roll quite dramatically I abandoned the winch maintenance on deck to seek a less precarious task. Chief Greenacre made an unexpected appearance at the entrance to the engine room as I was about to report to the 2nd Engineer for re-assignment.

'Hi Chief,' I greeted him with a nod, 'getting a bit rough out there for winch work.' I said, as we both swayed with the movement of the ship.

'Really, Six-er,' he said almost with a sneer. 'That's okay, I've got something else for you to do.'

With a beckoning finger he bade me follow him and took me out again on to the lurching sea-swept deck. 'There's something wrong with the port storm light atop that aft mast, I think it's loose. Get up there now, take a shifting spanner and make sure it's secure.' He marched off to his cabin leaving me no room for discussion.

It was the first duty he'd ever assigned personally to me, could I be seen to flinch? It may have been psychological, but the ship now seemed to be rolling even more. I was finding it difficult to stay upright there on the deck never mind climb up, maybe 100 feet, on a narrow ladder to work with one hand while holding on with the other.

I contemplated informing the 2nd and seeking his or one of my fellow engineer's advice, but didn't want to be seen questioning our most senior officer so I collected the spanner and made my way unsteadily to the mast. The dipping, rolling and lashings of spray made a climb – which even in port would be taken with care – perilous, to say the least. Gripping on for dear life while my stomach lurched as violently as the ship I finally scaled the ladder and inched towards the lamp. I could find nothing visibly wrong with the fittings, nothing broken or loose. Pausing for a moment before attempting the descent I could now see the 2nd Engineer and Scouse George below looking up at me.

'Sixer, what were you doing up there?' The 2nd asked.

I took a moment to answer as most of the contents off my stomach seemed to be forcing their way up into my mouth. 'The Chief sent me up to check the storm-light,' I eventually muttered. Both looked at each other and shook their heads.

'Okay, George, help him to his cabin. Take a rest Six-er.'

'I couldn't find anything wrong with the storm….'

'Okay, okay Jimmy,' George interrupted, shaking his head again.

Later, over a few beers, opinions differed among my shipmates; that I had been the victim of his warped sense of humour; that he was demonstrating his authority; that he was testing my resolve. All however concluded, that it was totally unnecessary and therefore irresponsible on his part.

We were now effectively on the way home and I was told that if I witnessed excessively exuberant or frivolous behaviour, or indeed felt compelled to act in such a way, this was perfectly acceptable. It was a well known condition called *'the Channels'*. The longer the duration of the trip the more likely one was to display symptoms of this temporary affliction.

Conveniently, our final Port of call on my first trip was Dundee which permitted me to make a short journey home to Glasgow for my first leave. I spent at least two days relating a sanitised version of my experiences to my relieved and excited parents before I could justify leaving them on the third night to swagger into the pub to release the unexpurgated edition to my mates.

I rejoined the City of Birmingham some weeks later in Birkenhead to begin preparations for another voyage. The Chief and 2nd Engineer had remained on board and were there, not exactly to welcome me but to recognise I had returned, by giving me a demanding work-schedule. As we as yet did not have the full compliment of engineers I was obliged to work double watches. Chief Greenacre appeared on several occasions during those long shifts to bark out, almost incomprehensible, orders. His attitude towards me was beginning to rankle. I had come to expect no sympathy from the 2nd in dealing with this, as empathy was obviously not his thing and in any case he was somewhat intimidated himself by his immediate superior. I did however expect that I as an inexperienced junior would get guidance and instruction on how to carry out these grunted commands; in this I was also to be disappointed.

By the third day, tired and disillusioned, I collapsed on my bunk at the end of the watch. I could only have been sleeping a couple of hours when I was awakened by my cabin door crashing against the bulkhead and the booming voice of Greenacre summonsing me back to the engine room. Before I became conscious enough to get both feet on the floor he'd gone but he could still be heard, through the door he'd left open, ranting on about my unfulfilled duties.

Like all bullies he'd probably been selective throughout his years – low level workers in need of a job, small introverted types anxious to keep their position and juniors such as myself, all got the rough end of his temper. Others such as the ex-SAS Scouse-George may not have been shown great courtesy but were certainly never antagonised. But this time Greenacre had miscalculated. Mix a robust Glasgow upbringing with tiredness, disgust, humiliation and anger and you get a 'blowing of the tubes'. In modern terms – I lost it. I pursued him down the alleyway and as he reached his cabin door confronted him, I'm told, brandishing a large screw-driver I'd picked up. I warned him that it could be his very last trip if he even thought of speaking to me again in the manner and tone he'd just used.(In this text I've omitted the expletives, for fear of giving offence, but be assured he would've received the full version). Two other members of the staff apparently made a cautious intervention and the Chief took to his cabin, deciding to remain there until I had left the ship. When I finally composed myself I decided, without prompting, that I should disembark as soon as possible as my position as 6TH Engineer Officer of SS City of Birmingham had probably become untenable.

I had no trouble in convincing my mother and father that I could not have put up with that treatment through another trip. But I was in no doubt that although I had called the Agent to put my point of view, the Chief Engineer's report of the incident would hold sway and my career in the Merchant Navy would be over. My mother tried gallantly to feign disappointment, my father though sympathetic with my position worried that another door of opportunity had closed at a time of rising unemployment in Glasgow.

To my complete astonishment only a few days after arriving home I was contacted by the agent and offered the 6th Engineer's job on the SS City of Bedford.

To this day I'm not sure if, in their need to fill vacancies, they had decided to overlook a youthful indiscretion or previous complaints of this Chief's behaviour had given credence to my side of the story. Dad was satisfied that my stance against the bully had been vindicated, poor Mum was once again forced to contain her disappointment and feign pleasure on my behalf at this recall.

Engineer Officer on the City of Bedford

CHAPTER 16

My encounters with the Chief Engineer Greenacre had been minimal but acrimonious, my contact with the C.E. on the Bedford during my tour of duty was to be even less but at least mutually respectful. The contrast between my on-duty superiors on the two vessels was to be even more dramatic. Whereas the 2nd on the Bedford had found difficulty in translating his wishes, or the Chief's demands, into actual words, Dave Sayers was a communicator. I was now, not only, given duties but also asked if I understood and if I required some assistance or guidance to carry them out. He also understood only too well that for a small group of people to be thrown together for any extended period of time in a restricted space in often trying conditions, they needed not only to be able to work together but also to live together harmoniously. He and his wife, who under the terms of senior officer's articles was accompanying him on this trip, did everything to make the social life of his fellow officers convivial. Like myself and 3rd Engineer Kenny Campbell, Kate Sayers was a Scot. She had been re-christened by her husband and was only ever referred to as - Haggis. Alastair and Dave the fourth and fifth Engineers made up our small coordinated group. The Ship was once again scheduled to sail into politically volatile destinations but the closeness and cooperation of the group was to make this less traumatic than it might otherwise have been.

As on my previous trip the first port of call was Port Said and then through the Suez Canal to Aden. This time, because of increasing security concerns, in Aden we were confined to the ship. This severely curtailed my crewmates' black market shopping plans although some purchases were made with the bum-boat traders.

The next two weeks were spent on the open sea and again much of it was spent on deck servicing steam winches. The watches I did cover with Davie Sayers were instructive and entertaining; he having anecdotes which included just about every aspect of a marine engineer's duties. When not working I mixed comfortably with whoever of my colleagues happened to be off duty normally also in the company of Haggis. Once again I was a little bit behind on world events. While I, Davy Williamson my fellow junior engineer and a few of the younger deck officers, listened to short wave radio it was normally for the music, sports or comedy. Naturally, we would cock an ear to the news reports especially from home but the ongoing details of foreign conflicts, international disputes and civil unrest can always safely be left to those few who seem to delight in the collection and dissemination of disturbing news. One junior Deck Officer seemed to have taken up this mantle. 'There's trouble up ahead. Looks like there's going to be another India, Pakistan war,' he insisted. Not cheering news, as we ploughed our way across the Indian Ocean towards Calcutta.

To reach Kalkata, as our pani-wallah called it, we had to enter from the Bay of Bengal and steam up the Hooghly River. The city on the south east of India was near to the border of what was then called East Pakistan, later to become Bangladesh. As a matter of fact our next port of call after Culcutta was scheduled to be Chalna on the Pasur River in East Pakistan and this was about to present a problem.

Clashes between Indian and Pakistani forces over disputed territory had increased to the extent that a major conflict did not look to very far off. We assumed that if there was any real danger the company, in constant touch with its local agent, would know about it and inform the ship's master to change course. In the absence of any message from the Chief Officer most crew went about their daily business, ignoring the increasingly gloomier predictions from the 'news disseminator'.

As we tied up at the dockside the Jeremiah appeared to have been proved wrong as there was no immediate sign of tension or conflict and we were not prohibited from going - *up the road* I'm not sure if I had any real preconceptions of India at this early point in my life, whatever they were they would not have foreseen the abject squalor and poverty I was to witness on my first day ashore in Calcutta. I'm reminded of the Monty Python sketch when a group of men try to outdo each other in emphasising and exaggerating their deprived start in life. The boy from the 'single-end' in Govan was suddenly among hundreds of thousands of people who on hearing from him of his humble beginnings could have uttered 'You were luckyyyy!'

By far the most distressing aspect of this first visit was having to ignore the outstretched imploring hands of emaciated women carrying screaming underfed infants and avoid the pathetic limbless or limb-contorted individuals who limped or crawled in front of us to beg for help. Their sheer numbers made it impossible to think how one might begin to assist and the veterans in my company advised strongly against making even a token gesture. Even the more commercial areas of the city could hardly be called salubrious and here again the sheer volume of people and the clamour they created was somewhat overwhelming even for a lad used to city bustle and industrial noise. The other disconcerting affect was on the olfactory system. The mix of humid conditions, aroma of exotic foods, low priority in personal hygiene and a primitive sanitation system made for a potent cocktail. After a few hours of exposure to the realities of life in India for the vast majority we briefly tasted the sheltered existence of the privileged at a private members club; basically a club for expats although very rich and influential Indians numbered among their members. We as 'Officers' of the Bedford had apparently obtained entry via the good offices of the shipping agent. No limbless beggars or pungent smelling vendors here, instead turbaned servants balanced silver trays and waited while members agonised over the choice of wine to accompany their dinner.

By the time we boarded ship after our day of contrasts, although no official announcement had been made, the tension previously predicted had begun to seep through from our company agents and senior officers to the rest of the crew; it had become apparent that all was not well.

According to the rumour mill, two problems had apparently emerged; the first was that we listed Pakistani nationals among our crew and the second, that we were carrying cargo destined for Pakistan. No official verification of those reasons was passed down but shore-leave was now suspended.

The days went by and a succession of Indian officials were seen to come and go and Police and Military personnel had now positioned themselves by the gangway and dockside.

There was no panic amongst our ranks only frustration at the lack of clear explanation, even from our own company. Everyone busied themselves with the routine maintenance that is an essential part of ship life. In off duty hours there was of course now a universal interest in the news items and no shortage of interpretations as to how the latest development would affect or status.

But one consequence of what was now in effect a ship-arrest, was, that all cargo destined for the vessel had been impounded. This included the ships stores, an important part of this being our the day-to-day food provision. Certain humanitary concessions had been made so we were permitted a supply of pre-prepared local food. We therefore embarked on a total curry diet. Hunger can inspire the most courageous culinary risk-taking but not repeatedly. I'm not sure how the others feel but to this day I have a resistance to curried food.

We never received an official explanation or report on what had taken place behind the scenes so I can only imagine that, this being only one of multiple incidents involving British subjects, our Government via British Foreign Office staff had intervened.

After two weeks being holed up in Calcutta our stores were released and we sailed for Chalna.

Not surprisingly I remember little of Chalna as most of time was spent in the toilet and after only a few days we sailed back to Calcutta hoping this time to enjoy a more balanced diet. Poorly as I had been, some of my colleagues had been even worse. When we had tied up Davy Williamson the 5th Engineer had to be taken ashore to hospital and would not to rejoin the ship until four ports later.

This time the restrictions on shore leave had been lifted but the berth where we had docked was an inconvenient place from which to go into the city and being myself somewhat weak from dehydration, due to food poisoning and excessive sweating in the intense heat. I decided after taking a short walk in the local area that I couldn't really face the city heat. Rather than take the extended trek around the dock road I cut across a piece of rough scrubland to return to the ship. I then contented myself with shipboard entertainment; the major attraction being the show which would be performed on top of the forward hatch – a contest between a cobra and mongoose.

How he managed to get the nod from senior officers and company agent to enact this on the ship I'm not quite sure but as the quartermaster said the man was a 'charmer'; obviously not only of snakes. The contest was well attended and the two protagonists, who had arrived incognito in the charmers' sacks, milked the applause - the cobra puffing itself out and spitting in arrogant defiance while the mongoose danced and darted around waiting for the moment. It was to be the snake's last performance while the mongoose would continue having found a part he could really get his teeth into.

I was intrigued by the spectacle but had to admit to the other guys that the very thought of snakes usually terrified me.

Kenny the 3rd agreed. 'Yeah, well none of us like them, especially cobras, and they're all over the place here in India. As a matter of fact the Serang told me that scrubland out there's crawlin' with them, that's why everybody takes the long road round to the gate.'

After the potential dangers of Pakistan and India our anchorage in one of the world's biggest and most beautiful natural harbours, the exotically named Trincomalee in what was then known as Ceylon(SriLanka), promised to be peacefully therapeutic. Off-duty we could take the launch to the nearest sandy palm-lined beach.

But even here I was to prove my mothers theory that I should never really be away from the watchful eye of a minder. On the last day before getting under steam for the short trip to the Ceylonese capital Colombo, a cadet, junior deck officer and myself decided that the deep blue sea surrounding our anchored ship was just too inviting. The plunge from the first deck down into the sea below was also an attractive challenge without any real hazard. I permitted my two shipmates to perform their high-dive first before I attempted to attain maximum points for artistic impression while executing my double twist and somersault but unfortunately finished with a belly-flop. I tried to silence my guffawing colleagues with a demonstration of swimming skills as they hoisted themselves out of the water and on to the suspended stairway. As I moved seamlessly from backstroke to butterfly to freestyle a chorus of warnings rang out from the ship and I moved my head to catch glimpse of a fin, then another one. I broke into a new stroke –the frantic splash-and-scramblestyle – and raised my arms for my shipmates to haul me up onto the stairway just as a large fin passed below. My two rescuers plus several onlookers began to dispute the species and even suggested that it might have been dolphins. I didn't bother to enter into this discussion I was far too busy downing the brandies and puffing my way through several cigarettes.

Another nine days was spent moving between what is now called Sri Lanka and ports of Southern India before we were off once again to traverse the Suez Canal and from Port Said embark on what was to be my longest period on open sea through the Mediterranean and across the Atlantic to Montreal; in effect almost one month at sea.

I was now beginning to understand why many veterans had told me they often preferred long sea voyages. A ship in port is often a hive of activity with the noise of agents, dock officials, customs officers and vendors to be added to the normal human traffic in the alleyways. Shouted instructions to dockside work-gangs and the barrage of steam driven winches taking and offloading cargo, sometimes over twenty-four hours, adds to the cacophony of sound as those who have just come off watch try to catch some sleep before their next shift.

A prolonged period out at sea affords a more ordered life as I was now finding out. For the first time in my short life I began to appreciate books of all types and listen, not just to Elvis and Buddy but, also to Ludwig, Frederic and Gustav. I also dabbled with writing. At first this was confined to letters. In those days telephone communications were primitive so we were obliged to have letters prepared before our next port of call to enable the agent to collect and send them at the earliest. But I now felt the urge to write about other things and though never disciplined enough to keep a diary, fortunately, from the point of view of writing this now, I started to scribble down notes on things I had seen and emotions I had felt.

Although I had now experienced turbulent weather quite a number of times and was happy to confirm I had felt no ill effect. But during our passage across the Atlantic we hit an extended period of heavy seas and this prolonged spell of pitching and rolling eventually took its toll. My head and stomach began to pitch and roll as well and was never so happy when we reached calmer waters.

By early October we had entered the Gulf of St Lawrence and steamed up the river by the same name to Montreal, from there we would make the short trip to Three Rivers then Quebec and lastly Port Alfred. Our schedule, after sailing halfway round the world to get here, seemed a little hurried. It gave us less than ten days to visit the four Canadian ports before re-crossing the Atlantic entering the Mediterranean and then via Suez return to the troubled Indian Peninsula.

In the window of opportunity I grabbed between my watches and sleep-time there was no shipmate available to go ashore with me. In the more exotic destinations, as I had found out to my cost, it's not always wise to wander into uncharted territory alone. But this was Montreal a civilised Western city and in any case not everyone had the same criteria when going ashore; those who had been in this port before normally didn't want to go sightseeing; some had a favourite bar, club, restaurant or indeed girl to visit. Sometimes, after the restriction and claustrophobia of a ship it was just nice to have space and be alone for a little while.

I had enjoyed the day – a mixture of sightseeing and shopping and had decided I would walk back to the dock area. Perhaps as a young man walking alone in that particular area I was unknowingly giving off a signal, I don't know and none of my veteran colleagues could later enlighten me. A car drew up by the kerbside and the driver opened his window and leant across his vacant passenger seat to ask me directions. I of course immediately informed him that I was a stranger to the city. Then, in what was probably a well rehearsed line he informed me that he knew he was near to where he wanted to go and had a city map but unfortunately had forgotten his glasses – could I assist him to plot his route from that point. He opened the passenger door while brandishing the map. I slid onto the seat and he spread the map over my knees while giving me the street-name I should be looking for. Not surprisingly I had difficulty putting my finger on the location, but he was having no difficulty, beneath the map, locating the inside of my leg. His revolting audacity had caught me totally by surprise so I probably didn't react as quickly as I might which emboldened him further. When I did, I'm not sure if I hit him once or twice, but I do know I then exited rapidly took the first corner at pace and keep going until I reached the port gates. Later, as I reviewed the events I began to wonder why he had thought I might permit that type of behaviour. I didn't have an effeminate walk that's for sure – walking on the streets of Govan would have revealed that at an earlier date. Nevertheless, I think for some time after this I unconsciously affected an unattractive macho swagger and aggressive scowl when walking around unaccompanied; until I realised that the only ones I seemed to be frightening off were the people I least wanted to - young ladies.

The next stages of the trip, which took us back across the Atlantic through the Mediterranean and on to Suez, seemed to pass without major incident. Although on such a long trip the individual traits and peculiarities of colleagues can become a source of irritation, for the most part, the team led by Davy Sayer was fairly unified. The only real worry as we made our way to the canal was the continuing strife in and around Aden. As it turned out shore leave was limited to daylight hours and within a restricted area. We left there after two days to repeat our passage to India and Ceylon, but on our return on December 1965 violence had reached a level where it was again unsafe for us to venture ashore.

But perhaps the most traumatic experience I personally was to endure in this Middle Eastern Zone was now upon me. After 22 years I was about to spend my first Hogmanay away from family, friends and Scotland. When I heard the first strains of Auld Lang Syne coming across the mess-room radio, emotion overcame my earlier resolve to take it all in my manly stride. My colleagues, no doubt concerned to see me in such a distressed condition administered, in copious amounts, the only known remedy for a distraught homesick Scotsman. I think we were well on our way through the 'Med' to the final port of call before I fully recovered from the remedy.

I had finally signed off at Gibralter after a trip which had lasted seven months. To Naval or Army veterans this would not seem such a long time, but it had been the longest I had ever been away from home and although I had enjoyed and benefited greatly from the experience I was more than happy to be going home. At this point I don't believe I even considered if I would return to sea or not.

CHAPTER 17

The first few days home was a mixture of pampering and debriefing. Mt parents were eager to indulge me in all my favourite dishes at meal times while waiting to hear of my adventures in the far off and turbulent areas of the World. My accounts were once again edited and sanitised. I'm sure my father, who kept up with all the latest news, knew more about the troubles in the areas that I'd visited but he avoided probing too deeply for fear of upsetting Mum, especially as I had yet to decide if I would sign on again. Naturally, being a worldly man and having regular contact with navy personnel Dad would also have known about the seamier side of a seaman's life but of course I didn't touch on any of those incidents.

The macho version of my experiences I was saving for the guys down he pub but it was to be a reduced audience. Sandy and Alan had taken off for London to pursue their dream of becoming actors and Jim McCarvill who had joined the Army had got himself in trouble and had been accused of going AWOL, was now likely to do time in Army prison.

By the third week after returning home I was already becoming aware that although I did not see myself as a career seaman equally I could not see me finding any work to interest me in Glasgow. Not surprising really, jobs were becoming scarce, and I had still not attained full qualification as an engineer and had no other experience or obvious talent to call on. After a period working in temporary jobs I was eventually persuaded by Rick to join him in the South of England where he'd taken up a new job. Having completed his apprenticeship as electrician he now had an opportunity to work on the planning department of a company working on the construction of a power station in Tilbury, Essex and he assured me that there would be other jobs available.

He was right. While he sat in the office and decided where electrical cables should go, I was employed in the team who would put them in their designated positions. Sounds simple, but the metal core plastic coated cables were hundreds of feet long, on average 6 inches thick and had to be hauled across a construction site through ditches and up the sides of the building. The veterans on the cable-pulling squad were fairly robust but noticeably there weren't many of them. It wasn't the kind of job that offered much opportunity for advancement or mental challenge and if my aching muscles were anything to go by the burn-out rate was probably high; nevertheless, for the moment, it paid my half of the rent. That rent was for a room which I shared with Rick in a semi-detached house in Seven Kings, the couple who owned it and their daughter inhabiting the rest the property.

Rick worked quite a lot of overtime and much of his spare time he spent with a new girl friend. A lot of this activity he unwittingly shared with me throughout the night as he had a condition which I believe is called somniloquy. I was about to say he suffered from sleep-talking, but he did not, it was I who suffered from his condition.

The tiring work and disturbed sleep would have been enough to prompt me to consider an alternative lifestyle but a new situation was arising which was worrisome. Our landlord was, not surprisingly, protective of his young attractive daughter. He had once or twice given her notice that she should not become over friendly with us. It seemed to escape his attention that the other female member of his family perhaps needed the same reminder.

She had started by being most concerned that I should have everything in the room that I might need. This progressed to offers of special cooked dishes, particularly when I was on my own and coincidentally she was too. At first I politely accepted her culinary offerings but the accompanying chats became less appetising; starting with a complaint that she was too often on her own, followed by the observation that her husband was much older, topped with a suggestion that she needed some fun in her life. I decided to go on a diet. A sudden necessity to work overtime almost every night meant I was seldom in the house to take advantage of the delicacies on offer.

About this time both myself and Rick were to face an extremely traumatic experience – the English World Cup triumph of 1966. Had we been in Scotland it would have been bad enough but at least we would have been among fellow sufferers but to have to go to work and hear the crowing. I almost packed my bags and took off for the auld country.

Actually, quite soon afterwards I was packing up. My landlady, miffed by my reluctance to sample her offerings began to find fault with my conduct and level of hygiene. Had she done so from the beginning it would have been understandable. Working on a building-site means muddy boots and dirty clothes and at times having worked long hours I collapsed into the bed not having cleansed myself properly. The bed linen was therefore in constant need of washing. On occasion I had also come in late and perhaps noisily. But these things she had ignored earlier. Now her husband was constantly being sent up to chastise me. I was sorely tempted to tell him why his wife had become so 'disappointed in me' as he put it. Instead, I decided it was time to move on, not only from the digs but also from the sleep-talking and cable-pulling.

During my time at Tilbury I had gone with Rick to London to visit Sandy and Alan, now living in Chalk Farm in North London and studying acting at the Central School of Speech and Drama. Although Rick didn't seem to share my opinion, to me their lifestyle was not only more attractive but more interesting and fulfilling. I now decided to take up their invitation to share their accommodation for a period while I considered my next career move.

Listening to my flatmates and their fellow drama students in the pub and at the apartment reawakened the desire in me to create and perform; a feeling I had enjoyed in limited form when singing with the band. It is something to do with being somewhere else even if only for a short while. This feeling I can also now recognise when writing.

I contemplated applying for an audition to enter Drama school but first I had to find myself a temporary job as I was rapidly running out of funds. I then spent a soul destroying period applying for a wide variety of jobs, none of them requiring any great ability or experience but all of them, in the opinion of the recruiters, beyond my capabilities. Eventually I was accepted for the exalted position of warehouseman at Marks & Spencers - on a trial basis. I was one of a team of four whose main job was to take in and check deliveries to the storeroom and, on request from the sales staff, move stock to the shelves. It was no more intellectually demanding than my cable pulling position but the physical input was not nearly as taxing. There were other clear advantages over the previous job – young female shop assistants.

Of my three colleagues two were, to put it diplomatically, veterans and the other though somewhat younger was a husband and father. The only other male was the manager of the store. So a young slim, but strong, hunk temporarily employed while waiting to embark on an acting career would have a field day among all these women, right? Well, not quite. Of the three women who most attracted me, one, when she found out I had been brought up as a Presbyterian, wanted to lure me back to the church while the other insisted on introducing me to her husband, who was also ex-merchant navy. The third, and most attractive, hardly gave me shelf space. I took solace in my studies.

On the advice of several student actors I had decided to apply, not only to the Central where Sandy and Alan were studying, but also to what some considered more prestigious, the Royal Academy of Dramatic Art. The audition for RADA, as it was known to all in the acting world, was to come up first, and it consisted of performing two passages, one from a classic work and the other from a contemporary. At this stage all the self delusion should have drained away and forced me to make a decision based on stark reality. I knew nothing of contemporary plays and far less of the classics. Save belting out a few rock songs and inadvertently making a hilarious stage exit at school I had never performed on stage and certainly not in front of professionals. On top of these obstacles I was advised to overcome another – an almost incomprehensible Glaswegian accent.

I should have done 'the Scottish play' as my choice of Shakespeare and pretended I was adding a bit of authenticity. Instead I chose King John because I'd heard it was one of the least performed of the Bard's work. For the contemporary I decided on Pinter's – 'The Caretaker'.

As I remember the audition was in much the same format as we see today in the 'X Factor' and 'Britain's Got Talent' except the judges were not celebrities and they didn't make their criticisms public. As it was after hearing my King 'Jock' they didn't recognise that X factor and though they were sure Britain had talent they couldn't detect it in me. I was quietly informed that it was unnecessary to assail them with 'The Caretaker' and that I could go. To say I was demoralised is perhaps an understatement; I decided I wouldn't even attempt to audition for Central. The news a few days later that I had passed my trial period as warehouseman and could therefore retain the grey nylon overall was insufficient compensation.

I was now marking time. For the moment I would stay at M&S where at least I had a steady wage and in time I'd decide what I wanted to do. For now I concentrated on the things I could do best - smoking, drinking, watching football, going to the occasional rock concert and pulling girls who somehow never looked quite as attractive as they'd looked the night before. One young lady who did look good, at any time of the day, was our next door neighbour in Chalk Farm, who at that time shared a house with a young photographer named David Bailey. Miss Katherine Deneuve and I would cross each others paths frequently as we entered and exited our respective residences, and I would flash her my winning smile. But with typical Gallic coolness she contrived to convey the message that she was un-tempted.

A lot of my time I still spent in the pub known as the 'Winch' which was the Central Drama students' local. When I mixed with them it still depressed me that I would not be part of that world though much later I'd became aware of the high failure rate and the much reduced expectations of the people who'd followed that career. Very, very few would achieve the real fame that they'd craved. Alan would give it up quite soon after I left London and Sandy would have a long grind before he attained a moderate level of success with the part of Golly in the series Monarch of the Glen. Of those we mixed with at those times perhaps the late Mike Elphick was perhaps the most successful.

Once again I was at a crossroads. With no immediate career prospects in London I decided that perhaps it was time to go back home. But before leaving London I, along with ten of thousands of other football loving Scotsmen, was able to give England a massive V sign. At Wembley in 1967 the newly crowned World Champions played against a Scotland team that included Law, Baxter and Bremner. The 3-2 scoreline in favour of the Scots confirmed their position as the team of the future. How far in the future we have yet to find out.

I returned home unsure of what I would do next and, in the absence of any immediate opening, signed on the dole. My old Penilee mates were all still around including Jimmy McCarvill who had spent a period in Army prison after having gone AWOL. After a few weeks I was offered a temporary job in the nearby Hillington Industrial Estate and with some money in my pocket again settled back into the life of - pints at the pub, sometimes followed by a night at the dancing, to see if I could pick up some undiscerning wallflower, Saturday afternoon watching the 'Gers' and on Sundays taking the field myself to show what Govan-ite the Blues could have had up front, instead of that loser Alex Ferguson.

It was Jim McCarvill who came to me with the information of a casino that had opened up in the City and were looking for young men to train as croupiers. Neither of us knew anything about casinos but the idea seemed excitingly different from factories and shipyards; where curiously the only real money I'd ever made had derived from gambling. The Regency Casino across the street from the Waterloo Bus station was owned by Reo Stakis a Greek Cypriot who had seen some success with restaurants and was now trying his hand at gambling. As we waited on the ground floor of the discreetly lit and plushly carpeted premises we could hear, from the open-plan level above us, sounds that were to become a familiar - that of a balls spinning and dropping into the sections of revolving roulette wheels.

I don't know if McCarvill was more surprised and excited than I was to be accepted for the training course because if my memory serves me correct we both took the decision with cool acceptance. This could well have been because we were advised that we would be continuously assessed and would only be retained if we reached the desired level of competence. Probably having been disappointed by our previous choices of profession we were showing caution. On the other hand maybe we were just displaying some Glasgow 'gallus'.

My parents were not sure how to take the news of this offer. My father was happy if I found any work whatever it was, because for him unemployment was just about the worst fate that could befall man and collecting dole acceptable only when all else had failed. But he knew nothing of this 'new' business and doubted if it would offer any real long term prospects. Mother also wanted me to find regular work – 'but in a gambling house?'

CHAPTER 18

The first stage of our training took place on a roulette table where it was explained that the currency used within the casino was the round tokens called chips. These so called, 'cash, or value chips' could be bought, by those wishing to gamble, at the cash-desk or directly from the croupiers at the tables. On each Roulette table they also stocked up to eight sets of chips each of a different colour which carried no value on their face. Players buying in at those tables for money or value chips would be given a colour which would identify their bets from the other players. The chip value at which the gambler wished to play would be indicated by placing a marker alongside a chip of this colour set.

Croupiers have to be able to collect, stack, count and distribute chips at speed with both hands, so the first tests were designed to assess our natural ability and then a series of exercises would be practised continuously to bring us to the required level of dexterity.

Basically eighty chips were spread flat in front of each student and on the signal 'go' they had to pick up, using forefinger and thumb, enough chips in each hand that when put together in one hand they amounted to no less than twenty. This was called a 'stack'; stocks of chips on the gaming tables are always arranged in 'stacks'.

Apart from the ability to pick up chips at great speed a croupier also, through constant practice, learns to feel when he/she has twenty chips in one hand and drops or shaves off excess chips before placing the stack in the desired position.

At the first mention by our tutor of the importance of manual dexterity I began to have fears that once again I would be found lacking;

the principal concern being my partially webbed middle fingers. As it turned out, those fingers play no important part in the manipulation of the chips, so one excuse for eventual failure had already been lost.

Almost the entire first week was spent on seeing how many chips we could pick up and place in stacks in a given time, usually the time between when the ball was spun and when it dropped in the number. We were also given homework. To enable us to arrive at a total when a player had a combination of winning bets we had to be able to multiply the number of chips by the odds paid on each bet and add the totals; once again speed was essential. A winning bet on one number pays 35 to 1, on the line covering two numbers a bet pays 17 to 1, a corner of four numbers pays 8 to 1, the line covering six numbers 5 to 1, and the section covering three numbers 11 to 1. So, a player having a winning combination of 5 chips x 35, 13 chips x 17, 15 chips x 8, 9 chips x 11, and 12 chips x 5 would be paid a total of 675 chips and if they were marked at a value of 50 pence the value of the payout would be £337.50.

Having learnt at school the 5, 8, and 11 times table we only then had to memorise the 35 and 17 tables. There are several mathematical tricks to arrive at totals but at this stage it was thought better to simply memorise the tables.

At each stage we were tested and having satisfied the criteria were permitted to continue. When we reached the final week to our delight, and perhaps our family's surprise, only McCarvill, myself and one other guy called Phil Dinardo had completed the course and been offered full employment.

My new work attire of black evening suit, white shirt and black bow-tie contrasted somewhat from the previous boiler-suit of the shipyard, engine room and cable squad and the grey nylon overall of the M & S's storeroom. Resplendent, in this new uniform I strode on to the floor of the Regency Casino to start my new career and was assigned as chipper to one of the roulette tables. I was probably a little nervous but having practised this basic function for ten weeks I didn't have too much difficulty performing the duty and after one hour was given a break. On my return from the rest-area I was confronted with my first real challenge when the supervisor instructed me to substitute the dealer on one of the tables. Though nervous I felt I was performing reasonably well considering it was my first 'live' game in front of real players. The dealer announces 'place your bets' spins the ball, and during the time the ball is spinning keeps a watchful eye on the placement of bets by the players to ensure they are not misplaced or over the limit. He may also be required to place bets which are beyond the reach of a player, change cash for colour chips, if there is time, and accept call-bets. When the ball is decreasing in speed and first begins to fall the dealer calls 'no more bets, please' and as the ball is just about to drop in a number announces more emphatically 'no more bets!'

Any bets place after this announcement are returned to the player as null and void, with the authorisation of the table inspector. The dealer then announces the result, for example, 'number fourteen, red, low and even!' The losing bets are then cleared away in a practiced sequence and the winning bets are paid in a strict order.

In comparison to most other cash businesses a considerable amount of money is put at risk by both players and the house and unlike those businesses, or other gambling activities like bookmakers, the speed and frequency of the wagers makes a paper record of each transaction impossible. This makes the activity vulnerable, not only to cheating but also to misunderstandings between the parties. Games are therefore conducted with strict procedures and dealers are taught to announce each action they carry-out. In those years they did not have the CCTV systems that gaming establishments have today so the table supervisor, called Inspector in the casino hierarchy, and the more senior staff were expected to be constantly vigilant. I had so far handled everything acceptably in spite of debutant nerves and was about to request players to place their bets before spinning once again when the Inspector bade me wait.

'Good evening Sir,' he greeted the large bespectacled man as he took a seat at the table. One of our Floor Managers then placed a tray of cash chips he had transported from another table in front of the new arrival who began placing bets to the maximum. I glanced at the Inspector who winked and signalled me to give him a little more time. I could see the Floor Manager had remained next to the Inspector and now the dealer who had been chipping for me was replaced by another senior member of the staff who whispered in my ear. 'He's one of our biggest players.'

The importance of the player, who now looked up at me with a challenging look, was more than emphasised by the sudden emergence of so many senior staff. My nervous system was now in overdrive. With trembling hands I reached for the roulette ball, 'p-p-place your bets, please!'

My spin was weak but valid and after only a few revolutions the Inspector, perhaps anticipating my loss of voice, announced 'no more bets.'

The number that had come up wasn't the worse from the house point of view but still gave our VIP punter a substantial return; this he recognised by giving me a thumbs-up sign. At the time, I expected to be replaced by a more experience dealer but learned later that, in the gambler's constant search for positive advantage, he had been attracted to the table because I was a novice. The management although inclined to replace me had not done so for fear of upsetting an important customer.

Having made the payments I reached for the ball as my senior, in the chipping position, whispered in my ear once again. 'turn the wheel a bit faster and spin the ball hard.'

Sweating profusely, I picked the ball from the wheel, 'place your bets please!' I nudged the wheel round faster and taking a deep breath attempted, with the much practised thumb and index motion, to spin harder than I had done before. The ball flew from my sweating hand, bounced from the spindle of the wheel and would have travelled half way across the room had its flight not been impeded by the lens of our high roller's spectacles. There was a momentary silence My table Inspector with a tactless adherence to procedure announced, 'No spin!' I stammered an apology as the player removed the spectacles, inspected the cracked lens and glared up at me, belligerently. Someone swept me off the table as another dealer took up my position before anything more could be said. As I left the floor, having been commanded to remain in the rest room until further notice, senior managers were surrounding the table in a damage limitation exercise.

Was this to be my first and last night? I sat there enduring a constant stream of jokes as all my new colleagues passed through the staff-room during the work and rest-break cycles. With them I seemed to have attained celebrity status but I feared by the end of the night I would have an unemployed status.

After more than two hours the Pit-Boss came in shaking his head and with a wry smile beckoned me. 'He's gone now, so you can come out. Chip on Roulette three, keep your head down don't say anything.'

Amazingly, I overcame this inauspicious start and within a few weeks was confidently dealing roulette although, the occasional appearance of the 'roulette ball victim' still prompted my removal for an unscheduled rest-period.

Both myself and Jim McCarvill, by observation and in our conversation with other longer serving staff, were becoming aware of the peculiarities of the Company's operational policies. Reo Stakis was by origin a Greek Cypriot who having been successful in the restaurant business had made a recent foray into the casino world.

As is often the case when a business people first open up in an adopted country he probably felt more comfortable appointing family and friends from the old country to management positions, irrespective of their knowledge and experience in that business. The Regency Casino was an example of this, the Manager was known by the anglicised name of Mr Peters and was said to be a brother-in-law of the owner. A man more ill-suited to the job of managing a gambling entity would have been difficult to find. I can say this now without fear of contradiction, after many years of experience running such businesses, but even then as an inexperienced lad I could plainly see his unease with every aspect of the job. Perhaps the most significant failing was his surrender to superstition.

Gamblers often fall prey to superstition and it is a damaging condition which can lead to even greater losses due to irrational decision making during play. Gaming Operators should not suffer from this disability; it reduces profits, and in some cases can ruin the business. The most damaging aspects of a management governed by superstition are the destruction of staff morale and customer trust.

My first sample of the harmful effects of superstition I had unwittingly experienced on my first day. The management pressurised to attain instant results and indoctrinated by Mr Peters that irrational forces play a part in achieving those results they had transferred the pressure to me, a mere trainee. My spinning of the ball and the wheel had been within regulatory guidelines and had achieved random results which may have been temporarily beneficial to the player. But the insistence on increasing the speed of ball and wheel would have had no effect on the result had it not made me nervous, causing the unfortunate incident that upset and could have lost them the player.

In spite of the idiosyncrasies of our bosses I was enjoying the lifestyle of a croupier, it had an excitement about it, on the table you almost felt like a performer and of course the salary was higher than anything I'd had so far. Only a few weeks after my lens-breaking feat there was further confirmation that I had been pardoned, at least by my bosses. I was scheduled to learn a second game. This time it was Dice or as it is called in the business, Craps. However, before that, I was to be present at another demonstration of our Boss's distorted thinking. A customer, who was an even bigger player than 'he of the broken glasses', had been coming in to terrify Mr Peters by playing maximum bets on Roulette. Over several nights he had fluctuated between losing a fortune and winning one; each time ending with a small loss. But this night his winning chips were piling up in front of him and panic was beginning to register on the faces of senior staff. In a futile effort to change the 'house luck' dealers, including myself, had been changed continuously; the ball and wheel had been spun, without optical damage, at varying speeds; inspectors had doubled as croupier; the roulette ball had been surreptitiously changed several times - all this ritualistic changing to no avail. By early morning the player, undoubtedly aware of all this activity and perhaps fearful of even more extreme measures, cashed in his chips and departed, leaving the Regency Casino with a sizable deficit in their weekly budget. Only a few moments after his departure one of the Cypriot managers discovered the cause of the house's misfortune; in the staff quarters someone, presumably to dry it, had left open a black umbrella. This triggered an immediate inquest, but the culprit failed to come forward. We were all reminded to stay vigilant and in the future report anyone seen committing such an act.

I remember the rain was pouring down on the way home and I was soaked to the skin. I'd lost an umbrella but the alternative might have been to lose my job and that would have been unfair; how was I to know the correlation between black umbrellas and winning numbers on roulette. This was something that had been left out of our training course.

Dice, at least in its modern form, is considered to be an American game and players there will say they are about to 'shoot craps' when they talk about playing the game. The table in casinos are large, rectangular and double ended. There are three dealers. One at the middle of one side of the table called the 'Stickman' and facing him on the other side, one dealer to his right and one to his left. Opposite the stickman a seated Inspector called the 'Boxman' and when the volume of the play justifies extra vigilance above him on a raised podium there will be another called the 'Ladder-man'.

The Stickman as his name implies is equipped with a stick angled at the end with which he manipulates the dice, offering them to 'the shooter' (the player who rolls the dice) ; he calls the total of the two dice when they come to rest and retrieves them in readiness for the next roll. The dealers facing him assist players to place their bets and change cash chips for lower denomination chips to place combination bets. When the Stickman calls the result they remove the losing bets and calculate and pay the winners. The game is played at an even faster pace than roulette so dealers have to be alert, ambidextrous and precise with their calculations.

Although, in training for roulette, I had become fairly proficient with chips I could see Craps required even more dexterity, so I continued to practise chip-work while learning the rules of the game and the bet calculations. Several people participated in my training including a Cypriot called Andreus who held the position of Boxman and seemed to be favoured by his countryman Mr Peters as the boss of that game although the other members of the dice crew, particularly a big humourous guy called Ian Cuthbertson made no secret of their disregard for his abilities. I was soon to find out why.

The Stakis organisation was now operating four gaming establishments. Apart from the Regency there was also the Chevalier in Glasgow and this was considered to be the company flagship. Outside of Glasgow they had a casino in Kilmalcolm and one in Dunblane. The Dunblane Hydro Hotel, which is less than an hour's drive from Glasgow, was, and still is, a magnificent structure built in the 1800's on 10 acres of beautiful landscaped ground. It had always been known as a health spa but Stakis felt it needed something else to attract a new market and increase its profitability. The casino had certainly done that and now with its increasing popularity more tables and therefore more staff were needed. So my first real taste of Craps action was to be in this unusual setting.

Some of the staff who had worked there for some time had taken up accommodation in and around the local area, but there was still some who preferred to travel to and from Glasgow by car; I decided that for the time being I would take up the offer to travel with them. One of several who drove there in their own car was a guy from Isle of Man called Lennie Quayle. Because the driver who had taken us the first two nights was scheduled to have two nights off, Ian Cuthbertson and myself decided to travel with Lennie. I remembered someone had told me that Lennie had at one time aspired to be a race driver and had also taken part in the Isle of Man T.T. races. We were to find out that the motivation had not left him. I'm still not sure if he was trying to impress us, scare us or was simply oblivious to our presence in the back seat. But no, he couldn't have failed to hear our exclamations, pleas and ultimately – our prayers. At the last roundabout before the turn-off into the driveway of the hotel he finally slowed right down to merely hair-raising speed.

Suddenly we were aware that a Police car was following, if some way behind. Lennie drove up the driveway, parked and with relief we clambered out. We had just about made it to the door when the police car screeched to a halt by the entrance.

'What's your fuckin' game?' asked the burly officer. Lennie shrugged and tried his best to look mystified.

'What kinda speed was that, and why didn't you slow when we came up behind you? The other officer put himself in Lennie's face.

'I didn't see anything on the road with me....'

'That's because you were never on the road, you were fuckin' airborne!'

We decided from then on to find an alternative chauffeur although we considered that the sanction from the Police might curb his pretensions to be a Formula One driver. The arrival of a sweating pallid colleague who he'd carried the very next night convinced us that he'd not yet been discouraged.

The action on the craps table in the early part of our first week was moderate with periods of inactivity. It gave me a chance to settle in and practise with the other members of the crew. I was now beginning to see that most advice that I was likely to find useful was coming from Cuthbertson, or 'Big Ian' as he was known in the casino. Andreus who was now officially in charge of Craps at Dunblane was already beginning to irritate me. The accuracy of his information could be immediately assessed by a quick glance to Big Ian; if his eyes were rolling I could discard the supposed gem of wisdom.

By the weekend the action began to increase as the occupancy of the hotel rose and the restaurants and function rooms filled with dances, weddings and company conferences.

when the action was at its hottest and particularly when we had players, such as those from American golf groups, who understood the game and bet on all the combinations. The periods on the stick though less demanding I also found strangely exhilarating perhaps because of the feeling of performing and orchestrating the pace of the action. The stickman initiates the game by emptying five dice from a 'dice-bowl' in front of him and, guiding them in a clockwise direction with the stick, offers them to the first player who wishes to 'shoot' and who has placed a bet on the section marked Pass-Line, or the section marked Don't Pass. The Shooter selects two dice and the stickman removes the other three from play. If the player has bet on the Pass Line, to win on the first roll ('come-out roll') he must throw the dice to hit the opposite end of the table and when they come to rest the total of the two dice must be 7 or 11. If the total is 2, 3, or 12 he loses immediately. If the Shooter does not get 7, 11, 2, 3. or 12 then obviously one of the other combinations will come up 4, 5, 6,8, 9, or 10. all of those being represented by a sector on the table. The number that comes up is called the Point. It is indicated by a big round marker and to win the shooter must bring up that total again before a 7 shows. No other combinations affect the bet initially placed. While waiting for the winning or losing total to show there are many other bets which can be placed which are based on the combinations that show on each roll. The shooter relinquishes the dice if a combination of 7 comes before the Point is repeated. Naturally all the other players on the table can bet on all the bet combinations offered while the Shooter retains the dice.

Like all other games in a casino the odds favour the house, some people misinterpret, or choose to misinterpret, this to mean that the house always wins. What it means is that because of the house advantage the probability is that the house will eventually win a percentage of the total money played. There is no time limit to this, so results can and do fluctuate. It is the time element which inspires the unscientific term 'luck'. It could be said that a player who happens to play when the results are going in a certain way has been a beneficiary or victim of 'luck'. Of course it always helps if the player manages his or her money sensibly, does not chase losses by continuously increasing the amount played or wagering on long odds bets. Naturally, the longer a player plays the more improbable it will be that he overcomes the odds favouring the house.

In my short time in the casino I had already decided, as had my more sensible colleagues, that 'luck' should play no part in the gambling manager's thinking. Unfortunately Mr Peters and his acolytes only too quickly abandoned all logic when there was a danger that a player might distort their profit expectations. The Casino Manager at Dunblane, his name was probably something like Loukas, had tellingly accepted the local staff's corruption of his name and happily answered to Mr Lucky. He at all times tried to live up to this name and insisted that his managers do the same.

Young Andreus, as he was called, to distinguish him from another Cypriot employee named Big Andreus, sometimes found it difficult to protect and live up to Mr Lucky's image. There were always gamblers who would seek to change the manager's epithet and craps' players were no exception. When the roulette result wasn't going to plan the ludicrous process of changing the spin, ball, and croupiers was set in motion, likewise on blackjack the croupiers were told to change their method of shuffling, cutting the cards and when that failed would be shuffled off themselves to the restroom.

On craps when someone was throwing the wrong combinations for too long the 'stickman' came under close scrutiny by Andreus, I'd already witnessed his paranoia in limited form as he mumbled incomprehensible instructions to the other dealers on the stick when a players won points. But one busy Saturday I was to see his obsession in it's extreme form.

Big Ian had been on the stick for some time when local player, somewhat merry from a party that had been held next door, took up the dice. He proceeded to make several points and in the process throw all the numbers across the boxes on which he, and several other players, had bet.

To rub salt in the wound this player had decided to re-christen Andreus. 'Hey Sammy, looks like I'm on a roll tonight!'

Andreus, sulkily chosing to ignore him, bade Ian hold the dice while I was sent to replace him on the stick.

Unfortunately I was unable to convert the stick to a wand and was soon receiving, to the accompaniment of Ian's rolling eyes, instructions on how to collect the dice, manipulate them with the stick and push them towards the player with a seven combination uppermost. Whatever I was doing wrong - perhaps pushing the wrong combination of seven – the player did not oblige and continued to throw every number except the seven, which would've lost him his bets and obliged him to pass the dice to the next shooter.

'I think I'm going tae clean youse oot, Sammy!' He winked at our Cypriot Boxman. I could see Andreus was becoming furious not only with the man's run of luck but also with his commentary.

'Six, Six! A winner Six!' I called as he made another point, and drew the dice to the centre of the table while Ian and the other dealer paid the bets.

Andreus glared across the table. 'Hold the dice there!' he demanded as he made his way round to take the stick himself.

'Oh ho! Sammy's on the stick now!' The shooter taunted him and then threw a seven combination as a winner on the come-out roll. 'You see Sammy, I can throw a seven!'

Andreus muttered expletives in Greek as he swiped at the dice wildly, dislodging bets that we had to replace, and passed them back for the smug shooter to throw again.

'Ten, the point's Ten!' announced Andreus, encouraged by the fact that a ten combination was statistically more difficult to repeat before a seven. The player undaunted, increased his risk by taking *odds behind the line* - which is a duplication of his initial bet and wins two for one if he throws the ten.

'Sammy, it's the big one this time!' he winked and threw the dice.

One dice landed showing five and the other seemed to spin for some time before also showing five. Our stickman seemed at that point to lose his voice, though the roar from the players would have probably drowned him out anyway. He seethed inwardly as he retrieved the dice and pushed them towards the player.

'Sammy, is that what you guys call *a straight back winner* ?'

'My name is not Sammy!' roared Andreus, then cringed as he realised he had advertised his loss of control to the entire casino. There seemed to be a shocked silence for a few moments and we focused our eyes on the table trying not to laugh.

'Sorry,' said the big shooter as he picked up his chips. 'Sorry... Sammy.'

The rest of us could not contain ourselves.

In spite of our boss's peculiarities I was enjoying the lifestyle and the salary. My private life had also seen a dramatic change. Up until then, during my two days off, a sizable proportion of my income had been spent on the consumption of confidence-enhancing liquid. In this way, by late evening I would be witty and attractive enough to swagger up to the girls in the bar or dance hall and offer them my company. My success rate seemed to be governed by whether the girls themselves had similarly consumed enough to see some value in my offer. Perhaps not surprisingly, having spent so much time in pubs in preparation for these advances, I had eventually formed a relationship with a barmaid.

Unlike many of the other girls with whom I came into contact Janette's appearance did not need to be enhanced by my consumption of several whisky chasers; even before my first drink of the day I found her stunning. Unfortunately, in my delight at being encouraged by this dark haired brown-eyed beauty I ignored all the signals that should have told me that a serious relationship with her would be ill-advised. For one thing she was married; even if, as she had discreetly informed me, that relationship was all but over. On top of that there was also the contrast in upbringing. Though I had come from a working class family whose first home was a single-end in Govan, my parents, in particular my mother, would have described us as *respectable* working class. The hard drinking and generally chaotic lifestyle of some of Janette's Gorbals-dwelling family, including the women, would have been categorised just a little differently. An early indication of their relaxed approach to questions of morality was their tacit agreement that I could sleep with their, still married and not yet officially separated, daughter in their spare bedroom. Even though I was aware and shocked by some of the family's behaviour, in my besotted condition I chose to ignore it. Also in my naivety during this period I did not consider why I was so readily accepted into this family. Could it be that I was seen to be working in a job that paid good money? A potential asset to a family, whose only official and regular earner up to that period seemed to have been Janette their daughter, and she had been married.

My lifestyle was now as chaotic as my new extended family; I could be said to be of no fixed abode. I was working in Dunblane and sometimes stayed in an apartment in nearby Stirling rented by my colleagues. On occasion I made it home to my parents' house but more often, especially on my nights off, I would stay with Janette at her mother's house. Needless to say I had not told my parents of this relationship. As far as they were concerned I stayed most nights at the apartment in Stirling.

Janette had now officially separated and had returned to live with her parents. Her husband had apparently not agreed the separation and continued to approach her and other family members. I was advised to steer clear of him as he could be trouble. Not the only one as it happened. Though I was still infatuated with her I was now beginning to realise the incompatibility between myself and other members of the family and their associates. She herself had been forced to intervene one night when her cousin's boyfriend, a thug even when sober, had in a drunken state tried to pick a fight with me in her mother's house. I was now considering getting a flat in Glasgow and taking her, and more importantly myself, away from all the family conflict. But I was now hit by a bombshell; Janette announced she was pregnant! Worse. She was unsure who was the father – me or her husband.

The events that followed this announcement are unclear. Not for obvious reasons, through the passage of time and the decline of my recall system, but because they were unclear even then. In my infatuation with this woman, and perhaps my fear that I would turn her against me, I failed to ask the pertinent questions and demand explanations. Our relationship stuttered on through her pregnancy. Curiously, she did not consider abortion although no obvious religious ethic prevented this option. She did not return to the marital home and although she kept contact with her husband did not sever her relationship with me. My obsession kept me as her stand-by right through the birth of her daughter Lorraine and for some time.

The spell finally came to an end on a New Year's Eve. We had seemed to be getting close again after a period when she had appeared cool towards me and we'd agreed to celebrate Hogmanay together at a party in her mother's house. Even her family could not have expected her to choose that night and that place to stand me up. As the bells tolled in the New Year, I waited alone amidst people with whom I had little in common instead of being with my own family and friends; she did not appear.

In my misery I could never have realised then, just how lucky I was to be in escaping from that lifestyle.

I turned to my parents and the comforts of home but they had obviously suspected something had gone wrong with my life. It was my father who finally addressed the subject he being no longer able to ignore my so obviously depressed condition.

Eventually, his subtle promptings had their effect and I broke down to tell him of my failed relationship with a married woman, her treatment of me and also my shame at having concealed all this from him and my mother.

I cannot recall Dad's exact words, there were many of them and over a number of days, but I still benefit from their effect. I began to slowly recover although I knew, and I believe my poor parents also realised, that I needed to make a complete break from my surroundings.

CHAPTER 19

Once again it was Jimmy McCarvill who alerted me to a new opportunity. He and several others from Glasgow had already made the move and were working at The Albion Casino in Salford, Manchester. I decided it was time to try something different and after making an application, travelled down there for the interview. I arrived at a casino located in a large barn-like building at one end of the local dog racing track and could see that even in early evening they were already doing considerable business on the tables.

After going through the usual preliminaries with a Manager I was shown out to the gaming floor for the expected table test. This normally consists of a simulated game where a few staff act as players. What I did not expect was to be asked to relieve the dealer on one of the operating tables, in fact a roulette which was at that moment the busiest table in the casino. Although surprised to have been sent into a live game, I felt a determination to show them that I could handle whatever was thrown at me. Which in this case turned out to be everything but the kitchen sink. At this point I imagined that the almost anarchic style of play by the customers around this table had in fact been orchestrated to test me to the full. I resolved to maintain discipline and control but after a few spins when the volume of protests at my handling of the game reached a crescendo I was taken off by the beleaguered Pit Boss, Eric.

'Bloody hell, you had us ducking there, I thought they were going to throw their chairs at us!' He said laughing, as we were joined by the Manager. My heart sunk, they would not employ someone who would upset their clients.

'Okay, as you can see, the players are a little different from what you've perhaps seen in Scotland but you'll be alright when you get used to it,' said the Manager as he led me, I was now almost skipping, back to the office.

The customers I was to learn, first from my colleagues later by personal experience, were indeed different. Or at least had been permitted by the management to be different. A large proportion of them were from the local Jewish community and some of the casino company's top management were also Jewish. It was said, by some staff, that this was the reason the players could do almost as they pleased. I was inclined to believe this myself, but through the years have learnt it's not always as insidious as it first appears. When a business draws most of its customers from the same tight-knit group one has only to upset a few of them for negative messages to spread rapidly within that community. Managers coming from the same background become only too aware of the opinion formers and tend to avoid upsetting them. It often leads them to make one concession too many.

In any case whatever the challenges I was about to face I was happy to be offered the job, and like my Scottish colleagues with whom I would now share a flat, I would learn to moderate my earlier dealing style to accommodate the new conditions.

Manchester for me was a completely new start and I quickly embraced the lifestyle. After work, even at four or five in the morning, there was no shortage of clubs eager to welcome high earning gaming staff. One in particular, the MiniClub had become a second home for the Glaswegian Diaspora which seemed to be increasing by the day. For the football fans among us there was also the Busby Babes at Old Trafford and we had timed our arrival just right – it was the period of Best, Law and Charlton. There was also no shortage of girls and this time I was careful not to form any lasting attachment to any one in particular.

At the Albion I was now working most of the time on the craps table which was the game I most preferred to deal. All was going well, or so I thought.

The constant demands of the Albion customers and their readiness to complain about almost everything were things that all the staff had to contend with, but on Craps, which by its nature is a more physical and vocal game, we attracted clients who seemed to imagine that their win probability increased with each rant at the dealers. One regular in particular, who had been identified to me as having a close relationship with the casino company's owners, appeared to believe that upsetting the staff of the table was the first stage of a winning strategy. I had seen him intimidate several staff during the time I had worked there and some of the older hands assured me that in the past he, who was known to be an influential man in the local community, had actually had dealers taken off the table, two had asked to be transferred and one had actually resigned. For quite some time I had managed to resist his attempts to unsettle me when I was dealing at the end where he was playing or when I was on the stick. On the nights when he appeared I looked upon his presence as a challenge and after a while became accustomed to his methods; they were for the most part childish and predictable. Scattering money that he wished to change for chips across the table just as the dice was being thrown thereby obliging the dealer to scramble to retrieve it lest it impede the game; tossing chips for change just out of reach of the dealer; at his turn to shoot the dice selecting three instead of two dice; shooting a succession of obviously illegal throws and protesting vehemently when the Stick and Boxman called 'No Roll'; aiming the dice at player's place-bets at the other end of the table obliging the dealer to constantly replace bets. These are just a few from the full repertoire of irritating tricks that he employed. All this was accompanied by an ongoing verbal campaign that became all the more intense as his audience increased.

 My determination not to react in any way to his provocation and coolly refer his protests and demands to the Boxman was obviously causing him some frustration. Whereas before his comments were mostly general his attacks became more personal. The 'Jock' was pronounced as a useless dealer, and advised to get back to Glasgow. My sexual preferences were questioned. He would take up a position by my side and make veiled threats. This lasted several nights until about the third night when I was on the stick and he began his campaign once again by grabbing the stick and making an illusion to my honesty and saying what he would do to me. Enough was enough!

 I wrenched the stick from his hand, stared him down and in my broadest Glaswegian, 'Think yu'r a fuckin' big man, we'll see if ye are – ootside in the carpark!'

 He stood open mouthed and did not respond to my challenge. At least not until I had been taken from the table and sent to the break room to await the Manager's call. By then he'd apparently found his voice again, but I was told, many of the staff and customers had a smirk on their face.

It was effectively my farewell speech. The manager sent me home on temporary suspension. I did lodge the complaint which I'm sure he had heard many times that the customer had been allowed to go too far, but his assurance that this would be looked into I took with a pinch of salt.

By coincidence a few of our Glasgow contingent, myself included, had already been sounded out as candidates for dealers jobs in the Casino on the Isle of Man. There had been a common connection as several Manxmen had worked in Glasgow and several former Stakis employees had been employed in the island's capital Douglas. I quickly made contact and was delighted to be told that I could start almost immediately as they were running junkets from America and were short of dealers.

I was therefore able to anticipate the Albion management's decision and have the satisfaction of giving my notice.

CHAPTER 20

The Palace Casino in Douglas, Isle of Man was by the very nature of its location a seasonal casino. The Island, its capital in particular, was a popular destination for British holidaymakers in summer, but during winter the casino saw very little business, the indigenous population being relatively small. As a solution to this the Manager of that period, an Italian by the name of Mr Volio Varnier, decided to embark on a Junket programme. Gambling Junkets are groups of usually foreign gamblers who,

in return for an all-expenses-paid package, agree to wager an amount of money over a defined period of time on the casino's tables. The deal is normally signed between the Casino and a Junket Operator, who is in effect the equivalent of a Tour Operator who has access to gamblers who are known to risk the appropriate amount of money necessary to qualify for this offer. The casino operator works on probability. If X number of players play a minimum per coup for X number of hours the casino's favourable advantage should see them win 20% + of the total money played, thereby justifying the outlay of the travel, accommodation and food and beverage for the players. Normally the players will deposit an agreed sum at the casino cash desk on arrival that they will draw against when playing. This guarantees their ability to meet the conditions.

I had been employed principally as a roulette dealer although the casino did have craps which in fact was the major attraction for many of the junket players. But for the moment they had a full crew of dealers while on roulette and blackjack they had been short.

I didn't mind at all working in the roulette pit because the system they used where the dealer worked by himself on the table and only called on the floating inspector-cum-pit boss if it was really necessary demanded more care and attention, but in some way was more of a compliment in that it assumed your professional competence. They also did not automatically assume that you would need a chipper, so you had to be quick and efficient enough to handle this task as well unless the volume of chips demanded an extra hand.

But by far the greatest difference was that table procedures had to be adhered to not only by the staff but also by the customers.

When I arrived in Douglas I was advised to find accommodation quickly as it would become more difficult and expensive when it got near to the tourist season. I took this advice and found myself in digs.

My landlords, only ever known as 'Old Jonnie and his wife', had previously accommodated casino employees and so were accustomed to the irregular hours of their new boarder. For them, who no doubt needed to supplement their savings and pension, it was a convenient arrangement to have a longer term tenant rather than have the uncertainty, and short term benefits, of holiday lets.

Apart from running the casino at the Palace Hotel the company also operated a small casino on board the five star luxury cruise liner the SS Andes. The staff of one manager and four dealer/inspectors would go for a full tour of duty which sometimes lasted for months. A trip was already in process when I joined the company and one of the dealer/inspectors on board was Phil Dinardo who had passed through the training school in Glasgow with Jimmy MaCarvill and myself. It was Jimmy who was to break the news to me that Phil was to be sent back prematurely - in disgrace. It seems it had been revealed that he had been having homosexual relations with a passenger and possibly also with members of the ships' staff.

I'm not sure if the news that Phil had been confirmed as a homosexual was so very much of a shock. He had certainly chosen not to announce his sexual preferences to any of us before, perhaps understandable given the macho Glasgow street culture of the late 60's early 70's. But I think in some ways we did think he was a little different and not only because he was of Italian descent. I'm sure if it had been some other bloke, and not him, our own inbuilt prejudices would have prevented us from showing any regret at his dismissal, but the point was – we liked this guy.

To have relations with a passenger and therefore a potential casino customer was of course against the rules, but as I imagined and was later to experience, the heterosexual staff spent almost their entire time in the pursuit of sexual relations. On a ship that had female entertainment staff including a dance troupe, even some unattached women passengers and visitors when the vessel was in port, it would have taken a young man of extraordinary self-control not to infringe this rule. They did, it was known to our superiors but never punished.

In the end, perhaps because of the obvious unfairness and the protests of others he was re-instated, not to the cruises but to the land based casino. To some extent the incident, although painful and embarrassing to him at that time, was to release him from what had been up until then a life of secrecy and subterfuge.

The Casino owners had acquired the rights to install, during the peak summer months, a small satellite casino operation in the Palace Lido concert and dancehall. These were low limit tables to cater for what were principally working class holidaymakers from the U.K. mainland. The duty manager felt that I would be ideally suited to cater for many of the clients in that first part of the season as it was 'the Glasgow Fair Fortnight'. On my way there to start the first shift I could already imagine the scene but even those negative images failed to capture the mayhem we would encounter.

Masses of boisterous, inebriated Glaswegians, spilling drinks, throwing up, tossing money and chips across the table, disputing regulations, contesting results, arguing with staff and other players, threatening violence. In other words – they were in true holiday mode. I was to learn very quickly that far from it being an advantage to be a Glaswegian, it was a great disadvantage. My accent marked me down as one of them, and as such I was expected to be complicit with their aims or, at the very least, sympathetic. When I was not, this was seen as an act of treachery.

Never was I so happy when summer of 1970 ended and I could return to the relative tranquillity of the main casino. By the end of that year there was even better news; I had been earmarked as one of the five staff who would operate the mini-casino on the cruises on board the SS Andes. Two of our Italian staff members Franco Bertola and Pietro would accompany me and to the surprise of all, given that his harsh critic the tall straight laced Patrick Gordon Walker would be our manager, Phil DiNardo was to be reinstated. But first, starting on 30th of December I would have a two week holiday in Glasgow; a chance to celebrate Hogmanay and then have twelve days to recuperate before setting off to sea once again. However, my presence in Glasgow was to place me at the scene of an event which was to be unfortunately memorable, horrendously so for many people.

The 'New Years' match' between Rangers v Celtic was to be held at Ibrox. Traditionally the match had been played on New Years'Day, but if I remember correctly it had been moved some years before to a day later as, it was thought, the excessive alcohol consumed during the celebrations might increase the likelihood of irrational and violent behaviour. So on the 2nd January 1971 I made my way to the match with some mates, a little guiltily, because I suspected my Dad who had introduced me to football and to Rangers would have liked me to accompany him. But for a lad in his twenties the prospect of a few pints and a laugh with the lads had triumphed over a day with my tee-total Dad.

It had not been a particularly memorable match and we were already making our way up to the exit when a goal by Johnstone of Celtic prompted us to make an even more hurried departure. We were already on the street when we heard a second roar from the crowd which I took to be the final whistle celebrations of the Celtic fans. I had decided to go home and dandify myself for a night out on the town, to drown my sorrows over the result. When I was almost home a neighbour, on seeing my Ranger's scarf, offered sympathy.

'Ah well ye can't win em all,' I replied. He at first looked puzzled then realised I hadn't understood.

'No, I mean aboot that terrible accident....' He could no doubt see I was still puzzled.

'They're sayin' there was an accident at the end o the game, an quite a few people might be deid!'

I'm not sure, in my shock, what I mumbled to him, but I then hurried to my mothers' house where I found her in a state of high anxiety.

'Dear God, what happened at Ibrox, where's your Dad?' I again muttered something in response and raced to the next room hear what was being said on her television. At that stage the number of fatalities was not yet known but the most frightening detail to emerge was exact location of the accident. The relevance of this fact was fortunately, at that point, lost on my mother – she did not know that my father's habitual stance in those days required him to enter and exit by Stairway 13!

I was trying not to cause her any further distress but at this point I'm sure it was showing on my face and in my behaviour. We had now put on the radio as well as the TV and as time passed it was being reported that the number of possible fatalities was increasing. My mother, as she usually did, was sitting by the window waiting for him to come off the bus at the end of our road. My spirits had reached their lowest point I just knew he was going to be one of the casualties and felt I had to prepare her for that tragic fact.

'Mum, this stairway….'

'Sorry Son,' she interrupted, as she got up. 'I'll go put on the kettle, he's just come off the bus now.'

The relief was unimaginable, but for many people their loved ones would not be coming home, the final toll was 66 dead, countless injuries and thousands grieving for the loss of family member or close friend.

As with most accidents and their subsequent enquiries there are still to this day some differences in opinion on the cause of the accident. From my father and some other friends' accounts and from what I know of football fan's behaviour, it seems entirely probable that the unusual sequence of events on the field was a contributory factor.

Like ourselves many fans had started to make their way out. The 89th minute goal by Celtic significantly increased the numbers leaving at the Rangers' exits, but directly from the restart Rangers scored an improbable equalizer and the roar from their own fans caused many to hurriedly retrace their steps. Then, almost instantaneously, the referee blew to end the match causing the usual stampede to get to buses and trains. This would have brought about a collision, unbalancing many people causing them to fall and trip others. The resultant tumbling mass of people could not be held by the old and inadequate stairs and barriers.

In Scotland the lesson was learnt and Ibrox and other major stadiums changed their designs and crowd control procedures. But a considerable number would still have to suffer before authorities worldwide started to take a more serious look at controlling football crowds.

CHAPTER 21

The Royal Mail's Andes was at that time one of the few cruise ships in the world still selling an exclusively first-class service. This was hugely beneficial to us as, according to the terms of the Palace I.O.M.'s contract, their casino staff would have full passenger accommodation and services. I had been scheduled to serve on the ship for three months this first trip of twenty days being the shortest. We left from Southampton and would sail down through the Bay of Biscay to the Canary Islands, later to the West African ports of Freetown and Dakar before turning round to head north, stopping at Madeira on our way home again to Southampton. It was nice to put to sea again, this time in a first class passenger's cabin and dining, not in the mess-room, instead at our own table in the restaurant and just to add to the contrast, when working I had swapped my boilersuit for a tuxedo.

Apart from restaurant and bars the ship offered a cinema, showroom with orchestra and entertainers. Quite a number of the entertainers and dancers were attractive females. Phil having been 'outed' on his previous trip had now been welcomed into what was a sizable gay community made up of service personnel and entertainers.

Our manager, suitably equipped with a double barrelled name, impressed upon us that the Andes catered only for people of the very highest category and as such our behaviour, at all times, had to be impeccable. After having had a look around during the first two days I was sure we could comply with almost all of that requirement, except perhaps the 'im' part.

Our first port of call was Teneriffe where we docked briefly before moving on in the evening towards the African coast. The casino did not open while the ship was docked at any destination nor usually during the manoeuvres in and out from port. Not being called upon to man the tables that evening we were therefore able to attend a party. Gordon Walker had said it was acceptable to mingle with the guests and take a little refreshment. I awoke next morning suffering slightly from an excess of refreshment and untangled myself from the showroom dancer I had been mingling with. I was sure this appointment on the Andes was going to be one of the most fulfilling of my career.

Freetown, Sierra Leone, seemed quite an unusual stop for 1st class cruise line passengers but I suppose it was thought to be exotic. Some of them and my work colleagues had never been in a 3rd World country before but their visit consisted mainly of short trips on the ships' launches to tropical beaches and some chosen sights around the city, so, they had only the briefest exposure to the horrendous levels of poverty in some nearby areas.

Having put to sea again after the brief stop in Freetown a few days later we reached the Equator. A ships' officer, filling in for King Neptune, passed sentence on those crossing the line for the first time, fortunately during my Merchant Navy stint I had already been initiated.

Dakar, Senegal on the Southern tip of the Cape Verde peninsular was next on the programme. In those days it did not have the prominence it was to achieve later that decade when it became the finishing line for the Paris –Dakar Motor Rally. But once again it was an intriguing look at a area of Africa still stamped by it's French colonial past and attempting to move into the new world.

When at sea, work in the casino could hardly be described as taxing, there were a few regulars who played substantial amounts and others who dabbled from time to time but at no time was there ever a high volume of play either on roulette or blackjack, the only games available. So in effect we were the only first class passengers who were being paid to make the trip.

The last port of call on our cruise was Funchal, Madeira. There are many things to do in this Portuguese resort but one thing that should be done, particularly now in todays super technological era, is the traditional toboggan ride. Originally a fast means of transport down to Funchal for people living in Monte, these sledges have been going since around the mid-eighteen hundreds. Sliding at high speed down narrow winding streets, the two-seater wicker sledges glide on wooden runners and are pushed and steered by two men traditionally dressed in white cotton clothes and a straw hat, using only their rubber-soled boots as brakes. The downhill 2km journey to Funchal takes about 10 minutes, reaching at times a speed of almost 50 km/hour.

By the time we docked at Southampton four days later there had been further opportunities to take refreshments and intensify our mingling, especially as Gordon-Walker normally retired early to his cabin. My colleagues and I could honestly say we had been bearing up well on this first arduous trip and were fully prepared to face whatever hardships we might encounter on the next much longer voyage.

As I had learnt during my time at sea in the Merchant Navy there is nothing quite like a longish period at sea with the same group of people in the restricted environment of a ship to test ones ability to maintain a tolerant and patient attitude towards all your fellow travellers, be they shipmates or passengers. I'm not talking here of inbuilt prejudices towards those of a different colour, creed, religion or social standing. I'm referring to the gradual build up of irritation and animosity over the others' approach and attitude to the daily conditions and activities on board. When individuals have continuous close exposure to each other without the relief of an entirely different environment, such as home after work or a weekend with family or friends, it is sometimes amazing how much tension can build, even in the supposed relaxing and luxurious splendour of a first class liner. We had made brief stops at Madeira and then Luanda, Angola, at that time still the capital of a tranquil Portuguese colony giving no hint of the horror that was to come later in that country. But a considerable amount of time had been spent on board and at sea, so we were hearing that one musician didn't want to play in the band with another, two dancers had been in a slapping bout, a barman refused to put the drinks up for one of his waiters. Some passengers had taken to using cabin service as they did not want to sit with others on their table. Pietro was doing his best to upset Phil and our manager continued to irritate all of us in different ways. It was therefore a relief to have reached South Africa where everyone would have longer periods onshore.

We had all read about Apartheid but we were now to see it at first hand, more than twenty years before it came to an end. As is no doubt the case in all societies with a repressive regime, if you are one of the chosen or at least the accepted few, and you can ignore the plight of the repressed, often the outward signs are, that their policies are effective. The areas we visited in Cape Town were clean, organised and to all intents and purposes safe. Safe that is, unless you played football on the beach.

We were free for a number of days and had already planned a wildlife safari up-country a cable-car ride to the top of table mountain and other sight-seeing expeditions, but on this first day the white sands of Camps Bay beach was the most enticing prospect. I had intended to loll in the sun and take an occasional dip in the sea to cool off but some of the guys from the ship had been challenged by another group to a game of beach football and I could not resist the chance to show my bare-foot skills. Although I say it myself I was indeed playing well when I slid in to make contact with a 50-50 ball and my opponent's heel came down on top of the small toe of my right foot. That in itself would not have caused such damage but below the toe was some beach debris including a piece of shell.

Two guys carried me groaning, with blood spurting from the sand covered wound, to the nearest deckchair. It was then seen that the toe was in fact hanging almost completely severed from the foot and any attempt to clean it would perhaps complete the amputation.

Transport was arranged and I was taken to the nearest hospital.

Several hours later I was back on board ship, the toe having been saved, and stitched back in place. However, I would now spend a fair proportion of the trip with an enormous white balloon-type covering on one foot and a walking aid, but in a strange way the injury was not to inhibit me from doing the things I had intended and in fact would seem to open up other possibilities.

The first item on my programme was ideal for one recently incapacitated, a tour by bus of a national safari park. Ironically, on our way out to the park we passed one of the townships where we got a brief glimpse of its inhabitant's conditions before going on to view the habitat of more protected species such as lion, gibbon and ostrich.

During the first part of the trip I had, not surprisingly for a Glaswegian, befriended the head barman Ginger and his two assistants John and Dave. They, and in particular Ginger, took it upon themselves to ensure that in spite of my injury I would still get about and arranged my next trip, a ride by cable car to witness, the magnificent view of Cape Town and its surroundings including the infamous Robben Island, from Table Top Mountain. Later, we returned to the Andes and evening cocktails with passengers and a number of local guests who had been invited to visit the ship. Ginger, on seeing that one young lady had noted my bandaged foot and walking stick, was working to get me the sympathy vote.

'Jim, I was telling Sarah, here you were so looking forward to getting around Cape Town but then had this nasty accident on the first day.' He said, presenting me to the young woman. During drinks I continued on Ginger's theme, that unfortunately I was going to be restricted. Eventually she insisted that the next day she pick me up in her car and show me everything. Everything, was exactly what I wanted, but to get there, the following evening, required me to dangle my large be-swathed foot over the end of the bed. Unfortunately, just as I was coming up to the moment of fulfilment, Sarah's pug terrier 'Tug' on seeing this bobbing white item, decided he would justify his name.

Not quite the climax to the evening I had planned.

The next day Sarah had planned a party at her flat for most of those who had taken cocktails at the Andes. Though some guests did not realise the significance, the presence of one of Sarah's guests, a black girl, meant that we were all complicit in breaking the absurd law in force in that country during those years. Later that evening I did insist on the segregation of one guest - Tug – who had still not learnt that the white thing at the end of my leg was not for his amusement.

After a poignant dockside farewell to Sarah and a promise, by both of us, to keep in touch, the Andes sailed off and we never again made contact. In some way I feel the one most disappointed by that was a pug terrier.

The Andes next trip was to be my last and although none of us knew it then this was actually going to be the ship's last year of operation as a cruise liner. Perhaps, because this cruise involved crossing the Atlantic and as such would spend more time at sea, the complement of service staff and entertainers, particularly young ladies, seemed to be much higher. This had been established by Franco who, of the casino staff, had arrived back on board first and had made a quick reconnaissance.

'There are some very nice signoritas in the dance group and also, I am told – masseuses…' He lingered on the word while doing the hand movements.

There was also a contingent of Phil's 'friends' so it would seem we would all have the opportunity for companionship. Actually, Phil's charm and sense of humour frequently attracted the attention of females before the more calculated approaches of Franco, Pietro and myself. As the time went on he became a sort of agent and matchmaker.

Naturally, as the trip was a luxury cruise the company hoped we would steer clear of rough weather, the navigational crew would of course try, where possible, to avert any regional squall but we were after all crossing the Atlantic, and on a timetable, so sometimes this wasn't possible. On the whole we did not meet with any serious deterioration in conditions but on occasion because of heavy seas and the consequential rolling of the ship we had to suspend play, partly because several of our better players were suffering from sea-sickness, also because some roulette players complained that the movement of the ship was affecting the spin of the ball and as such their ability to predict the winning number. The most difficult part for us was accepting this complaint with a straight face.

These early closures were accepted stoically by us even if it meant having to see out the rest of the night in the bar mingling with customers or improving inter-departmental relations with other staff or crew members. The extreme movement of the ship could also provide a credible excuse for lurching from side to side as you finally made your way to your bunk after a downing a bottle of Black Label and the squeamish look in the morning could also be blamed on heavy seas.

However, after one particular session when I lurched squeamishly out of a cabin, which was not my own, I ran into Franco.

'Aha, I wonder where you go last night,' he said with a look of delight. 'I don't believe it. You have been with Chi Chi Panda!'

This was the name he had given to the considerably overweight hairdresser with black mascara who had been actively advertising her availability since the start of the voyage, much to our dismissive amusement. Bribes, threats - there was to be no way to keep Franco quiet about this, so for some time whoever I ran into - our guys, barmen, crew, even a few male passengers – I got a nod, wink and 'Chi Chi Panda eh?'

Undoubtedly the high point of the voyage for many passengers and crew, including myself, was the visit to Rio de Janeiro. High points don't come much higher, for non-mountaineers than the Corcovado and Sugarloaf Mountain. The concrete terrace and balustrade built over two thousand feet above Rio on the Corcovado Mountain is just below the giant statue of Christ the Redeemer. Like everyone else we posed for photographs and as I stood there saying 'cheese' another group from our ship arrived and Chi Chi Panda, much to the amusement of everyone in my party, scurried to my side to be included in the shot.

'I didn't realise she was coming up here.' I said, in an aside to my colleague, as we looked up at the giant statue whose outstretched arms seem to encompass the entire region.

'Well Jim, you should know she can't resist anyone with his arms open.'

The Sugarloaf with its incredible views of Rio and the shoreline below was our next stop,

followed by an eagerly awaited descent to one of the most famous beaches in the world the Copacabana. If as a young man you have a passing interest in sun, sea, drink, food, football and women – this place is worth a visit. The skills of many of the beach footballers would have been absolutely mesmerising if I had not been continuously diverted by bikini clad beauties; and this was before topless bathing became acceptable.

The following evening proved to be as memorable, if not more so. A visit to the Maracana Stadium had always been on our agenda but to my delight some of the ship's officers had obtained tickets to the game between two of Brazil's top football teams Flamengo and Botafogo. In those years the stadium, with a capacity of 200.000 standing fans, was the biggest in the world, although as we took our place on the terraces the attendance was said to be a mere 155,000. You do not need to be a football fan to enjoy a match at the Maracana, the Brazilian people's love of colour, music and dance creates a theatrical spectacle that would excite anyone. The bonus for me as a lover of the game was, that on the field would be players of the calibre of Jairzinho, Roberto, Paulo Ceasar and Zico; all members of the Brazilian International Team.

For once the final score in a football match was irrelevant, having sang and samba-d my way through this match surrounded by Brazilian beauties, with flowers in team colours in their hair, football was never going to be quite as exciting again. In fact it was beginning to look as if the rest of the cruise would be an anticlimax.

It could not be all excitement and pleasure we were supposed to work sometimes although even the casino activity could hardly be said to be arduous. As with the previous trip most players were amusing themselves after dinner although one player betting maximums on roulette was giving our manager palpitations.

Off duty, but between ports, I continued to promote inter-departmental relations by liasing with a girl from the dance troupe. But just before we reached the next stop-over in West Indies I established a friendship with a very attractive girl passenger called Diane. She was, as some of my colleagues were quick to tell me, a little bit different from my usual female companion in that she was sober, charming, well spoken and educated, and accompanying her mother on the cruise. All those points, my barmen friends observed, were inhibiting factors if I wanted to 'deepen' the relationship, not least the latter.

I joined them both for drinks on several occasions at Diane's behest and surprisingly found no difficulty in communicating with Mum, so much so that when we arrived in Barbados they invited me to accompany them on a trip to the beach.

There was no doubt that I was attracted to the young lady but from then on, for the few days around the West Indies ports and during the voyage home across the Atlantic, it remained only a friendship, although occasionally it seemed to be taking the form of an old fashioned courtship; once again to the amusement of my colleagues. It had commented several times that she seemed a bit 'posh' for me and it was likely to be only a shipboard flirtation. However, as we tied up at Southampton and I said my fond farewell, to my surprise, she gave me her phone number and address in the south of England on the promise that I would contact her.

I was now once again unsure of where my future lay. The Andes apparently would not sail again as a cruise liner and the casino company had not concluded any agreement to operate on another vessel; we would therefore be returning to the Isle of Man. While life on the island was pleasant, I could muster no great enthusiasm for dealing in a casino that could offer little activity in winter followed by a brief frenzied summer wrestling with drunken holidaymakers. More importantly, the company's lack of any apparent ambition to expand meant that the possibilities of promotion would be limited. I was already hearing through Phil Di Nardo, and a network of former casino colleagues, that London was the place to be for job opportunities; this appeared to be my best course of action and coincidentally near to my new found friend, Diane. I would take the opportunity afforded by an extended leave to have a look there, but first I would take a quick trip home to see my parents.

CHAPTER 22

Mum and Dad were now in their sixties. Only now do I have some idea of what that meant, although being that age today has quite different connotations than it had for them in that earlier period and in that working class environment. Mum had stopped the part time work that she had in the bakery shop as her arthritis was beginning to trouble her. Dad was still in Fairfields Shipyard, though at times he looked weary. Nevertheless he would still seize on the opportunity to get his 'two nights and a Sunday'. This meant overtime payment for additional hours on Tuesday and Thursday nights on top of the eight hour shifts Monday to Friday and the double-time payment for all day Sunday. Add travelling time between Penilee and Govan twice a day, and the climbing 100 ft up and down from the crane several times each shift and this was by anyone's standards a long and tiring week. They were happy that although I wasn't returning to work in Glasgow I was, for the time being at least, not going to be on a ship on the other side of the world.

On my return to London I wasted no time in arranging an interview for the place which seemed to be on the lips of everyone – The Playboy Club. To obtain a job in the 'Bunny Club' male applicants did not need to exhibit the same qualifications as females.

This was fortunate because my vital statistics would not have measured up to their exacting requirements. My gaming experience however did find favour and my career took on a new shape.

The London Playboy Club was located in a building on Park Lane originally intended to house offices. The recent conversion had taken into consideration clauses in the Gaming Act which isolated gambling activities from other forms of entertainment; hence the separate nightclub entrance alongside that of the casino. At that point there were two main gaming floors although a third VIP level was already in the planning stage. The Playboy concept, without gambling, was created by Hugh Hefner in America and introduced to Great Britain by his acolyte Victor Lownes and he had recently seized on the opportunity, afforded by the law and conditions in London, to branch into this new even more profitable activity. The primary attraction of course at the club was the young, shapely and attractive females, sporting a pair of large ears and dressed in skimpy outfits that had a vague association with rabbits in that they had an attached bushy tail.

As a 27 years old single man, being surrounded at work by young curvaceous females did not in any way divert me from what was normally uppermost in my mind – it simply intensified it.

Although there was no shortage of women at work I still toyed with the idea that I might convert my shipboard flirtation with Diane into something more serious and with this in mind had already made contact to advise her of my plans. We agreed that we would meet when I had found myself a permanent residence and settled into my new job.

After a period of time, during which I stayed first with some of my old Scottish mates and then with a former colleague from Isle of Man, I finally rented an apartment in Inverness terrace, Bayswater.

I should have realised from our first reunion in London that the relationship with Diane was a non starter. When feet are firmly planted on dry land the exotic backgrounds of tropical beaches and moonlit seascape are replaced by the mundane considerations of everyday life. She was from an English upper middle class family with ambitions for their daughter. I imagine the message had got home that the young fit, white-tuxedo clad man who had done his best to charm both her and her mum, in the nightclub and restaurants of the luxury liner, was in fact a rather rough Glasgow boy who'd now got himself a job in a Girlie gambling club. Her message to me was of course couched in the sensitive and diplomatic tones one would expect from a well brought up young lady, but it was clear. I was free to look to my work colleagues for romantic companionship.

Of the places I had worked so far, Playboy was the most interesting and exciting. Not only, because I was surrounded by beautiful girls but also because it was a club with international image in an excellent location within a city that had fully earned its epithet 'Swinging'. The term is normally applied to the 60's but for some industries the real dividends from that image would come during the 70's.

My starting position in the club was Inspector and I was normally assigned to Roulette or Blackjack. The equality legislation was of course not to come in until much later so almost all senior staff, from top executives through management to pit bosses and down to inspectors, were male. All dealing positions, apart from a few men who were training for higher positions, were Bunny Girls. Curiously, the Dice game was still thought to be a purely masculine environment and was therefore fully staffed by men.

This gender demarcation was repeated in the extensive catering side of the business where almost all wait staff were Bunny girls and those above male. It was of course company policy that most direct contact with clients would be made by the Bunnies but the predominance of males in senior positions reflected the inequalities of that earlier period.

Bunnies had to adhere to a strict code. Having been selected principally for their physical attributes the first thing they had to ensure was that they maintained this attractiveness or as the company called it 'Bunny Image'. There was then, to some extent, an incompatibility between the new Gaming Act for Gt. Britain and Playboy's basic concept. A fundamental aspect of the new law was that casinos would cater to existing demand and not stimulate gambling, while essentially Playboy used female allure as a marketing tool. Aware that this might be used by critics, the company strove to present a wholesome image including a strict code of behaviour for Bunnies that discouraged over-familiarisation with clients and prohibition of relations with male clients outside of work; the first rule was loosely adhered to by most girls, while many religiously ignored the latter.

Another condition, one almost universally imposed by casinos, was that there should be no romantic liaisons between male and female gaming staff. This ludicrously impractical edict has been treated with disdain throughout the industry. The chances of it being honoured in Playboy were perhaps even more remote than some places, given their policy of hiring beautiful young women. It's been suggested that, for a period of time, one way the company had of ensuring compliance was to hire only unattractive men; on that I couldn't possibly comment. Except to say, that if so, then obviously some good looking men slipped through the barrier.

My apartment in Bayswater had become a reception centre for displaced Glaswegians, one of whom, Tam Brady, having started with

Stakis in Glasgow and then followed a similar career path to myself, had now also taken a job with Playboy. The Bunny Club would also the be the new workplace of Phil DiNardo who, needing temporary lodging while looking for his own place, had moved in to one of my rooms.

Tam gave his qualified acceptance of this arrangement 'It's okay, as long as he disnae bring any pansy mates in here.'

During my time away from the Glasgow streets, in England and abroad, I'd realised that to reduce the necessity to repeat everything I said, at the very least I'd have to slow down the pace of my speech and avoid Glaswegian colloquialisms. Tam could or would not make any such concessions, therefore I, and occasionally Phil, often had to act as his translator. But this was not the only problem, in speech he also had an unfortunate brusque delivery and this, to those unused to it, had the effect of making many of his comments seem aggressive and his instructions, to Bunny croupiers on the tables, like threatening ultimatums. If nothing else this made him somewhat unpopular and limited his capacity to infringe the - no fraternising with the Bunnies - law. I myself took at least a week before I was able to break this cardinal rule but before long it became apparent that the only way to apply that law would have been to put Phil DiNardo in charge of the male recruitment programme.

We now had Sandy in the apartment which at least from time to time took me out of the casino environment and back to his thespian world. But the working hours of gaming staff to a large extent determines their social calendar, particularly when they are young and in a vibrant city such as London. When we finished in the early hours of the morning there were many night clubs still open and only too happy to welcome the late arrival of relatively affluent young casino employees. It was therefore not uncommon for me, and a companion, to happily stagger back to the apartment in mid morning. I would then rise late afternoon, establish the identity of my bed partner, see if she needed transport and then prepare myself for the evening shift.

The job itself was intriguing. Unlike my most recent places of work it was continuously busy and by comparison with other casinos, that had almost the same players or at least people from a similar background each night, the Playboy's patrons came from as wide an ethnic and cultural catchment as I had seen anywhere. If it ever needed to be confirmed, gambling and girls was a good marketing mix.

The modern American business model, in particular as it applies to places of leisure and entertainment, was also in evidence. The traditional and conservative style exemplified by Monte Carlo and aped by most European casinos had been replaced by minimalist décor and canned pop music. The polite but reserved acknowledgement of customers converted to a friendly smiling welcome and to more suitably accompany the bunny costumes even the compulsory black evening wear of the senior male table staff had been shed in favour of a brown jacket and orange shirt; even I, who welcomed innovation found this a garish step too far.

Formalities in communication had also been Americanised, all staff from the most menial to the most senior were encouraged to be on first name terms. Thus, Mr Lownes Chairman and Chief Executive was to me simply, Victor.

It's easy to be dismissive of these policies but, although as with all large companies there were some troublesome and irritating individuals, in general the working environment was agreeable. It was also exciting and challenging because the Playboy's international brand image attracted personalities from the world of film, television, and sport.

One such personality was to play a leading role in one of my early experiences on the tables in that club. In all activities there are unrecognised, but self appointed, experts and card games against the house seem to attract a fairly high proportion of these. I was inspecting a Blackjack game that had attracted one such know-all. As a fairly frequent visitor who played substantial amounts he could be considered a valued client, but was also categorised as a potential nuisance in that he continuously offered unsolicited, in most cases unwanted, advice to other players. This could be a source of extreme irritation, could cause disputes and provoke other customers to leave the game. An Inspector had therefore to strike the balance of permitting him, as a recognised client, a certain amount of leeway while being prepared to intervene should he begin to annoy other gamblers.

This particular night, as he sat playing on the third box, he had as usual been urging accompanying players, particularly the person playing the last box, to take, or refuse, additional cards on their hands; making disapproving comments when they had not followed his advice. I was therefore obliged to diplomatically point out that each player had the right to exercise their own discretion. Thereafter, he loosely complied with my advice but contrived to make his thoughts known by body language and a series of mumbles and grunts. When the player on the last box departed with a look of disgust I was considering an ultimatum when I was distracted by the arrival on that position of a new player.

Astoundingly, no one else on the table turned to identify Joe Frazier the recently crowned World Heavyweight Boxing Champion.

Playing only his second hand since arriving at the table he decided to stay with a soft total of seventeen permitting the dealer to take the next card, a Queen, to make her total 20 and beat every player's hand.

If you don't know the game it's not wise to call the last box. Or words similar, were grunted by our resident expert.

'Hey hideous!' The Champ leaned threateningly across the table. 'You talking about me?'

For once, our card technician was racked by indecision. If he did say something it was drowned by the guffawing of myself, the dealer and the other players. He managed to shake his now starkly pale head in denial and after only a couple of hands decided he would not go the distance and retired, to the amusement of everyone at the table.

After that initial period of nightly boozing and birds I was beginning to slow down just a little. I was consuming less, started playing football again and had taken up with one girl who seemed a little different than most of the current Bunnies, being a slim dark haired beauty, less hips, more hippy. I was becoming fond of her but, as with previous relationships, I wasn't entirely sure if she, like me, was looking at our affair as a potentially long term relationship.

It's now difficult to say if I misread the signals and what might have become of it had I not thought she was going cool on our relationship, but in any case another girl at Playboy who made no secret of her interest came on the scene and eventually after a coming together at a night club we came together at my flat. News of this coupling with Bunny Odette or, to use her real name, Sylvia was to reach my other lady friend and convert her from occasional, to former girlfriend.

Sylvia was from Leeds and shared a flat with several other girls who had come from the north having been attracted by London's glamorous image and enticed by Playboy's promotional campaign. When I think back now I find it difficult to imagine what we actually saw in each other. As a young girl I suppose she was cutely attractive, certainly not among the most beautiful girls in the club but, being no matinee idol myself, perhaps I seemed to her more likely to stay around. Also perhaps, a supposed common bond, of a northern working class background. Whatever it was, in the early days of our relationship it seemed to be working and was even to survive the test of a sudden and unexpected appearance of my first real love.

The announcement of Janette's arrival in London came from Phil DiNardo via his sister who had apparently known her in Glasgow. My initial resolve to demonstrate that I was over her and had moved on was broken, not by a yearning to recover a lost love as she may have imagined but by the usual enemy of restraint, alcohol. Phil had made his flat available and not wishing to be rude, or because I was planning to be rude, I took up his offer. For the short period that Janette was there I think we spent our time giving confusing signals to each other but in the end it must have shown that although I found her attractive and desirable I was no longer in-thrall. She was to say before she left that in a way she no longer knew me.

Though Sylvia retained her room at the girls' flat she had more or less moved in with me.

At Playboy, the manager of the floor on which I worked and with whom I had a good relationship left to take up a position in Australia, however I continued to enjoy the challenge and gain from the experience. As well as studying the technical aspects of the job I was also witnessing the behavioural peculiarities of people caught up in the gambling fever. It is not essential to have followed an academic career in psychology to recognise warning signals in a person's body language. When you are inspecting or supervising a table those gamblers who seem compelled to glance up or toward you are always worth paying a little extra attention to, from a security stand-point. But sometimes nervous tics and peculiar betting patterns indicate problematic tendencies that can be disruptive to the game , the other players and of course ultimately to themselves.

The roulette game had been busy for some time with all eight sets of colour chips being played and several other players playing chips of a fixed value. One player, at the far end of the table from where I stood, had been taking note of the results and was so obviously frustrated that the numbers he'd played in a particular section of the wheel had so far failed to come up. Several times when I looked towards him he quickly and suspiciously averted his eyes downwards. Once again he and the other players placed their bets, the croupier spun the ball and I watched for his reaction. Face strangely contorted and eyes bulging he kept his hands below the table as the ball completed its revolutions. Could it possibly be? I wasn't sure. The croupier announced – 'no more bets' and the ball dropped in a number, so I was obliged to watch her complete the procedure of clearing losing bets and pay winners. One of the winners, of a modest prize, being the said gentleman. The Bunny called 'Place your bets' and spun again. This time as the ball circled the cylinder I swiftly moved behind the dealer to the end of the table to catch the straining, crimson faced, google-eyed punter lift the underside of the heavy table ever so slightly.

'New system?' I asked. He looked away and then feigned surprise that I should be addressing him.

When he had cashed his remaining chips a security agent escorted him to the exit and instructed reception to cancel his membership.

This incident was still the talk of the rest room when on the very same table only a few days later I was to witness yet another example of compulsive behaviour. No warning signs were this time evident. The player sitting on the first seat next to the wheel had bet continuously on the same number for a considerable time without any return. The failure of his number to appear after so many spins, to some extent compelled him to continue, as players always fear that the moment they stop the number will come up. At this point the croupier Bunny cleared the table of losing bets that yet again included his, and as she swept them back a chip fell to the floor obliging the male trainee, acting as chipper, to bend below the table to retrieve it. He rose abruptly, stared at me with a look of amused shock and signalled that I should look below the table. I asked the croupier to pause and quickly bent to see a puddle on the floor. My immediate thought was that a drink had been spilt but the chipper was now whispering in my ear. 'That guy was pissin' on the floor.'

This time I made no attempt to bring the misdemeanour to the attention of the player and gladly passed the information to the floor manager for him to deal with as he saw fit. I believe the customer was discreetly advised that he seemed to have had an accident and his embarrassment was sufficient to send him off never to return, as far as I know.

I'm sure it's a common theme, when people are attempting to recall the motivating emotions and circumstances that brought them together, that it's difficult to imagine what it might have been. Failure of previous relationships; desire for continuity, stability; imagined common bond, such as, both being working class northerners. Whatever it was we were now in effect living together as a couple. And soon a series of events would lead to what, I can now say, was an unfortunate decision for both of us.

In anticipation of an eventual move to one of the many foreign operations that were now recruiting gaming staff in London I had decided to leave Playboy. My relationship with a Playboy Bunny could then be legitimised, though to be honest this was never a serious concern as we were far from being the only couple in their employ to be conducting an illicit affair.

A position in the first Australian casino, which was to be in Hobart, Tasmania, had already been offered to me by my former colleague, and Playboy floor manager, Ron Hurley. The project was still at a very early stage of the planning process so, exciting as it was, I did not want to fully rely on that development. I had also heard in the wind that the owners of the Olympic Casino in Bayswater, just round the corner from my present apartment, were also planning to open casinos abroad, and as they were recruiting staff for their London casino, and paying well, I decided that all round this could be a convenient stepping stone.

An additional convenience of working at the Olympic came in the shape of Mike Bennett who had also been approached by Ron Hurley to eventually take an even more senior position in Hobart than the one I had been offered; through him I could be updated on the progress being made on that project.

My friendship with Mike had only recently been cemented, by of all people, a referee.

The occasion was a football match between Playboy and Knightsbridge Sporting Club, where Mike had previously been working. As I remember we had both been previously warned by the official for what he considered to be over enthusiastic challenges on other players. When we both clashed later and vigorously and animatedly protested to each other, and to the man in black, he invited us to leave the field. We trudged to the communal dressing room and after a brief period sitting opposite each other in silent contemplation we broke into a grin and an embarrassed shaking of our heads.

'We might as well go for a pint?' or words to that affect, won me over completely and that's exactly what we did.

For me the work in the Olympic was to some extent a return to my earlier years with Stakis, in that the owners and managers being also Greek, demonstrated many of the same traits. It was quite evident that any member of the table staff wishing to progress with the company had to be careful not to impose, on certain members, the same rigorous procedures they were expected to apply to most other customers. My previous experiences therefore assisted me to blend in more quickly.

However, my stay at the Olympic was to be a very short one. After only two months the news came through via Mike, from John Haddad a Federal Pacific Executive, that progress had been made with the Tasmania project and, as a promotional enterprise prior to the opening, a casino would be set up on board a cruise ship and this would call at major tourist destinations in the Far East to promote Australia's first casino. My employment *Down Under* would therefore start with me going back to sea again. The bonus was that Sylvia had also been offered a job on board as croupier.

At this stage she seemed to become a little daunted by the prospect of moving to the other side of the world and during these discussions about commitment I somehow got carried away, asked for her hand and she accepted. The necessity then to tie the knot quickly left no time to consider the fact that this was a girl I still barely knew.

Sylvia's mother had died when she was young and her father Vincent Arthur Musgrove had already indicated he could not possibly follow the tradition of the bride's father financing the wedding. A Glasgow registry office was chosen as the venue; not the preference of my church going mother but she consoled herself by planning, with my father, the reception and compiling the guest list. In the end no one from Sylvia's side attended as her brother and father were, they said, unable to come. Mr Musgrove did provide the princely sum of £5 as a wedding present.

The Playboy male staff football team

CHAPTER 23

Therefore as Mr and Mrs Wrethman we were contracted to work on the MV Kota Singapura which translated into English means *Lion City*. But the newly-weds would be immediately separated since the first stage involved Mike and myself taking off for Singapore to meet Haddad , discuss the set-up and operation of the on-board casino and learn what benefits, in terms of publicity, they hoped this venture would give, the soon to be opened Wrest Point Casino in Hobart, Tasmania.

At the Malaysia Hotel while we awaited the arrival of Federal's executive to arrange our first visit to the ship, we discussed how we, and the four casino staff including Sylvia and Mike's partner Patti, would operate this small casino. To assist us with catering administration and security the company had apparently designated three people from the Australian side including, we were told, a Mr and Mrs Paul Reid and Peter Jules Bible. The latter was first to join us and for me from that moment on he would epitomise an 'Aussie'.

Peter or 'Jules', as he was alternately called, a six foot-plus, solidly built, heavy jowled ex-policeman lumbered into the hotel foyer to announce his arrival and make a fair attempt at crushing every bone in my fingers with his handshake. I was soon to be aware of his particular talent for the descriptive phrase; many of them, if judged by today's politically correct standards in UK, would render him liable for prosecution. At the first meeting in the crowded reception area we were informed that a bunch of 'slopeheads' as he called the local inhabitants, had delayed his arrival. We managed to shush down and curtail the full description of his encounters, to avoid any accusations of insensitivity.

But we would learn you could not keep him quiet for long. I myself was not to be immune; from an early date I was christened 'Mumbles', apparently because, unlike himself who had a permanently thunderous delivery, my low voice tone combined with my still fairly broad Glaswegian accent, made comprehension, for him, at times difficult. No such problem arose with Mike Bennett a voluble wise cracking Londoner who, like Bible, gave the impression of being permanently upbeat. In the company of those two, my position would always be that of 'straight-man'.

The Kota Singapura was a nine thousand ton diesel powered motor vessel that had berths for around three hundred passengers with access to four decks and, when at sea, was manned by two hundred staff and crew.

As the rest of our team would arrive over the next few days, one of the first items on Mike's to-do list was to arrange everyone's accommodation. Mike and his wife Patti would need a double cabin as would Sylvia and myself; then two single cabins for Stevie Callaghan and Julie, the other two staff who had been recruited by Mike. Then of course there would be another two needed for the Australian contingent. It was a small group but we would initially operate only three tables, one roulette and two blackjack.

This was not going to be anything like my previous cruises on the S.S.Andes, as I could already see that the Kota Singapura's facilities, service areas and quality of cabins would never attract high income passengers. But it was the cabins offered to the staff that was to become the first major stumbling block to the continuation of the project.

When the cabins originally allocated to staff were shown to us by Haddad I detected a look of amused disbelief on the face of Mike but, when it became all too clear that the Federal executive was serious, he lost no time in dismissing the possibility that we would accept this accommodation. Even had we all been single males, the positioning and size of the cabins would have been inadequate but as we both required married quarters they were totally unacceptable. At one point it looked like our wives might be welcoming us home instead of we meeting them and the others at Singapore, but Haddad's intransigent stand softened.

The cabin issue having been resolved, we set about the preparation of the casino which would be located in a salon next to what would be the night club. Once again the décor could by no means be described as plush but then we would have been surprised if it had been, given the general standard throughout the ship. While Mike and Jules checked what equipment was already available and supervised the installation of lighting etcetera, I volunteered to shoot off to the customs depot to sign and take delivery of equipment that we'd been advised had just arrived.

Dealing with customs officers in any country is never likely to brighten your day but when you add the Asian look of inscrutability to the normal officious attitude of a Government official you somehow feel that it's going to be a long, long day; and it was.

Having provided the documentation, I was asked to wait. After about fifteen minutes I was again summonsed to the desk and when asked for identification submitted my passport. I waited, as he scrutinized both the documentation and the passport looking up at me every now and again, presumably to compare my actual appearance with the passport photo. I was instructed again to take a seat as he took my passport through to another office. He returned some time later to escort me through to the other section where I was positioned in front of another desk manned by two uniformed officials. The silent scrutiny of the document continued punctuated by an occasional comparison of my facial characteristics with those of the passport photo.

'I'm sorry, is there some problem?' my frustrated enquiry was met with a hand signal which I read as – Wait, be silent!

I waited silently for a few more minutes and then had a document pushed in front of me that I should sign to say that I was responsible for the consignment, identified by number, that I had requested to take into Singapore. At last, I thought, and scribbled my signature. One of the men then escorted me to yet another room and signaled to take a seat at a table.

Time passed once again and I was about to enquire how long this procedure would take when a uniformed official entered accompanied by another, I had not seen before, who carried a folder.

'You are James Hamilton Wrethman, British passport number…….? He read out the details of my passport and brandished it for me to identify.

He then asked me to establish that I had stated and signed that I was responsible for the consignment No …. and that I intended to take it into Singapore. I agreed but was beginning to recognize a legalistic tone in his questioning.

'You are aware that organization of gambling is an illegal offence in Singapore as is the importation of equipment used for the purposes of gambling?'

My stumbling reply in response to this, that the equipment was in transit and would be used on a cruise vessel, was brushed aside and he continued. 'You will be held here until further investigations have been carried out.' As he rose I, probably incoherently, attempted to explain my relatively junior position in my company organization. He stopped to address me again. This time, to inform me that I should be aware that this was indeed a serious offence and, if found guilty, I could incur a lengthy period of imprisonment. While I gave justification for the moniker Bible had given me of 'Mumbles', they both exited and, to my further anguish, locked the door to seemingly commence my imprisonment. After a very brief period of reflection I decided I couldn't just wait until they decided to come back; I began to bang on the door. I prepared myself for their displeasure at my action but was somehow surprised when they eventually opened the door and with visible restraint listened to my appeal for permission, as an accused party, to make the traditional phone call.

It was to be some hours later, following my call for help, before I was to walk free. My message having been transferred from Mike to John Haddad who in turn insisted the Ship's charter company make representations and supply documents to Customs Authority. The incident did of course give additional bantering material to Bible and Bennett, not that the two B's ever ran short.

Sylvia, Patti, Julie and Steve arrived and with Paul Reid and his wife already on board we were now fully staffed and ready to sail to our first port of call, Fremantle.

It wasn't long before the first minor crisis befell the Kota. In the area connected to the casino, passengers could enjoy a drink and listen to some live music provided by the resident band. Unfortunately not all members of the band had arrived before we sailed and, as this included the lead singer, their daily performance of popular songs became somewhat limited. Sensing this could diminish the entertainment value, and eventually reduce numbers who might visit our casino next door, Mike, who could play guitar, invited me, who had sang with him on occasion, to stand in for the missing band members. Hence we became not only casino managers but also entertainers. The relative success we enjoyed can, of course, be attributed to the fact that the customer base was not the affluent cocktail dress and dinner-jacketed clientele seen on my previous cruises but younger, less demanding, travelers looking for a bit of fun and happy to join in with our popular rock songs. Our versatility may also have brought some success to the casino as people did later gravitate to the tables, but the client numbers and level of play could hardly justify the confidence exhibited earlier by our company Executive. This could hardly be seen as a major advertisement for the new Tasmanian casino nor would we build a future client base from the travelers joining the sing-a-long on this ship.

After approximately one week we tied up at Fremantle and were able to make, not only, a brief tour of the port city but also travel the short distance to the fourth largest city in Australia. Perth is a beautiful city that overlooks the Swan River where it expands on a coastal plain before flowing out to the Indian Ocean. With this first brief experience of life 'Down Under' I began to understand the attraction of immigration to Australia for guys I'd met in the Merchant Navy who had been there during their service.

Unfortunately, we had little time to sample all its offerings, including the white beaches, because we had to return to Fremantle to make ready for our second voyage on the Kota.

Table play on the second leg of our project showed no dramatic rise although there were perhaps a few more passengers on board. Day to day activity was for the most part enjoyable principally due to the presence of the two B's who seemed to compete with each other for punch lines. Patti did her best to accommodate this eccentric pair while also giving support to my wife Sylvia who did not seem to be entirely comfortable with the radical change to her previous lifestyle. At this stage I wasn't sure if, like me, she was experiencing a creeping realisation that perhaps she'd taken up the marriage option a little too soon, or she was simply having difficulty, as we all were, of adjusting to somewhat chaotic events in the first period of this project. There were further tests to come, the first major one erupted when were approximately two days away from Singapore. I was never fully aware of what brought about this crisis and accounts tend to vary, but what I am clear about were the consequences. Basically it would seem an accusation had been made by a senior catering manager that restaurant waiters had been involved in some kind of fiddle. The individuals accused quickly garnered support from their colleagues in the kitchen to mount a vociferous rejection of the charge. As the confrontation continued, service in the restaurant became paralysed, leading to further, management intervention, heated verbal exchanges between the two sides then escalated to physical confrontation. As more crew members became involved, and the ships' senior officers were mustered to exert control, all the passengers and non commissioned individuals such as casino and night club entertainers were advised to confine themselves to their cabins.

Rather than wait in our individual cabins we decided that it would be more congenial, and ultimately safer, to congregate in the two adjoining double cabins where Mike, on guitar, and I as lead vocalist, could treat everyone to some old favourites while Jules assailed everyone with old jokes. After a while when the absence of any information became somewhat worrying, Mike, Jules and I decided to make a tentative sorties in opposite directions to see if we could find out what was going on.

We did not need to travel very far before being advised to return. Our cabin de-briefing revealed information that, to some extent, we edited so as not to alarm the ladies. We had heard, the ship's Chief and 2nd Officer, had felt the need to arm themselves, order all rebellious staff to their quarters and as an additional safeguard had called Coast Guard control to come out to ensure the ship's secure passage to Singapore.

To have managed to get his team off the ship alive could be said to be a result for Mike, but not quite the result originally projected after two trips of the casino cruise ship. For our employers a reassessment was surely now essential but we, for the moment, could relax in the hotel and now and again go out to enjoy the charms of Singapore such as the Tiger Balm Gardens and the Thian Hock Keng Temple*.

We had no idea how long the ship's owners, the charter company, seaman's association, worker's groups and companies such as Federal Pacific, would argue over the causes and the handling of the rebellion. Then the culpability and compensation issues, we imagined could take forever. But even if a temporary resolution could be found it was difficult to imagine the same officers, crew and personnel working together.

At this point Mike was instructed by Haddad to travel to Hong Kong to inspect another vessel on which we might operate a casino. His assignment effectively promoted me to Head of Casino Operations on the Kota Singapura, a stress free, temporary and meaningless positional advancement I thought, until 24 hours later when, lucky me, it was announced that the disputes and difficulties had been resolved and we should prepare for the return trip to Fremantle.

In spite of our preoccupations the voyage proved to be trouble free but from a business point of view the casino was also almost profit free, the play on the tables being at a very low income level. It seemed pointless to continue and a call from Mike when we were reached Fremantle not surprisingly, confirmed that the company had decided to refocus their campaign, and our efforts, on the cruise ship now docked in Hong Kong called the Eastern Queen. The switch would be complicated in that it required some of us to join Mike on the new vessel in Hong Kong, sail with it to Singapore and make ready the casino area for the transfer of all the equipment from Kota Singapura. The Kota had of course to return to Singapore from Fremantle and it was necessary contractually to operate the casino to the completion of this trip and then make the transfer. It was decided that I would fly with Sylvia and Patti to Hong Kong to join Mike, while the rest of the team would continue with a reduced operation on the Kota, making preparation to dismantle all equipment as they approached Singapore.

There were no passengers on our preparatory trip to Singapore but it was already fairly apparent that the Eastern Queen's capacity and services would not vary greatly from our previous vessel and so it was difficult to imagine any dramatic improvement in the quality of customers. The casino area was also similar in dimension and style as was the restaurant where it was hoped the influence of our Australian catering expert Paul Reid would ensure a higher level of service for our casino guests.

We tied up well in advance of the arrival of the Kota and, knowing more or less where it would dock, could see that the considerable distance between the berths of the two ships was going to complicate the transportation of the equipment.

This was confirmed the following day when she did tie up on the other side of the port which meant, the removal of all the equipment could not, as was originally hoped, be manually carried from one vessel to the other, thereby avoiding the need to completely dismantle all tables; we would now need a large vehicle to transport them.

Mike and I waited by the dockside as the passengers disembarked before able-seaman Bible could pipe us on board to prepare the equipment and discuss just how we might transport it to the other vessel. But first we were interested to hear how, with depleted numbers, they had fared on their last voyage on the Kota.

Fortunately, as only Steve and Julie could deal, the two gaming tables had been sufficient to satisfy demand. Peter Reid and his wife handled what little catering was required while Jules Bible, although knowing almost nothing about the games, strutted his stuff as boss-man.

In answer to Mike's enquiry about the financial result Jules said Steve had handled the finances which the latter, to our astonishment, now illustrated by having the takings brought out. Each day's income was clearly identified by the container in which it was carried; a large soup-plate. Steve's innovative form of bookkeeping from that day on was known as soup-plate accountancy.

When we had recovered from this hilarious episode we began to prepare the equipment and investigate just how we might transport it to the other vessel. It was suggested that some of the heavier items might be winched off the ship to a large barge and ferried across the bay to the other vessel where again it could be hoisted on board. This could remove the necessity to completely dismantle the tables thereby saving time. With my merchant naval experience I was somewhat sceptical about this however when we found difficulty in renting the second of two large trucks necessary to transport everything that day and were told a barge was available we reluctantly decided to take up this option.

After two days during which we almost lost the tables and Bible to the bottom of Singapore dock and nearly broke our backs carrying heavy equipment up the gangway of the Eastern Queen when no one could be found to assist, either to winch them up, or help us carry them on board, we finally got everything on deck; but decided to go and get pissed before even contemplating the assembly of the tables.

Life on board the Eastern Queen was of little difference to our previous ship and the amounts played on the tables was, if anything, even less than we had seen on the Kota. Then, in line with Paul Reid's professional opinion that everything about the entire enterprise seemed to be jinxed, events took a course that would support his professional assessment. The first was a dispute between a customer and waiter, in the dining area adjoining the casino. At one point as fellow passengers supported the customer's position and the waiter's colleagues rallied to his side, the seemingly improbable prospect of another mutiny became a frightening possibility. Fortunately, although the matter was finally resolved, the entire incident, in an area annexed to the casino, did nothing to create the kind of relaxed atmosphere that would assist us to promote our business.

Two nights later when we had attracted a number of new players to the tables almost without warning the ship began to roll heavily. From my previous experiences at sea I expected this to motivate the bridge officers to temporarily change course and meet the disturbance full on. Instead our roll became even more pronounced. The instability forced us to close the roulette game and Patti and Sylvia dealing blackjack were having great difficulty. Then a dramatic lurch to starboard brought a seated woman screaming and clutching her small chair as she careered sledge-like across an un-carpeted part of the floor to crash into small tables and chairs and then the bulkhead. The contrary lurch brought the debris then cascading across the gaming area. The casino activity was thus terminated without the customary –'last three spins' more like the last three rolls.

The lady was fortunately, and surprisingly, not as badly hurt as we feared she might be, but not surprisingly she was keen to get back on dry land. The storm quickly passed, we cleared the debris and were able to reopen the tables the following day hoping this incident would be the last of what had been a catalogue of misfortunes. It was; a few days later the ship, after failing an inspection in Perth, was refused permission to sail. With this latest setback Federal Pacific finally called it a day. Steve and Julie signed off immediately, the Australian contingent returned to their home base and Mike, with Patti, would wait in Australia for the commencement of the Tasmanian project. Sylvia and myself, although having been promised employment in Australia's first casino, were for the moment in limbo, as it was not yet even near to completion. After a few days it was announced that the Eastern Queen would be permitted to sail and, although the casino would not operate, Sylvia and I could retain our cabin to return to Singapore and from there arrange a flight home.

For the first time during our assignment on those two boats nothing dramatic happened so my wife and I were able to relax and enjoy the voyage and contemplate what future we envisaged. With all the drama that had unfolded I doubt if she, and certainly not I, had considered how our relationship was developing. We had not devoted much time to each other and although it had to be said that the difficulties we had encountered would have tested the resilience of the most adaptable person I still felt that she of all our party had contributed the least and complained the most. I did not of course say that to her and believed that when we arrived at a more settled lifestyle she would return to the good natured and more positive girl to which I had first been attracted.

The most immediate question was how we would handle this interim period. The job in Tasmania still appeared to be my most attractive opportunity, but when could I start? If it would not be for some time, how and where would we live? When we arrived at the Singapore hotel Johnson Kwok, the local man who had assisted us when setting up on the Kota, was there to meet us and relay a message from Mike. It seemed the start of the project in Tasmania could be a matter of six or seven weeks; in which case it would be pointless to return to find work and accommodation in U.K.; on the other hand, to stay in our current hotel in Singapore was prohibitively costly. We considered travelling back to Australia but Johnson Kwok and his charming wife Lucy presented us with an alternative solution.

They invited us to a temporary stay at an apartment they had taken but had not yet moved to in a relatively new estate in Singapore.

Tao Payoh, was one of the earliest satellite public housing estates in Singapore and the name, which in the local language apparently means the 'Big Swamp', refers to the land, reclaimed and developed, on which part of it was built. The importance of this development to the economy and the social well being of the local people was emphasised when it was twice included in Queen Elizabeth 11's visits to Singapore.

Our presence did not quite create the same level of excitement as that of the British Head of State but it did generate intense interest, as up to that moment it would seem that no Western expats had been known to reside in that area. The development was the first prototype in Singapore, being not just a public housing estate but a neighbourhood with its own shopping and community centres in leisurely and generous open space.

Part of that space was taken up with community dining areas that offered all day long cheap and appetising local food. This removed the difficulty we would have had to shop around for Western food or learn what local produce to buy and how to cook it. However we could never have anticipated the level of interest the attendance, of a white western couple, at the community centre might provoke. Though somewhat disconcerting to have people stop and direct the attention of their children to you, we imagined that the interest would rapidly diminish; not so, in fact we seemed to become a sort of attraction with people coming from other local areas to see the 'foreign residents'.

I now waited with anticipation to hear from Tasmania and plan our new home, but the news I was to receive necessitated a more urgent plan.

In the absence of what seemed like any reliable postal delivery service, and a postal address in my own name, I made a periodic call to my parents to be answered by my mother in a distressed state; my father had been diagnosed with a serious illness. Her description of his condition was somewhat confusing but one thing was clear he had been serious enough for him to be taken to hospital.

It was now necessary for us to return to UK so that I could be in Scotland to see my father and give support to my mother. There was no question of Sylvia remaining in Singapore and, although she would not have wished for this to be the cause, I suspected she would have, in any case, preferred earlier to return to UK.

CHAPTER 24

I'm now unsure if the postponement of our new life in Australia was, to Sylvia, a great disappointment or not. She had never quite demonstrated a great enthusiasm for the entire project nor had she blended particularly well with the people with whom we had come into contact in our travels so far. I suppose it could be said she merely, coped. Now she was going to have to cope with another set of experiences and conditions.

In times of family crisis an only child status gives added responsibility. In this case my mother in fear of losing her husband and with difficulties to manage and finance her day to day affairs looked upon me as her only salvation. This is not to say she received no offer of help from friends and other family members, but perhaps her Protestant stoicism would not allow her to seek 'outside' assistance. On visiting my father I learned that although he would remain under close observation there was no immediate threat to his life. I also received notification from Ron Hurley that the project in Tasmania was now about to start and if we were to take up the positions originally offered we should make immediate plans to return to Australia. Some decisions you make in life, in retrospect, seem more crucial than others and this seems to be the case with my decision to inform Federal that we could not now accept the positions in Australia's first casino. There seemed to be no other option for me as I did not feel I could leave my father, or my mother, until I was confident that he would make a full recovery. I was not so much supported in this decision by Sylvia, as unopposed; I believe she had no great desire to return to Australia. So we agreed Sylvia would travel south to visit her father while I remained in Glasgow to be close to dad and assist my mother.

As my father continued to improve from what was considered to be a stroke it was obvious that he would not return to work as a crane driver. Apart from the possible effects from the physical exertion of having to climb a hundred foot step ladder several times a day there was also the fear of what might happen should he have a reoccurrence while operating the massive crane. He hoped that he might be offered a less demanding position but I feel the company, already facing a diminishing order book and difficulties to reduce the workforce, grasped the opportunity and obliged him to accept an early retirement due to ill health.

I myself could not continue much longer without an income so fortunately my old friend Jimmy McCarvill who had first encouraged me to join him, in trying out the gaming industry, was once again on hand to point me in the direction of a new opportunity. This time it was a small casino in Greenock owned by a local entrepreneur, that Jimmy had heard, was looking for experienced staff.

The operation was small, the majority of the players being local businessmen and quite a few of Italian origin; a demographic peculiarity that stems from an influx of Italian immigrants between the wars.

But the level of business hardly seemed to warrant the number of staff employed, which included several former colleagues from my early days in Stakis casinos. There did not seem to be any great prospects of promotion, but in any case I viewed my employment there as simply a temporary means of earning a living. I couldn't really imagine Greenock as a long term home and was sure Sylvia, when she finally joined me, would be even less likely to settle in that part of the world.

My stay there was to be even shorter than I anticipated. When inspecting the tables I could already see that no strict operating procedures had been introduced and certain customers seemed to have license to infringe rules that were in place; curiously, unlike most casinos that applied this flexibility in policy, some of them were not high rollers.

One of my former colleagues, picking up on my criticism of some of the company's methods, agreed that it was not the most professionally run operation and those who could do a professional job, like him and I for instance, were poorly paid. It was to be the first of several discussions along the same lines. I began to get the impression he was preparing to suggest some form of protest.

I had passed up on a number of offers to go for a drink after work because of my fairly long drive home but after one particularly tedious night I agreed to stop for a quick one. After some preliminary chat he got to the point, 'I was never going to get anywhere in Greenock with my rigid attitude. I would only get in the way of other people trying to make a few quid. I should loosen up and if so could possibly make myself a bonus.'

The message was clear, it was time for me to look elsewhere to earn a living.

A return to the company that had introduced me to a career in the Gambling world I could never have predicted but at that moment in time it was a most welcome opportunity. This time at Reo Stakis Casinos I would be employed at their leading club, the Chevalier, where I would reunite with some old workmates. Reflecting their origins, senior positions were still held by Cypriot managers and Mr Fivos Scolarious held the top spot of General Manager; he had his own peculiarities but thankfully his management style was far removed from the idiosyncratic Mr Peters of Regency Casino fame.

The lifestyle I was leading could only be described as transitory as I monitored my father's condition, gave comfort where I could to my mother and arranged temporary accommodation for myself and my wife. Sylvia had not complained but neither had she demonstrated any great desire to relocate to Scotland. But that matter that had been of greatest concern now seemed to be taking a more positive turn. The improvement in my father's health had recently been illustrated by his renewed concern for the form of Glasgow Rangers and now the doctor authorized his release from hospital.

With my Dad comfortably back in the care of my relieved mother, almost coincidentally, my next career move came on offer and once again via my old pal Jimmy McCarvill; this time, as assistant to him at a new casino to be opened just outside Dundee. The new appointment once again required me to travel alone, find accommodation and settle into the job before bringing Sylvia to yet another 'foreign' destination. The owners of the Thistle Casino, at Hilltown on the outskirts of the city, were local businessmen known as 'the two Stan-s' Petrie and Duncan, who had only recently acquired the gaming licence and had given Jimmy the task of equipping, staffing and opening the club. Apart from myself, McCarvill had recruited other former colleagues from Stakis including Jimmy Brown as Pit Boss/Inspector with whom, during this interim period, I would share accommodation. The house, provided by our employers, where we would live, was a classic grey brick Georgian mansion in Broughty Ferry an area on the west side of the River Tay and just a few miles from the bridge of the same name.

It was Jimmy Brown who was to be first to feel the full impact of my appointment.

He had been housed at Panmure Terrace prior to my arrival and although aware that he would, for a period of time, share accommodation with me, he had not been given the date I would move in. He was therefore unaware of my presence when he returned from a short break in Glasgow to find he could not open the door because I, without thinking, had put on the secondary lock. I did not occur to him that in his absence I may have arrived in which case he would have rang the doorbell. Instead worryingly, and for him unfortunately, he succeeded in levering open the sash window on the ground floor lounge window. The strange noise alerted me to that room, where in the fading light of early evening the leg of an intruder suddenly appeared through the partly opened window. Decision time! I couldn't wait or hope to warn him off ; I ran towards the widow and met the crouching figure with an uppercut! My disappointment at not landing it as effectively as I'd intended was quickly alleviated as the recognizable figure of Brown screeched with fright and fell back groaning on the front lawn. I raced out to assist my colleague who was suffering more from the fright and fall, than the actual punch. His recovery didn't take too long; I suspect, knowing something of his background, this was by no means the first time a member of his household had floored him.

The Thistle Casino was to be a brief episode in my career and I cannot really say that my experience there added greatly to my professional management knowhow although it did offer me additional experience in balancing personal duties and responsibilities. For various reasons , my wife, still in England, had not yet joined me and in our frequent telephone calls I sensed a tone of reluctance. My parents were still adjusting to my father's early retirement and recent ill-health and they tried, without success, to convey that they did not expect me, on my day off, to make the drive across country to Glasgow. The job itself was demanding, in the sense that a small casino in an outlying area has limited possibilities and the marketing restrictions within the British Gaming Act prohibited any of the normal promotional initiatives that might expand the client base.

Sylvia finally joined me and for the first time since our marriage our day to day life had a feeling of continuity and normality. Jim McCarvill's wife, also recently arrived in Dundee and likewise from the North of England, gave Sylvia someone with which she could communicate on equal terms. I was also encouraged by the news that my father seemed to be recovering and had once again taken up an interest in long walks and on visits to Ibrox. But in spite of the apparent stability in my life, or because of it and the fact that I could now concentrate my thoughts on my chosen profession, I could not deny the feeling inside that my employment in this small operation had been nothing more than convenient and transitional phase in my career.

As the time moved on, my desire to look for a new challenge was reinforced by Sylvia's gradual but obvious disillusionment with life in Dundee. So a message from an old Manchester colleague that an opportunity was about to arise in that city was a little too tempting to ignore. The Oxford casino was a small newly licensed casino in the centre of the city owned by a man who I knew as a client in my previous Manchester employment at the Salford Albion. Although having less seniority than I'd had in Dundee I was commanding a higher salary with the possibility of promotion if the business was successful.

After the first two months the prospect of expansion and my personal advancement seemed a long way off. Although the casino was conveniently located in the city centre the facilities on offer by such a small unit could not really hope to compete with the larger well established casinos. Once again it was apparent that the restrictions of the British Gaming legislation seriously inhibited the small companies coming late on the scene as they prohibited them from running promotional campaigns that companies in other sectors of the economy would mount to announce their arrival on the marketplace.

A prank played on one of our colleagues is perhaps the most memorable event of my time spent at the Oxford. It partly came about because the slow growth of business permitted us too much time to indulge in banter and speculation. For some of us it was speculation on how business would go and where we might go if it did not reach initial expectations. For Steve, a recent recruit to the gaming business, his speculation centered on football pools and what he'd do when he 'inevitably' determined correctly the eight results that would capture the Littlewoods' Jackpot. Sitting in the staff room, pen in hand and deep in thought he'd select the draws for that weekend then ceremoniously wave his coupon and announce 'this is the one!' before slipping the copy into the top pocket of his dinner suit. At that period almost all football matches took place on Saturday, so the second part of the weekly ritual took place that evening in the rest room when he'd race in to extract the copy coupon, compare it with the results and, with a look of incredulity, discard it in the litter basket. To the rest of us, his apparent certainty that it was only a matter of time was a source of constant amusement.

I'm not sure who first suggested the cruel prank but have to admit complicity as I was present during its set up and implementation; it consisted of someone having a blank coupon and filling in the appropriate football results as soon as they were known. Then, before Steve arrived in the rest room, exchange this certain 'jackpot' winner for the copy in the top pocket of his dinner suit which he'd conveniently and carelessly left in an unlocked locker. The joke relied on him not remembering exactly what teams and results he had selected. On cue he arrived and made for the restroom and I, being already on the gaming floor supervising the opening of a table, hurried to complete that task and follow him in to see the reaction. The owner Jeff was also present on the floor which at this early hour had only a few customers present. I only just got to the door leading to the staff quarters when I heard the roar of exultation and, as I entered, Steve brushed by laughing and called back to all of us 'You're all welcome to a drink, I'm off to the pub, if not, see you at the Mini Club later!'

'Steve, Steve! Hang on it's a ….' a chorus of people implored him. I paused but then realizing what was happening I moved to catch him up as he moved out across the floor, towards the owner.

'Steve…! Wait….' I stretch out an arm to catch his shoulder; too late.

'Know what you can do with the job? Stuff it…I'm off to celebrate!' he waved the copy-coupon at his Employer, and chuckling strode off hurried off towards the door leaving the baffled owner looking to me, and others coming up close behind, for some explanation.

The owners' amused reaction to the reluctant admission of guilt by the instigators, and complicity by the rest of us, and his magnanimous offer to ignore Steve's unofficial notice of termination surprised everyone. But it depended on the pranksters finding a way of breaking the unwelcome news to the victim while risking serious consequences and then follow that onerous task by convincing the unfortunate Steve to make an apologetic return to work.

After apologies and a few unpleasant discussions a truce was agreed and Steve returned to the Casino but an atmosphere of unease remained and only really diminished because one by one the main protagonists, seeing there was no real future at the Oxford, moved on to other employment; something I was once again contemplating.

I now am quite sure that my relationship with Sylvia would never have worked under any circumstances but the almost nomadic lifestyle we had led since our marriage would have tested any couple. We now decide that we would return to London where it was hoped she would also find work although once again we would be separated while I found work for myself and accommodation for both of us. She went to Leeds while I became a temporary guest of an old Glaswegian work colleague and his wife who now lived in North London. I had at one point thought to shop around for a position as at that time, in the capital, business was growing rapidly due, in part, to the residual effect of the 'Swinging London' image but more importantly to problems in the Middle East, and in particular Beirut, which had forced rich Arabs to look for a new playground and they seemed to have chosen London. Of all the casinos, my former club Playboy seemed to be in the best position to exploit this unforeseen potential gold-rush. My personal take from this gold-rush was a contract valued at £ 70 per week and an agreement to work up to 88 hours within every two weeks. So, I was back working with the Park Lane Bunnies as Inspector of Roulette and Blackjack and housed in a new apartment near Hampstead Heath with the former Bunny Odette, now Sylvia Wrethman, with whom I hoped I could begin to establish a more stable relationship. However, we were to see that the recent disruptive lifestyle wasn't really the reason for our differences, in fact, the difficulties encountered in our travels and the immediate necessity to deal with them had perhaps concealed the truth that our characters were basically incompatible.

Her response to any disagreement, and they were fairly frequent, was a slamming of doors and crashing of any item within her reach. This would infuriate me and when I reacted angrily she would then lock herself in the bedroom. Though I did not really need much excuse this atmosphere justified my decision to go with the guys for drinks after work rather than go home, which of course fuelled even more acrimonious exchanges and was also to bring about another unfortunate episode.

An extended session at Gulliver's Night Club was followed by a visit to Covent Garden Market where the bars were open continuously.

I finally decided mid-morning having consumed several litres of alcohol to make my way home and stupidly oblivious to the dangers to myself and others thought nothing of taking my car. I was somewhere near Hammersmith when I was pulled over by a Police patrol. I'm not sure if it was a procedural tactic to observe my comportment but their requests brought out the worst in an inebriated Glaswegian.

'Can you step out of the car?' I responded to this reluctantly.

'What's in your boot? '

Apparently, I then faced up to him, 'My foot, you want tae feel it?'

This didn't endear me to the officers. Twenty four hours later I finally got to my happy home minus a car, a mode of transport would be without for some time until my suspension for 'driving under the influence' expired.

Not too long afterwards I would also be without a wife when we finally decided we would both be happier to go our own way.

CHAPTER 25

Single again, and without a car, I looked for accommodation near to my place of work to avoid the necessity, in the early morning when I finished work, of taking taxis, the only form of transport available at those hours. The cost of accommodation in the West End would of course have been prohibitive if two Bunnies working with me had not been looking for a third person to share the rental cost of a large premises in a Mews in Park Lane just round the corner from Playboy I was therefore happy to move in with Bonnie and Maggie.

The return to my former place of work had certainly been timely from the point of view of remuneration but more importantly job interest. The club had been successful when I'd last worked there and had continued to prosper from its image as a venue that attracted famous sports and media stars. But now, even the income from affluent members was being surpassed by the enormous increase in revenue from rich Middle Eastern visitors to London. Wealthy males from Arab states with no access in their part of the world to gambling facilities and clubs staffed with attractive females found the Playboy a temptation to great to resist.

This had made the company's intention to extend the operation to include tables with higher maximum bets all the more urgent. The floor above the ground level reception which in British terminology would normally have been called the 2nd floor became the 1st floor VIP salon owing to the company's American origin and ownership. This new area offered a large restaurant and gaming area with high limit roulette, blackjack and punto-banco. Curiously, the existing gaming salons on the two floors above continued to be referred to as the 3rd and 4th floor.

Having returned to the Bunny Club as an Inspector, within a few months I was being used as a relief Pit Boss and with the opening of the VIP had been proposed as a Unit Manager on that floor. The term Unit Manager, it was said, had recently been introduced by Derek Bernard who as assistant to the Casino General Manager Bernie Mulherne was in charge of Training and Development. His reputation with many casino employees was that of a pedantic bureaucrat in love with regulation and procedural detail and this latest innovation, the changing of the title Pit Boss to that of Unit Manager, was seen as a way of implying higher status to those individuals while keeping their salary at the same level. In some cases the title was also used to justify additional responsibility. This was certainly the case with Unit Managers in the VIP level where I was to work at the request of its Night Manager, Peter Byrne, but as this was an actual promotion I had no complaint with my job's title, nor with the level of responsibility.

In effect, apart from the two previously mentioned executives Mulherne and Bernard the casino table operations were managed by three senior managers. The tables being open from midday until 4 a.m the following morning this necessitated two complete shifts, the day - from midday until 8 p.m - involved the management of the VIP and the 3rd Floor only, while the night-duty from 8 p.m until 4 a.m. involved all three floors being in operation. The two levels on dayshift were managed by Tom Norton an Irishman with the traditional 'gift of the gab'. The later shift with all three floors was divided between the obdurate Jim Madison, who handled only the 4th Floor, while the VIP and 3rd were the responsibility of Peter Byrne.

Having already worked under all three I was happy to have been allocated the position under Peter who, even at this early stage, was in my opinion the most professional of the three.

My duties involved the allocation to the tables of Inspectors, the majority of whom were male, and dealers who were almost entirely Bunny girls. This was done at the start of the shift and each time they returned from a twenty minute rest period; given when they had worked a minimum of one hour on the game. Knowledge of the staff and their ability on each game was of course essential. It was also necessary to observe the volume of play, the type of player and the demands of individual players, to assess what staff would be best suited to allocate to that table.

The Unit Manager had also to ensure with the individual game inspectors that the stock of cash chips(table float) which had been credited to each table at the start of the shift remained at a sufficient level to facilitate payment of winning bets. An insufficient amount of high value chips would require him to order an additional stock (Fill) from the cash desk and supervise it's delivery, and verification of the amount by the staff of that table. Each hour, Inspectors would estimate the current result of the table and this I would verify and collect to then calculate the estimated overall floor result. Results could be assessed fairly accurately by counting the amount by which the stock of chips had diminished and reducing this from cash taken and recorded when it was deposited in the tables' 'drop box'.

Along with these administrative duties, the Unit Manager had also to identify and familiarize himself with the players, greet and take note of the regulars and newcomers preferences and requests, and if necessary, intercede in any disputes that occurred during play to ensure compliance with regulations and table procedures without damaging customer relations. Security of the operation was of course another essential duty of the Unit Manager in a business that dealt with such a large amount of money. Unit Managers/Pit Bosses had to be continuously on the lookout for behavioral indicators in both staff and customers that might suggest dishonest intent. In those days the CCTV technology in existence was at a very early stage of development so physical surveillance was all.

On the VIP floor, even more so than the other areas, all necessary procedures had to be carried out in such a way that they did not interfere with the essential objective of creating an environment that would encourage members to play as long, as often and as much as possible; so a fundamental aspect of the job was that of public relations.

If P.R. was essential in the work of Unit Managers it was even more so in the work of the Floor Manager particularly given the culture of the Middle Eastern clients and other foreign VIP's who expected to be recognised and treated preferentially by the most senior manager present.

In Peter Byrne, the Playboy, and myself, could not have asked for a person more suited to the task of dealing with individuals, sometimes volatile, often demanding but most certainly crucial to the profitability of the business. The other managers, in my opinion, had either insufficient charisma to handle customers or displayed excessive reverence to the high rollers. However, shortly after being given the title of Unit Manager I was included, with Peter and other managers, in a programme that offered additional insight into the skills of managing employees and clients. This consisted of a course, organised by Derek Bernard but I suspect instigated by a higher authority, the main part of which was a seminar on Transactional Analysis, a theory by a Psychiatrist, Eric Berne. The basic message being, that everyone's psyche consisted of three persons – the Child, the Parent and the Adult. The Child, can have us react as if being threatened, put upon or treated unfairly. The Parent, when shown, can show dominant and overbearing tendencies. The Adult is likely to be more receptive and understanding. The theory expounded was, that when one is responding to another you must first recognise what, of the three, they are currently displaying. If it is not the Adult, which is the most desirable, from the point of view of your continued relationship, then, as our tutor told us, by strategic use of the proper language you must – 'Hook the Adult' in the other person. We were then given a series of examples of what adult approaches would act as a 'Hook'.

It could have been no more than a week later when our recently acquired knowledge was to be put to the test. A new Arab client had been playing on Blackjack, but by his conduct had displayed that he was not properly conversant with the rules. Having received a request from the table inspector I politely intervened to explain to him the procedures; this was met by a grunt, in his own language, and a dismissive wave of his arm. Just at that moment Peter Byrne, who had come to request me to perform another task, arrived and indicated that he would talk with the gentleman. I left him to it and moved towards another table but had not gone very far when my attention was diverted by the shouting and screaming from the area I had just left. I turned to see Peter shrink back from the enraged arm-waving Arab who now threw chips across the table before storming off towards the door, conveniently as our security would have had to remove him in any case. Coincidently, Derek Bernard who had been dining in the restaurant at the far end of the room witnessed this behaviour and now joined us. 'What caused all that?' he enquired.   Peter shrugged, looked at me with a half smile. 'I was just trying to Hook his Adult'.

The private side of my life could not be said to be uneventful as there were no shortage of young ladies at my workplace always ready to break the Playboy's 'no fraternising' rule and of course at nightclubs and drinking holes we frequented after work there were also girls from other London casinos. I had however, reduced my alcohol consumption and was not staying out quite as late as before, perhaps because I had no one at home I wished to avoid, but also because I had returned to sport, football in particular, but also the occasional cricket match.

Back home in Scotland my mother was delighted to report that my father, although having retired from full time work at the shipyard after his bout of ill health, had recovered sufficiently to resume his daily walks and his position as steward at Ibrox with his beloved Glasgow Rangers.

But bad news had come from Hobart Tasmania of the death of Phil DiNardo who, had been hospitalised with a disease from which he had failed to recover. At that period not so much was known of HIV and our first reports were that it was a form of blood poisoning. Later it was said to have been Aids which of course would have been understandable given his lifestyle but I'm not sure if it was ever officially confirmed.

Before my change of plan I had looked forward to working with him again in Hobart although from what I hear, perhaps I was fortunate not to witness the rapid physical decline and passing of an old friend.

The level of play on the tables of the VIP was increasing by enormous amounts mostly due to rich Arab players many of whom had previously entered only with cash in thousand-pound plastic envelopes. Now, even those amounts were insufficient to satisfy their gambling instincts of some players and they had arranged with the casino to have a facility to sign cheques. The Gaming Act was very clear, and under no circumstance could a licence holder offer their members anything that could be categorised as 'credit'. A facility to sign cheques could only be given once a player had requested a maximum limit and had authorised the casino to solicit references from his/her bank. When this had been done and the amount authorised had been set, the casino could then accept cheques up to that amount but, only on the condition, the money having been lost, that the cheques were banked on the next banking day. Myself and other senior managers under the supervision of Peter Byrne adhered strictly to this regulation, but even in these early days there were signs that not all floor managers were sticking to the letter of the law; something that quite some time later was to have a disastrous effect on Playboy.

Without doubt the Playboy Club during this period was one of the most exciting and entertaining places that anyone could hope to work, there are not many places where in the course of your work shift you could come into contact with a Hollywood star such as Tony Curtis, the most famous footballer of the day George Best, or Tennis superstar Illie Nastase.

One person, whose artistic creations were sought after then but are even more valuable today, played a part in one of the most amusing incidents of my time at the club. I had that evening been paying particular attention to the needs of one of our high rollers, an oil rich Arab sheik who played the maximum bets on at least two or three boxes on Blackjack. Unlike the practice in casinos in other jurisdictions with less regulation we were unable to give this player exclusivity although he had let it be known that he preferred to play alone on the table. Peter had agreed that while seats were available at other tables both he and I would attempt to diplomatically steer other players to those tables and in fact to further discourage play at the Sheik's table we reduced the number of seats.

Our tactic had worked well and our VIP player seemed content although he was in fact losing quite a few thousand pounds. Peter had been called upstairs and I had been occupied with a client at the cash desk for quite some time when a touch on my arm diverted me.

'Meester Manager!' I turned to face the Sheik. 'Meester Manager there is a tramp on my table.'

I looked over to the blackjack table to see the familiar figure of Lucian Freud sitting on the end box in his scruffy paint splattered clothes while the Bunny dealer shuffled the cards in preparation for the next shoe. This situation did present a problem; Lucien was a VIP member who, although unlikely to play in quantities as high as the Sheik, was nevertheless a valued customer by virtue of the amounts he did play and the frequency of his visits.

'Actually Sir, this gentleman is a very famous artist who has no doubt come here directly from his studio, that is why he is covered in paint. His paintings are very valuable and are sold for large sums of money.'

He listened to my words intently then nodding, what I hoped was an understanding, slowly made his way back to the table where the girl and Lucian now waited for him to cut the shuffled cards. After finishing the matter with the other member I approached the potentially problematic table to find both players now in friendly communication. I happily left them to it, to report the situation to Peter who had just returned to the floor.

It was to be more than one hour later when seeing the immanent departure of Freud both Peter and I approached to bid him farewell and thank him for his visit, which we knew in the end had resulted in a loss although at one point he had been winning.

'Ah thank you gentlemen,' he said good humouredly. 'Well it's at least been profitable tonight.' Before either of us could find a response to this doubtful assessment he continued. 'The Sheik has agreed to buy two of my works, without even seeing them.'

I did not negotiate an agent's fee.

No one could possibly deny the success of London's Playboy Club, but only those who worked there, and were part of the management structure, such as Peter Byrne, myself, and others who were not sycophantic followers of the Chairman Victor Lownes and his cabal, could see that a large part of this success was fortuitous and was achieved in spite of the dubious policies of its most senior executives. It is probably true that the original decision to open a Bunny Club there was a rational business policy timed to exploit the 'Swinging London' image of the 60's which in many ways marked the liberalisation of Western European societies; but the originator of the Playboy concept Hugh Hefner, could not have anticipated the conditions that would make the casino one of the most successful in the world.

No one in that organisation could possibly have predicted the surge in oil prices that would create so many Middle Eastern multi-millionaires, nor the escalating conflicts in that region that would motivate them to look for places in the West to enjoy their wealth. Fortunately no other capital in Europe by that time had the facilities nor the popular image that London enjoyed.

It was already evident that the Chairman Lownes, appointed by the company's originator Hugh Hefner, had taken a lead from him in the sense that he not only considered the organisation a business to generate income but a personal playground.

Playboy Bunnies were not obligated to attend his private parties, on the premises or at his country residence, but it was generally known that girls who did were favoured by those in senior positions who also wished to win approval.

This situation created clear divisions, between Managers and supervisors who approved of this behaviour and cooperated, Senior staff who were aware of it but chose to ignore it, and those, like Peter Byrne and myself, who refused to cooperate and by eventually speaking out against it would make themselves unpopular.

But in spite of the potential problems in the workplace both my professional and private life was, for the moment, satisfying. Many people looking back at that period will be surprised by this because in by the end of 1973 we had just embarked on what would go down as perhaps the most turbulent time, both politically and socially, in post war British history.

The Conservative government of that day faced surging fuel prices as aggressive Arab regimes sought not only to, exploit their resources, but punish Britain for its imperialistic past and supporting Israel. This increased the already high rate of inflation and made it essential for the government to look for ways to decrease consumption and costs, the latter it did by limiting wage rises. The miners union seeing the Government's vulnerability and increased reliance on coal then used industrial action to force their demands for wage rises. This put further pressure on the Tory regime and as production of electricity fell below industrial requirements they implemented a policy which to this day is known as the 'Three Day Week', in effect, it limited all businesses, except essential services, to electrical supplies sufficient only for three days operation. This being in the winter period of long dark nights the country was essentially plunged into darkness for much of the time.

It was a testing period for many people but I personally managed to get through it, bolstering my spirits by such things as an occasional candlelit dinner and drinks, with a Playboy Bunny.

Actually the casinos in general managed to function by using temporary lighting, at times powered by their own generators. Ironically, some of the beneficiaries, of oil policies which had helped damage the UK economy and brought about the hardship and restrictions, would at night be losing thousands of pounds on the tables of London casinos while complaining about inconveniences they had encountered during that day.

The Tories lost the next election narrowly to Labour and although there was no improvement in the economy they restored the working week. But now residents of London were to face an even more immediate threat than just a drop in living standards; the Provisional Irish Republican Army or IRA had targeted England's capital.

Several bombs had gone off in the city and all management and staff of businesses and public places had been put on alert. At Playboy the reception and security staff had been told to advise all visitors on arrival of new security measures which obligated them to identify the contents of their bags and/or packages and where possible check them in to the cloakroom. Senior floor staff were also advised to be vigilant at all times and report any suspicious articles or behavior.

Not surprisingly, during this period there were to be many false alarms some of them, it has been said, perpetrated by the IRA or their sympathizers to intensify the terror, others, not surprisingly, by malicious idiots hell bent on causing disruption. In the case of casinos there was of course always the possibility a player, feeling aggrieved by his losses or some supposed unfairness shown towards him by a casino employee might make a bogus alarm call.

The company had been advised to formulate an evacuation procedure that would be followed in the event of a credible threat. We, on the floor, were not informed of the criteria to be met to justify such a decision nor did we know who in fact would take that decision; we were told that - on the command from a senior executive - all games would stop and customers would be advised to leave the building as quickly as possible by the public entrance unless for security reasons an alternative exit was designated. Staff would then follow closely behind.

Within a few weeks the building had already been evacuated twice after threats which were obviously proven to be false. I had not been on duty on those occasions which had seen both clients and staff ushered out of the premises and on to Park Lane where traffic had been temporarily brought to a halt; the sudden appearance on the street of scores of shapely Bunnies in their distinctive costumes drew much attention from a curious male public; perhaps giving a further incentive, for some individuals, to make false alarm calls.

But one particular night I was not to miss the drama. Peter had received a call from Bernie Mulherne to inform him that they had received an alert, that an explosive device had been placed somewhere on the premises and that all departments should now make an swift and immediate search for any suspicious container while also making preparations to evacuate.

We alerted inspectors to be prepared to announce last coup on each table while I and three others, trying not to cause panic amongst customers and staff, attempted a discreet but hasty search under and between tables and behind curtains. After a few moments, Peter signaled from a position near to the Punto Banco table that a leather satchel had been found, of which, no one claimed ownership or knowledge. As the security staff, present on our floor, assisted staff to inform clients to make an immediate exit, Peter, as instructed, called the number he had been given to report the find. He was told, perhaps unnecessarily, that no one should touch the package and to clear that immediate area of people. A few moments later, while our manager received a return call from Mulherne, the Head of Security arrived with two other security staff, gave hurried instructions to his and other employees to clear the immediate area where the satchel lay, but keep the passageway to the door clear. Then, as every heart on the floor missed a beat, he picked up the supposed explosive package and, with one of has assistants on either side, walked briskly across the gaming floor, through the restaurant and out to the main stair and down to the street entrance. Peter nervously informed us that the call from Bernie was to tell him that it was feared that, given the nature of the warning received, there seemed to be no time to make a complete evacuation. Even more that before, everyone now prayed that the bravery shown by the security chief and his staff would not be at the highest cost to themselves. As some employees and clients made their way gingerly to the windows to get some indication of what was happening, the telephone rang again; I was nearest. I recognised immediately the distinctive delivery of Derek Bernard who, when I had identified myself, began to ask if I had seen the bag that had been found when the alarm had been given. When I described it and where it had been found, he said he now understood and rang off. Peter, I could see, was trying to read the puzzlement on my face but when I told him the content of the call he was no wiser.

Still in limbo we waited, hoping not to hear a bang, the telephone rang again and we jumped.

This time Peter answered. 'Oh no! You've gotta be fucking jokin!' His eyes closed, he shook his head and after a few moments he put the phone down. 'That bag was left down here by Derek Bernard before we opened today, it contained a new product for cleaning roulette wheels he'd been trying out. He forgot to mention he'd left it.'

A short time later when we had reopened the tables and most of the players, curiously unfazed by all these activities, had returned to play. We were standing, Peter and I in the middle of the gaming floor when the head of Security strode across the restaurant floor to the gaming area, closely followed by his assistants, holding the satchel which when he got a little nearer he hurled in the air to land closely by our feet with an announcement which sounded like 'Here's your fuckin' bomb back!' He then exited through the staff door.

I suppose there was some justification in blaming two shifts of gaming supervisors for not detecting the unaccompanied satchel earlier, but we never did hear what words passed between Security and Derek Bernard, the latter's forgetfulness having exposed them, not only to the terrifying experience of having to handle a suspected bomb, but also the humiliating experience, after having stopped all traffic and brought police and national security services to state of full alert, to have the bomb disposal team return to them the company's bag of new cleaning materials.

In the aftermath, although the Security Head's action in the first instance can only be seen as heroic, the ludicrous outcome permitted his department's large army of detractors to return, from the uncomfortable position of having to consider him and his assistants as heroes, to their long standing view of them as insidious buffoons. This animosity stemming largely from security's mandate to snoop on employees, in their private life, to ensure compliance with the rule on no fraternization between male and female staff. The script describing the removal of the satchel from the gaming floor was therefore rewritten for all those who had not been present. It now had the Head gingerly pick up the bag, hold it at arms length, wincing and grimacing as he shuffled across the floor, both assistants walking as far apart as possible with fingers in their ears.

In spite of all the drama and disruption the club continued to attract large numbers of famous, rich and influential people and each day provided talking points for our after work drinking sessions. I was now looking for another apartment where I might conduct a private life free from the scrutiny of two female colleagues who might be tempted to give accounts of my liaisons in the 'rumour mill' that was the Bunny restroom.

The new accommodation at Eardley Crescent, Earls Court was ideal in many ways being still close to central London while being nowhere near as expensive. It was also walking distance from my new interest at Stamford Bridge, Chelsea F.C.

I had watched several of the London teams but perhaps what influenced my choice was the fact that Chelsea played in blue like my first love Glasgow Rangers, with whom in fact they had a long standing relationship; also they had in their lineup two of my favourite players Scotland's Charlie Cooke and Peter Osgood (The Os).

I myself was now playing regular football again, with the re-formed Playboy team, which had entered the Hotel and Catering League Division 3, a highly competitive tournament. This was an incentive for me to further reduce my alcohol intake and make another attempt to stop smoking, a habit I had first acquired during my Govan shipyard days. Ironically, the day chosen to finally forego the dreaded weed could not have been worse. I had just had a two day break from work and had not heard of the new public relations initiative of the Playboy hierarchy, so I arrived to find small containers of free cigarettes at every gaming table in the VIP room. Customers were therefore lighting up even more than usual, blowing smoke everywhere, but even worse, many of them with whom I had an amicable relationship would dangle these containers in front of my face and insist I join them in partaking of a freebie. Although during the next few days there were several moments when I almost succumbed, fortunately the strength of my desire to reach a level of fitness for sport overcame this temptation.

From my regular calls to home I could detect that my father had made an amazing recovery. He was now working quite a few days per week with Ranger's Football Club and with the season drawing to a close he and my mother were planning to go on holiday. Having just taken up my new apartment and the colleague with whom I had intended to share the rental had not yet moved in, I therefore had a spare room; I decided to invite my parents to spend some of their vacation time in London.

For their first visit to the capital I planned the full tourist programme, taking in Buckingham Palace, Houses of Parliament, Downing Street, Tower of London before finishing off on the last night with the most daring of all – the Playboy Club. For a modest man of humble origins like my father the club would certainly be a new experience; for a woman of strict Presbyterian conviction a Gambling Club staffed by scantily dressed girls presented, at the very least, a challenge. For her the most difficult part was to abstain from criticism of a place that had given her son a position on its management structure, with a high salary and lifestyle than she could never have contemplated for a boy, brought up on a sink estate, who had left school at 14 years.

After a brief tour of the premises I took them to our table in the VIP restaurant, arranged by Peter Byrne, and amused myself with their astonishment at the sumptuousness of the dishes provided and the attention given to our table by staff and management.

Had I been attempting to portray myself and my family falsely as being people accustomed to such service this pretence would have been destroyed when after the main course my mother, anxious to be seen as helpful, rose to take the dish from father and myself, scrape the remains on to hers and make ready to assist the waitress to clear the table. As kindly as I could, I bade her sit down and leave it to the staff who, along with the nearby maitre'd, were doing their best to suppress laughter at my discomfort.

The success of the brief holiday I had arranged for them would later be confirmed by other family members and friends who would tell me of the stories my parents had related to them of their wonderful experience. My status as a 'Manager' who could command such attention in his place of work they had also proudly announced.

This image had of course been largely manufactured by Peter Byrne who, having also come from a modest working class background, knew how pleasing and amusing it would be to transport my parents into this new world.

Our actual status at Playboy was of course not so clearly defined. The division I had observed at an earlier date even before I entered the management team was becoming more and more apparent. The strict adherence to the letter of the law on which we had originally been told the company's licence to operate depended, did not seem to apply to the management personnel outside of our VIP and 3rd Floor night executive team headed by Peter Byrne. The 'flexibility' employed by other managers, in permitting 'friendship' between some Bunnies and affluent players and in the administration of cheque transactions, at times left our team open to criticism from VIP customers and this was no doubt relayed to the very top. Although no one could openly criticise Peter for complying with legislation there was no doubt those at the very top of the company favoured the other approach and would have preferred that he were not there. For a brief period I had the distinct impression that I, as a newly promoted manager, was being courted by those at the top perhaps with the intention of ensuring that I would be their man within the dissident Byrne's team. I was invited to several one-to-one sessions with Bill Gerhauser who, as number two in the company, was effectively the chief operational officer in Playboy as Victor Lownes the all powerful Chairman seemed to dedicate most of his time to fraternising with his Bunnies and rich and famous contacts.

The message I was getting from the meetings with Gerhauser was, that I had a great future with the company and to raise my suspicions even further that this courtship was political motivated I was then invited to one of the Chairman's famous parties at his apartment above the Club.

Perhaps the person with the most difficult task at Playboy was Bernie Mulherne. It was obvious that he, as General Manager, would also have preferred to comply rigorously with the Gaming Act but knowing the wishes of those above him he performed a precarious balancing act of turning a blind eye to deviations and a deaf ear to criticisms from the likes of Peter Byrne and at times from his bosses. He had been the one to first convey the message that Gerhauser wanted me, as a new recruit to management, to exchange views with him on the tasks of casino staff. I asked Bernie, always a friendly and approachable man, why I had been selected for these sessions and now been invited to one of the Chairman's bashes. He showed some surprise to hear of the party invite then commented with a smile, possibly ironic, that it was gesture made from time to time to promote staff relations.

Promoting relationships was what I had heard these events were all about and, on my arrival there, the presence of certain Bunnies with a reputation for this sort of thing seemed to confirm this. With the free flow of drink and encouragement from the top executives their promotional activity with some of the VIP guests increased.

If this taste of so-called 'life at the top' was designed to seduce me it had failed. As a young single man I enjoyed food, drink, dancing and attractive females but this was contrived; I was no part of this scene and in a strict sense it was not an acceptable policy to sponsor this type of relationship between owners, management, staff and members.

Through my own attitude in meetings with Gerhauser and after more frank discussions I would have with Bernie Mulherne I think the latter helped get the message through to them that I was not really a candidate to join their 'inner circle'. I therefore became fully established as a member of the 'reluctantly tolerated' senior staff and management group.

As I had first intended when I took the flat at Earls Court I was now sharing with a Playboy workmate Roger Pennycate with whom I had reached agreement not only on the terms of the lease but also on a pact of mutual discretion should either of us succumb to the temptation of inviting a Bunny to share our amenities.

This was only necessary because of the ludicrous and hypocritical rule still in force that male employees could not have a romantic liaison with a Bunny. It was of course being applied selectively as it was well known that almost all of the favoured managers and senior staff had affairs with any Bunny who made themselves available to them. But those of us who were not in the 'inner circle' had to be careful as it could be used against us should the security department be able to prove we were conducting an 'illicit relationship'.

The blatant hypocrisy was even more difficult to take as the procurement of Bunnies to entertain rich Middle Eastern clients was discreetly encouraged and this not only infringed the internal rules but was in fact an illegal practice.

A primary agent in this activity was a person known to all staff as Little Abdul. The small Lebanese fixer, who would later figure in condemnatory reports by the licensing authorities, had more or less a free run of the place although he was at that point supposed to be simply another club member; it was of course common knowledge that he was a frequent and favoured guest of our Chairman at the club apartment and at Lownes's private home. This gave the arrogant little guy another reason, if he ever needed it, to shuffle around the club pressing his insidious attention on Members, Staff and of course the Bunnies. Nevertheless, even he was aware that on the VIP and 3rd floor night operation he would not get the same freedom and cooperation that he received throughout the club at other times of the day and in other departments at night. His dislike of this situation was at times all too apparent in his attitude towards Peter, myself and other members of our team.

In spite of the internal politics, like everyone else who worked there, I continued to be enthralled, not only by the frequent presence of film, television and sports celebrities and the flamboyant excesses of oil rich Arabs, but also, to observe the intriguing, amusing, and puzzling behavioural traits of the other disparate individuals who visited us each day.

It has been said that gambling can cause normally rational people to make illogical decisions and one regular player of Punto Banco, a Mr Jack Meyer, seemed intent on proving that theory. This gentleman, I had been astounded to learn, had recently retired as Master of a Public School having originally founded the prestigious institution more than thirty years before. This was undoubtedly an unusual background for a casino gambler but very soon we would see he had still retained a compulsion to educate those around him. Often, after three successive hands in favour of Bank he would benevolently impart, to other players around him, the result of his statistical analysis; that the next coup would be in favour of the Player and as such they should bet this option with an increased stake. The frequency of error with this assertion, the derisive response from other regulars and indeed his own record of losses on the table did not seem to deter him from repeatedly expounding such theories.

While one player gave food for thought another offered actual sustenance. Mr Kam was owner of a popular Chinese Restaurant in London's West End who would celebrate an infrequent winning night by gesticulating to all table staff and managers that they were included in his invite and then announce ; 'To-nite flee lob-siter !'

His offer of course wasn't made entirely without commercial motive as it invariably came at the close of a Saturday shift which, by law, finished earlier than any other at 2.a.m Sunday morning. It was common knowledge that the majority of staff would then take off for the West End of for food, entertainment and above all drinks. Therefore his late catering facility, licenced to provide alcohol, was as good a place as any to relax after a shift. So a sizable group of us from the VIP level of Playboy would avail ourselves of his offer to provide free lobster and other delicious items on the menu, while he benefited from considerable increase in the sale of alcohol.

On one particular session I myself with colleagues, male and female, had substantially improved Kam's revenue intake on alcohol even before giving thought to the food. We then decided that the advice of never to drink on an empty stomach was worth following and with suggestions from the head-waiter began to sample various dishes. I had enjoyed several items and did not really feel I could consume much more when the waiter returned.

'Hello Sir, Mr Kam.' he directed my attention to the owner at the far end of the room. 'he ask if you like cat?'

I waved my hand and shook my head negatively while stifling a sudden bout of indigestion. Only recently there had been reports that some Chinese restaurants were serving items prohibited in our country.

'No, is small cat ...kitten?' his look of assurance had no such affect.

My colleagues were showing a mixture of emotions from hilarity to nausea.

Another waiter now came with a large cardboard box and lowered it for me to see, scuttling about inside, a small black kitten.

'Stop, stop, enough!' I rose in protest, just as a Chinese girl who worked with us as a Bunny came to my side.

'Jim, please,' she smiled. 'They have not explained properly. Mr Kam's cat has had kittens and he looks to find a home for each one.'

A little embarrassed to have implied that our VIP client would permit illegal practices in his restaurant I pretended I'd understood and been making a joke. I then agreed to foster the feline and ordered a few more drinks to toast the addition to my family. At some point in the night I was asked what I would call this female who would now live with me. Of those Bunnies in attendance there was one girl who I , and I'm sure everyone else including her, thought was unlikely to have anything compatible with me; I announced my new feline partner would be called, Simone. I had no idea at that moment, nor did anyone else, how symbolic that would be.

Not only did Bunny Simone seem incompatible with me, she appeared to some extent out of place at Playboy. Educated at an all girls English public school she carried herself with an upright posture and spoke with an RP accent which gave her an air of sophistication not entirely in keeping with the stagy, flamboyant and coquettish image that many expected from a Playboy Bunny. The confident and assertive demeanour and tendency to speak her mind could also sometimes be seen as challenging, particularly to male supervisors, including myself on occasion. However, it had to be said that where she did qualify, with honours, was in the position's principal requirement of physical attractiveness. Attractive or not, at this stage I considered inviting only the small, black, furry, feline Simone to share my home, confident that she would not reject my proposal.

CHAPTER 26

A major factor in the success of Playboy UK, in a gaming industry that was by law, prohibited from advertising, had been its success in keeping itself in the public eye. This to a large extent it achieved by exploiting the general media's obsession with Bunny girls; the patronage of newsworthy celebrities and participation in news-making activities such as charities.

But a policy, once again initiated from the top, marked the beginning of a tendency to make news for the wrong reasons. The fact that even the favoured managers on the day shift knew nothing of the policy to remove the dice table, and make the male staff of that game redundant, was an example of the autocratic approach being taken by the two top executives. Representations from the floor managers to the Casino Manager Bernie Mulherne only served to establish that he himself had once again been bypassed.

With no justification or clarification coming from either Lownes or Gerhauser, other than an unconvincing inference that it was a financial decision because of a recent fall in the level of play on that table, the dice crew mustered crucial support from other gaming staff and a substantial group of Bunny girls, and called for industrial action.

'Playboy Bunnies go on strike' was too good a headline to be missed and as such was used by several National newspapers not to mention the news programmes on TV. Although many managers including Peter Byrne and myself were in sympathy with the dice crew and the striking supporters we did not believe it in our interest to join them on the street; we did however make sure our opinions were heard by the Bosses.

Apart from the legally questionable action of serving redundancy notices on the male dice staff, the company by their action had awakened an army of Bunnies with their own grievancies. A policy which had always ruffled tails and ears was Playboy's guiding principle of recruiting, promoting, assessing and terminating the employment of girls based on their physical appearance. Employment protection legislation would bring all this into question but apart from anything it could always be questioned on the basis that the assessment of anyone's physical attributes can only ever be subjective.

It was now becoming a little clearer, if no less justifiable, why the closure and redundancies had been initiated. It seemed that it had come to the ears of Gerhauser that some of the dice dealers had been promoting the idea that gaming staff should be have a representative voice ; one in particular had approached the Transport & General Workers Union (TGWU). Apparently, on hearing this, Lownes gave orders that they should all be shown the door.

What had seemed to him an easy and incisive solution to a minor irritation had now caused a major crisis. To quell the immediate problem the Playboy executives agreed to discuss the problem of the dice closure and staff redundancies. But the underlying question, of employees representation, which Lownes had endeavoured to eliminate, was now firmly on the table with the TGWU making a case to be the voice of the 'workers'.

It could be said that there was almost unanimity in one opinion – that each person should have a fair degree of employment protection. The differences lay on how to provide that protection. A sizable group thought there should be an elected staff committee, another fairly large number thought a Trade Union such as TGWU was the best option, while a hard core continued to believe that staying within the regime's chosen few was the safest and most lucrative option.

Peter Byrne took up what, he admitted himself, was a incongruous position for a manager, he supported the option of Union membership, mainly because he believed that it needed the strength of a major Trade Union to stand up to the autocracy of the Playboy senior executives. I myself could see that reasoning but having had some experience of Union practices I found it hard to imagine them being a positive influence in the longer term. A period of (anything but quiet)reflection was now proposed with a plan to hold a ballot of all employees to decide the issue of whether or not they wanted representation.

Apart from my normal duties as Unit Manager a great deal of the time was of course spent listening to diverse political arguments and proposals. Even the usual diversions of drinks after work and illegal fraternisations with Bunnies could be affected. A sociable banter in the pub would turn into a slurred argument on employment legislation, then later when I was getting close up and personal with one of the girls I'd get the erotic suggestion that I should become shop steward. As I was to find many times in my future career, the only activity that seemed to divert minds from current turmoil was football; the Playboy team was currently positioned to finish high up the league and had progressed through several rounds of the cup.

The company had now announced when voting would take place and that before that day there would be a pre-ballot conference where representatives of staff, Union and the Company could put their case and answer questions. Business would be suspended to permit everyone to attend and to accommodate the expected numbers it would be held in a conference room at a nearby Park Lane Hotel.

For once the executive heads of Playboy had assessed the situation correctly. As the young, attractive, well paid, and modern thinking majority of Playboy employees listened a veteran trade unionist put the case for TGWU recognition by droning on about traditional worker's rights and solidarity. The look of boredom on Bunny girls faces and the rising noise of conversation while he continued with his socialist mantra was already indicating to us that the battle was over.

When he sat down to a mere ripple of applause Victor Lownes, who had wisely chosen to let the Union man speak first, rose to prearranged cheering from his acolytes and with confidence began his address. His words had been more carefully chosen to placate and appeal to the majority of the youthful audience with a few jokes hurriedly added to emphasise the difference between the modern thinking of the majority of young employees and the outdated jargon of the trade unionists.

Everything was going more or less to plan for the top brass of Playboy and Lownes, used to being surrounded by servility, was enjoying the fact that his detractors would seem to have been silenced; all except one.

In answer to previous suggestions that Playboy did not respect employees, and in particular the girls who worked as Bunnies, he was waxing lyrical about just how well all the girls were treated when suddenly one emerged in the central passageway to loudly refute his claim;

it was Simone. In rushing to silence and usher her out of the hall, Lownes' henchmen provoked those who had been unaligned, and dissidents who had previously sunk into silence, to mount opposition. All this eventually forced the Playboy top brass to bring the conference to a premature end.

The outcome of the ballot which followed the conference was predictable. It could be said that the Playboy hierarchy triumphed, in the sense that the Union did not win recognition, but the TGWU had not lost because staff felt they did not need representation. No, they lost because they had failed to convince them that they were the people to represent playboy staff's interests.

But in all this, Lownes, and Gerhauser had been forced to accept that they could not treat all people as they pleased; there would always be those who would oppose autocratic policy, such as the now reinstated dice crew, Managers like Peter Byrne and girls with the spirit of Simone. So, what now existed was an uneasy truce that permitted the Club to continue on course as one of the most profitable casinos in the World at that time.

For myself, although the attitude of the owners was an irritation, I continued to enjoy the nature of the work and the environment where it was carried out. Unlike Peter, my senior in the management structure and also friend and mentor, I had not yet changed my view and still considered casinos and gaming as a convenient, exciting and well paid job. He viewed it as his chosen profession and as such was even more frustrated by the attitude and conduct of his employers, who having landed themselves in an almost ideal business situation seemed hell bent, as was to be proved later, in destroying that opportunity.

He continued to campaign for change and although I supported many of his views did not, either at work or at home, have his level of commitment; he being married to Maria a beautiful Kenyan born woman, while I was still footloose.

In actual fact, my feet were the part of my anatomy that seemed to be getting most action.

I was playing football regularly with some friends of mine but turning out sometimes twice a week for the Playboy football team that was now challenging for the top spot in the division, which would mean promotion; we had also reached the Semi-Final of the Benoist Cup.

The importance of encouraging employees to participate in sports and social events I was just beginning to realise. The involvement of Bunny Girls in public events was of course actively promoted and often financed by the Playboy hierarchy because of their high publicity potential. But most of the events, particularly sports, in which the male staff took part was organised by enthusiasts and self financed. However, it was evident that the communal spirit engendered by these activities had the effect of making the participants less likely to be disenchanted with their workplace or easily distracted by other opportunities; I myself being a prime example.

For large organisations there is an additional benefit from team sports such as football; often individuals from different departments and management levels learn to work together for the common good.

Our team at Playboy included a manager, inspectors, croupiers, a chef, waiter, reception and doorman. So when we won the final match of the league season to secure the title and promotion, the success reverberated throughout the company.

But for me the most exciting achievement was to reach the final of the Benoist Cup because that match was to be played at the famous Stamford Bridge, home of my adopted team, Chelsea F.C.

Dissapointingly the match itself was not captured live on video but an album of photographs assists me to boast of my 'time' at Stamford Bridge. The day may not be on film but it is stored in my memory bank and starts with the arrival at the ground, getting kitted out in the Chelsea change-room, followed by a team talk before the procession on to the pitch to the acclaim of the crowd (total number unrecorded), a lengthy warm up and then the kick off.

The team we were playing against was another gaming company, called Charlie Chester Casino, named after the original owner, a famous English comedian. But it was to be no laughing matter ; at that time, they were one of the strongest sides of the three Hotel and Catering Football Divisions. Indeed, it was said that the recruitment officer, a soccer enthusiast, consciously chose male employees on the basis of how well they could play football. I'm not sure how true that was, but curiously there were a number of former professional players within their pool. While in Playboy we could count on only one; a former Spanish player, Jose Gomez.

Sadly although we acquitted ourselves well, and I myself came near to scoring twice, we lost narrowly.

Professionally, I was now considering what I should do to further my career. Enjoyable as it was, to work in the glamorous Playboy environment, it was now clear that, like my colleague Peter Byrne, I could never conform to the wishes of the top brass; but unlike him, I did not want to spend my time and energy in a continuous war of attrition. I began to look at alternatives.

However, there were always distractions, the latest being the build up to the Wimbledon Tennis Championship which saw us, in the VIP lounge, playing host to top ranked players such as Jimmy Connors, Illa Nastase and, the first black man to reach the top in tennis, Arthur Ashe. The somewhat eccentric Nastase had been a source of entertainment to the staff but it was the ever-friendly Ashe who caught our attention and our support as he progressed through each round to eventually reach the final. Less than 48 hours before he stepped on to the centre court we were able to personally congratulate him on his achievement and wish him luck in the final. However, like almost everyone else, we found it difficult to imagine he, good as he was, at thirty-one years old would beat the top seed and current World number one, another customer of ours, Jimmy Connors.

Ashe's 6-1, 6-1,5-7, 6-4 victory over Connors is now a piece of tennis history.

Hob-knobbing with celebrities and sports-stars is all very well but it was not furthering my career; I now therefore became serious about finding another position. One of the main competitors of Playboy was Ladbrokes and on obtaining an interview I was surprised to be introduced to the Boss himself, Cyril Stein, already a leading figure in the gaming world and destined to become an industry legend.

Ladbrokes Casino Leicester doesn't sound in any way as exciting as the Playboy Club London but the position offered, that of General Manager, was a promotion even I had not anticipated. Notice of my resignation was, as Bernie Mulherne stated, reluctantly received; but only by him. Those above him were only to happy to see the back of a manager with an independence of spirit and would now hope that others such as Peter Byrne would follow my lead. Bernie genuinely hoped that things would change for the better and there would be a future for managers with a more professional approach. However, in wishing me well with my new position, he also reinforced my own view that this was an ideal opportunity for me to break into senior management ranks.

A farewell session at the Coach and Horses followed by top-up drinks when those who earlier had been working joined me at a local night club is as much as I can remember about my going away party. But only a few days later as I prepared to leave for the Midlands an event reminded me, if it were necessary, that not all was celebratory in Swinging London. The IRA extremists set off a bomb at London's Hilton

Hotel, only a few doors down from Playboy Club, killing two people and injuring more than sixty.

Frightening as the close proximity of this atrocity was, for myself and my former workmates, the full impact was to feel even closer when we learnt that one of those who had died was the father of a Playboy colleague.

CHAPTER 27.

Before taking up my position at Leicester I had a number of meetings at Ladbroke's Head Office to enable me to familiarise myself with company policy and ambitions. It was clear from those meetings that my new employers took a much more formal and businesslike approach to the management of their operations than I had seen at the Bunny Club. It was also apparent that they had been unsatisfied by the previous G.M. of the Leicester Casino and were now looking for me to improve results. Confident as I was with the operational side of the business for the first time I began to realise how ill equipped and inexperienced I was with the administrative duties of a senior executive of an operation.

Up to this point in my career I had dealt mainly with on-floor activities, staffing the tables, training and supervising table staff, applying and reviewing security procedures, being involved in most aspects of customer relations including, monitoring the quality of catering facilities without participating in their provision. Now all aspects of the business had become my responsibility, not least, the overall financial result. With no formal training in accountancy or bookkeeping I was obliged to rely on the existing chief accountant and his staff to continue with the accepted procedures while I embarked on some home studies to ensure that I at least could understand and participate in the preparation and control of budgets and accounts.

Not unnaturally, this being the first time I had total responsibility for an operation, at first I found myself working almost night and day; foregoing even my days off. My social life amounted to an occasional after-work drink with the Casino manager, Les Cooke; who curiously had been a policeman before he entered the casino business. As I became more confident in his and other senior gaming staff's ability to run the gaming activities, I was able to control my obsessive urge to be constantly present on the floor and concentrate on the planning, marketing and overall administration of the business. As a distraction I also occasionally took myself off to Filbert Street, then the stadium name of Leicester City who at that time were in the top division in England with famous international players such as Peter Shilton and Frank Worthington.

I also felt the need for some female company but as the only regular contact I had with young ladies was with those on my staff, and that sensitive and dubious option I had to avoid: instead I invited a former girlfriend from Playboy to come up from London on her days off.

The casino could hardly be said to be in a prime location and Leicester in the East Midlands did not have the population, income per head, or rich foreign visitors that made London such an economic power. Foreigners who did come to Leicester were immigrants which even in those earlier years marked the city as one of the most ethnically diverse in UK. The casino however did have a hard core of members and even after only a few months of my guidance we were beginning to see an improvement in attendance figures, cash-drop per customer and, most importantly on the bottom line. As always, due to the restrictions on advertising in the British Gaming Act, the promotion and expansion of business had to be done in more subtle ways than those employed in other industries.

Apart from the constant battle to win new clients there is always the difficulty in gaming businesses that the essential task of extracting a result can cause customer dissatisfaction. This of course gives fuel to the critics who like to portray casinos and other gaming businesses as activities which fleece the poor, vulnerable, unknowing speculator. It is therefore absolutely necessary to ensure that the message reaches members and potential customers that the casino does not compete against them; it provides the facilities and safe environment where they can, by choice, enjoy the challenge of gambling on games with a known risk factor.

The accumulated amount lost by the players, which on average rarely surpasses more than 20 to 25% of the total money wagered, is then used to cover all corporate costs including gaming and corporate taxes before any profit can be declared.

It is of course crucial in a professionally run operation that all aspects of the product, from parking, reception, environmental comfort, food and beverage, table and cash desk facilities and services are of the highest order to provide the client with a total experience. This had become more and more obvious the longer I worked in the industry but now I needed to ensure all my staff fully adhered to this philosophy.

Of course it is difficult to have players understand and accept the vagaries of chance when at times the budget and plans of casino managers can be seriously affected by an unpredictable run of negative results. Probability calculations give the casino management insight into what is the likely financial return on games over a period of time; but what cannot be determined exactly, is the period required and the amount of money wagered to arrive at that result. Even with an allowance for a margin of error in the budget, a substantial win or series of wins by a big player can cause some tension in the management ranks. In those days, without the hi-tech security equipment they have today to verify that a player's winning run is bona fide, all sorts of concerns and suspicions would arise. I was already learning that in the event of a negative run the General Manager had, as a matter of course, to look at, and hopefully rule out, the possibility of illegal activity and also consider that inefficiency played a part, but had to carry out these necessary procedures without de-motivating the staff concerned.

The long hours, absence of social activity and pressures in securing the projected results had begun to have some negative effects; I was taking little exercise and on finally reaching my apartment after work each night I would take, what I called, 'wind-down' shots of whiskey before going to bed. I then broke a rule I had made earlier – that of not having an affair with a member of my staff; Liz, an attractive blond girl from Birmingham had not long started on the gaming department when we met by chance in a local club when we were both on our night off.

Difficulties or not I did seem to be attracting some notice at Ladbrokes Head office, and for the right reasons. At a periodic meeting with the area head of the casino sector he informed that, if I was interested, I could be considered for a position at their new project in Knightsbridge London, the Park Tower Casino. This exciting prospect, although still a long way off and by no means certain, was a tremendously motivating force. I was advised not to mention it to the staff at Leicester. Though no one was to learn of this offer, including my new girlfriend Liz, they might possibly have wondered where I had suddenly got the renewed surge of energy and enthusiasm.

However, less than six weeks later, a call from my old friend Peter Byrne in London was to change the entire course of my life. He had been offered the job of managing a casino in Lagos Nigeria by Joseph and Michael Atrib, two Lebanese clients of the London Playboy Club. The two men, who I also knew from my time at Playboy, lived and operated several businesses in the Nigerian capital and were about to acquire the rights to a casino. Being regular visitors to London casino operations it seemed like the obvious place to find the people they needed to manage and staff their new venture.

Unfortunately for them Peter, their first choice for General Manager, had recently become the father of twins, so he and his wife Maria, a former Bunny ironically of African origin, not surprisingly had no wish to disrupt their family life to take off for Nigeria. On declining their offer he reminded them of my presence in the Playboy management team, my subsequent promotion to an even more responsible position with Ladbrokes and suggested they interview me for the position. Accepting his personal recommendation, which goes a long way in their culture, they asked him to enquire if I was interested.

There can be no question that the amount of money likely to be offered was a crucial factor in my agreement to see them, Peter himself had been tempted by that aspect, but for me without the family commitments that he had, there was also the exciting prospect of taking over a new project in an exotic foreign destination; first I had to convince the Atribs that I was the man for the job.

My first meeting was to be with Joseph Atrib at the Royal Lancaster Hotel in London. Of the two he, the elder brother, was the one with whom I had most contact in my days as Unit Manager in Playboy's VIP salon. He greeted me warmly and began by describing their project. The casino, was situated in a leased space within the Federal Palace Hotel on Victoria Island, an area of Lagos connected to the mainland by bridges. They would take over the rights to run the casino from the previous operators a company of Italian origin who had several casino projects in West Africa. Joseph assured me that they had very good Government contacts, an essential in Nigeria, and had already secured the licence to operate. I gave him my CV and proceeded to establish my credentials to manage the venture but was getting the impression that being known to them and recommended by their chosen candidate I had to some extent already been accepted.

This was confirmed soon afterwards by an unusual question. 'Jim, how much salary will you need?'

Not the sort of question one is usually asked by a prospective employer and I was somewhat non-plussed. I had been given some indication by Peter the amount of money they were prepared to pay him. But would they expect me to command the same as they would have paid their favourite? I could overprice myself or brand myself as inferior. I decided to go for it; explaining that having no knowledge of the tax or transfer regulations of Nigeria I would like to have a guaranteed net income out of the country of £15,000 per year, also two return airline tickets per year, a company car, local costs and accommodation paid; Atrib nodded, gave no indication how he felt about my demands, said he would consult with his brother and that we should meet the following day. On my way out I felt I had out-priced myself but the next day I was delighted to hear they had agreed to conditions which by the standards of that period put me among the top earners in the industry.

In my agreement with the Atribs what I had not established, nor even discussed, was the level of autonomy I would have to manage the operation. Unfortunately, it was only after agreeing financial terms, settling on a start date and handing in my resignation to Ladbrokes, that I began to find out some of the difficulties I was to face such as, the pre-conditions they had agreed with the previous owner and the staff they had recruited prior to my appointment. This would be an early warning, of their culturally ingrained philosophy, that as owners they should make operational decisions and decide on all policies even although they would employ an experienced General Manager.

The first evidence of their inability to separate ownership and management was when Joseph Atrib, with a self-satisfied tone, announced that some time before my appointment they had recruited two former Playboy Bunnies; he obviously expected me, a former Playboy manager, to welcome this news. Before I could ask the first question that came to my mind he gave me the answer to my second. 'Cleo and Beverly', he said, and waited for my expected approval.

'Joseph, why did you employ them before you had a manager in place?'

'People say, including Peter, that casino need minimum ten experienced gaming people. We have three Italians from previous company and two others, we add the two girls and the husbands to make nine.'

In my naïveté I had imagined that the Atribs, making their first venture into casinos, would want their appointed manager, with his experience, to form a suitable team to take over the running of the business. In this instance, unlike my previous recruitment by Ladbrokes, I did not anticipate a situation where I would inherit an entire staff none of whom I had personally selected. In a confused state I was of a mind to inform them I had changed my mind about taking the job. I did not go that far but did inform Joseph that, while I could accept that they were obliged to retain certain members of the previous company's staff, I was a little unhappy not to have been given the option, at least, to select my own candidates from U.K. casinos to complete the team.

After a pause his eventual comment left me without a suitable response. 'We think it good to have some pretty girls to brighten Lagos casino. Peter he say, these two girls are good'.

Whether Peter actually endorsed their idea or just didn't oppose it, that I didn't know, but he having recommended me it seemed pointless to continue with this discussion. Under these circumstances I dismissed the doubt I had about asking for a position for Liz, my current girlfriend and she was added to make up the team to the proposed number.

With no reliable information about the other expatriates I had inherited and wanting at least to have an aide who had been brought up in the relative discipline of the UK gaming industry I agreed with the Atribs that Jeff Tomlin, husband of Beverly one the former Bunnies, should be my Assistant Manager. To further complicate my position Ladbrokes insisted I work an extended notice period with the result that the Atribs' proposed take-over date would take place with their entire inherited and recruited team, but minus their manager.

CHAPTER 28

Anyone, in those days, arriving at Lagos airport for the first time could be forgiven for considering if their decision to go there had been a wise one; this was chaos as an art form. No attempt was being made by any official to organise the hordes of people passing through the control points. I would later hear that this was a marketing strategy to encourage people to 'pay' for chaos-avoidance services. Fortunately for me, those services had been secured by the Atribs, and their trusted lieutenant Karouze was waiting to guide me through the four checkpoints, past the armed military guards and out to the welcoming Joseph by his waiting limousine. The journey from the Airport to Victoria Island and the Federal Palace hotel was, I was surprised to learn, going fairly quickly; the continuous stop-start, being usually an almost continuous stop at this time of the day. I was told, the traffic situation was known by everyone as the Lagos 'Go-slow'. In reply to my question on how the first few weeks of their ownership of the casino had gone, Joseph's non-committal so-so head movement I took to mean he didn't want to talk in his assistant's presence; I therefore concentrated on taking in my first view of the Nigerian capital.

Lagos consists of three separate parts, connected by bridges. The Mainland, where the Airport is situated is the largest, most densely populated and least attractive part of the city with vast areas of squalid rudimentary shacks and derelict buildings. This is connected by three bridges to Lagos Island a more business orientated part of the city that accommodates many of the foreign firms and banks. At this point we were moving along the Marina towards one of the two bridges that connect Lagos Island to what would be our destination, Victoria Island, and the Federal Palace Hotel.

After a somewhat unusual check-in procedure and some confusion over whether my bags had been sent to the room, Joseph showed me the direction I should take to reach the casino from the reception but told me to take time to get settled in my room and come down when I was ready. The cleaner had not yet finished in my room but I asked her to come back a little later, unpacked my bags, had a quick shower, changed into my working suit, with collar and tie, and made my way down to my new workplace. On my arrival downstairs in what was the casino reception a large man rose from his chair with a questioning look which quickly changed to welcoming when I identified myself. He pushed and held open one side of the double door for me to enter into the large rectangular salon that at first sight was, to say the least, visually disappointing. Knowing the casino had been operating for some time under the previous owners it was difficult to imagine why in the first instance they had not created a more attractive public space and if it was because it was necessary to get it opened quickly, why they had not improved the décor at a later date. Now the Atribs for some reason had done the same.

The lower half of the walls were covered in a dark brown wood paneling and the upper part in some sort of ochre coloured hessian material. No pictures or decorative features had been added to spoil the Spartan effect. The only colour that was evident was from dashes of red in the aged carpet and the green baize of the gaming tables. The general lighting and the lights above the tables had suffered from the same lack of imagination. There was no time for any further appraisal as Jeff strode down from the far end of the room to greet me. 'Jim, Welcome to Lagos and Federal Palace Casino!' His look told me that he could see, and agree with, my first impression. My question on how things were going was also more or less answered first by his facial expression and body language and then 'It's a long story.'

He told me the Atribs were waiting for me in the office, which I had not known was the door on the other side of the casino reception; so I left Jeff's long story until later.

I was greeted warmly by Michael Atrib, it was the first time we had met since my days in Playboy. Though Joseph had conducted all our negotiations and discussions it was clear that I would not be there without the agreement of his brother. In fact it had been said before that Michael, the younger of the two, was in fact the dominant force in the family's business dealings and this would become more and more obvious. At this first meeting I attempted to establish my position and proposed that during those first few weeks I would acclimatize myself to the conditions in Lagos, study the existing market, their current method and style of operation, staff capabilities, working procedures and security and as soon as possible come back to them with a report, proposals and financial targets. Not for the last time I was to get a response similar to, 'Eh…Jim…you know… things are… different here, it is not like London.' What we did establish was, that for the time being until I settled, and my girlfriend Liz arrived probably in two weeks time, I would remain in the hotel. Thereafter I could move to my own rented accommodation on Victoria Island and have a company car with driver. At that point as we approached the casino opening time and the staff began to arrive we exited the office to go out to the gaming floor. The Atribs, to take up what was their accustomed daily meeting place on a baccarat table positioned in an alcove at the far end of the gaming salon, while I re-acquainted myself with former colleagues and was introduced by Jeff to the rest of my new team.

The negative assessment of the setup and the personnel, that Jeff was to give me on that first night, I was soon to consider as somewhat more positive than my own. However, in those first days, as I began to assess the difficulties I had inherited, an event was to take place which would overshadow all my current problems.

I had been invited to make the short trip, from the Hotel to the Atribs's house on Victoria Island, to discuss some of the first items on my list of problems. They had arranged a car and driver to pick me up from the Hotel, but at the appointed time there was not only no sign of the driver but there seemed to be traffic jam on the main road obstructing any entrance to, or exit from, the hotel grounds. This had provoked general consternation and an animated discussion between drivers, passengers, hotel staff and even some of the street beggars. Even in my short time in Nigeria I knew that the notorious Lagos Go-slow did not normally extend to this area. Unable to establish from the heated exchanges and the multiple theories what exactly had caused this pile-up and therefore how long it might last, I moved back inside to the Hotel reception. There I also found anxious clients and staff but did eventually establish that the situation had been caused by the closure of all roads to and from the Islands and Mainland by the Military Authority. As yet, no one knew why, but of course there were no shortage of terrifying suggestions. Unsure of what to do I waited downstairs, ordered some coffee and remained alert for status reports. Later that morning a Lebanese man, that I knew to be one of the Atrib's people, finally appeared and ushered me to his car, assuring me that although the bridges were still closed we could get to 'Mr Mike's house'.

In the light of what was happening in Lagos the original purpose of my visit seemed, for the moment at least, to be pointless. At the Atrib house Joseph greeted me with an apologetic gesture. 'Jim, sorry, but as you know, there is some problem with the Military Government and we wait for some clear news.' At that point Mike Atrib entered, gave me a nod of recognition and turned to usher in a Nigerian gentleman I had met once before in the casino office, announcing solemnly 'Bankoli has some news for us…'.

'They have killed the President!' the Nigerian solemnly pronounced. 'This morning they shot Murtala Mohammed in his car in Ikoyi!'

A flood of questions followed his announcement, many of which at this stage no one could answer, not even Bankoli Oki who until recently had been the Lagos State Attorney General and Commisioner for Justice. One thing was in no doubt, there was a coup attempt taking place by a rebellious faction within the Military ranks, this much was certain, said Oki , because a radio broadcast had been made after the assassination by one of the coup leaders, a Lt Colonel Dimka. Among other things he had said that state affairs would be run by Military Brigade Commanders and that all borders, airports and sea ports would be closed until further notice and a curfew would be imposed.

What we did not know was, if any serious resistance to the rebellion had been mounted, what would be the likely outcome and what consequences there might be for ourselves. At this stage the assistants, of the Atribs, were assigned to the radio and television to listen for news bulletins while another attempted to reach contacts in other parts of the city to get updates from those regions.

It was eventually established that no restriction existed on Victoria Island to prevent my return to the hotel so I was driven back to the Federal Palace where it was agreed we would all meet later to assess the situation. The return journey was slow due to a traffic build up near Federal Palace. On finally reaching the hotel carpark the sight of fire and smoke in the vicinity of Ikoyi gave us, and many others who congregated on the hotel grounds, cause for great concern.

As we waited for concrete news rumours intensified our fears, particularly as many of our staff, including some of our expats, lived either on Ikoyi or the Mainland and therefore could not be reached because of the closure of the bridges; furthermore, as I had quickly learnt, telephones, even in less turbulent times, rarely worked in Lagos.

A further report, from one of Atrib's people who had been on the roof of Federal Palace, of seeing explosions just across the bridge in the Marina area had me wondering just how long it would be before they moved across to our side.

Later Joseph Atrib arrived to inform me that the coup had failed and that although there might be still be some disturbances on the other side the main dangers were over, the road bridges were opening again and they had sent some people to bring our foreign staff across to the hotel and out of harms' way. Later, when they were all finally together at the casino, I could have organised a 'My experience was scarier than yours' competition.

Over the next few days we attempted to get back to normal, if that word has any meaning in Nigeria. The full story, or a least the interim administration's version, of the assassination and attempted coup was now coming out on newspapers, television and radio. The coup had indeed failed when the rebels failed to remove all the targeted heads of the existing Military Government and win sufficient support from the others. Nigeria's new leader Olusegun Obasanjo, who had narrowly escaped being assassinated, had initiated a nationwide campaign to arrest the plotters and their supporters. One aspect of the ongoing investigation that would cause some concern for the British expatriate community was that General Gowon the former head of State, who was exiled and living in Britain, had been accused of being implicated in the plot and because of this Britain had been asked to arrange his extradition; the British Government's refusal to do this was being used by some as argument for action against British interests and possibly British subjects.

In spite of all these concerns and distractions we reopened to the public and I attempted to get to grips with my contractual obligations. If the recently arrived British staff had been disillusioned before, they were certainly even more so now. This frightening event coming on top of their, well advertised, disenchantment with the day to day living and working conditions in Lagos it was obvious it would not take very much for them to pack up and go home. Curiously, although I could see many difficulties in running the business I had taken on, the seriousness of the event which had just taken place seemed to diminish the importance of the mundane problems I might encounter in managing the Federal Palace Casino. I now looked forward to having the company of Liz who, if the Airport was functioning again, would arrive in a few days.

Of the four British staff I had most sympathy for Jeff Tomlin. He had been given the job originally because of the Atribs primary wish to employ his wife Beverly; later, in the absence of an alternative, he had been nominated by me as assistant Casino Manager; he was then obliged to start without my presence and support and received no recognition or assistance from the Atribs. While he would not have been my first choice, his failure to assert control was due he said, to their cultural prejudices and attitude to business and not to any deficiency on his part. As for the two young ex-Bunny women, although employed for the wrong reasons they could nevertheless, because of their earlier casino training perform the function of gaming inspector satisfactorily. However, the fourth member of the team Gordon Berry, had always been a problem even in his London days, having limited intelligence and a disruptive personality. His employment was due entirely to Joseph Atrib's desire to employ his wife the former Bunny Cleo now using her real name, Sonia.

If the selection of the UK contingent failed to live up to my expectation it had to be admitted that most of the individuals who made up the rest of my supervisory team made the Brits look like ideal employees. Only one of the three Italians that the Atribs had retained from the previous owner could be said to be an asset. Aldavino Pertile, or Nino as he was known to everyone, was not only to prove himself valuable to the company but was also to become my long term friend. Unfortunately the same could not be said for his compatriots. One of them was the former casino manager who displayed a barely concealed opinion that he should have been retained in that position, although in effect he had only experience of working on French roulette. The other more senior and somnolent colleague could be said to be passing his retirement in the casino. To add to this array of talent the Atribs had employed a veteran known to everyone as 'the Doctor' a gentleman of supposedly Greek origin who had apparently been around casinos for many years; doing what exactly, was never made clear. As he sat inspecting two Blackjack tables, any confirmation, of a transaction or procedure, requested by either croupier would oblige him to loom down to within a few inches from the table, and squint through his thick lensed spectacles before giving approval. When I asked Jeff if he knew anything of the Doctor's gaming experience he said that on asking the same question of Joseph Atrib the reply was 'Here in Nigeria there are a lot of suspicious people around, the Doctor is an old hand in these parts, we keep him here because he sees things'. Jeff agreed with me that he was undoubtedly an old hand but he had great difficulty seeing anything. To complete my team of inherited professionals we also had the Lebanese, Makram. He was by far the most vigilant of the group. Unfortunately, as I was to realise fairly quickly, he was not only alert to the activity on the tables but also every overheard comment, observed movement, or even body or facial expressions displayed by a work colleague, one of the owner's team of personal assistants or even the Atribs themselves. To any of the observations he could then apply his interpretation and discreetly feed this information whenever, and to whoever, he thought might use it to provoke reactions in others. Ideally this would be to his professional benefit, although often, it seemed simply to be for his malicious amusement. Added to this squad of foreign supervisors there was one Nigerian called Abdul. If I wanted to be what is today called, *politically incorrect* I would have called his promotion to Inspector a token gesture.

This team was expected to supervise, direct and instruct Nigerian employees from underprivileged backgrounds with limited basic education who had been brought up in a society with low levels of discipline and morality. Even in more developed societies croupiers exposed to large sums of money, at times being squandered frivolously by the more fortunate, can succumb to temptation and commit illegal acts either in collaboration with players or by stealing chips themselves. Here in Lagos with a high level of potential risk, an expat team of doubtful ability or commitment and no sophisticated security equipment that was now installed in most Western casinos, I could see that I'd accepted a challenge somewhat more difficult than I anticipated. However, a factor that increased the temptation for others to cheat might also be seen as an incentive for me to continue; from my early observations and calculations I could see that the potential turnover, and therefore profit level, was higher than I could have imagined. Anyway, to consider my career move as a success, I had only to surmount those internal difficulties and any new ones I encountered, overcome the trials of living in Lagos such as shortage of food, power, telephones and manoeuvrable roads, and survive threats such as corrupt Police, diseases like Malaria and possibly the occasional Military Coup.

Joseph Atrib, seemingly anxious to get me settled into Lagos, escorted me to the house I would share with my, soon to be arriving, partner. The detached building was in Okrika Close, a cul-de-sac in Ikoyi. It consisted of a separate ground floor property and from a side door on that same level a stairway to our upstairs apartment which had a sizeable lounge with balcony overlooking the street, kitchen and, from a large hallway, access to two bedrooms, a bathroom with shower and another balcony at the rear of the property. I was introduced to Steven who, in keeping with local tradition, would be our houseboy; accommodated, in what we would consider primitive conditions, in a basement closet at the back of the property. To Joseph's surprise when he announced the arrival of my car, I resisted his assertion that the houseboy should double as my driver, stating that I preferred to drive myself. I did however accept his strong recommendation that Liz should not ever, in Lagos, drive it by herself.

My expectation of Liz's arrival centred around my personal physical needs and companionship outside of work but I had overlooked the additional burdens her presence would put upon me, such as helping her acclimatise to the strange and somewhat threatening environment that was Lagos and assisting her to adjust to the often confusing arrangements at the Casino; neither of which, in the my short time there I'd been able to do myself. As with my own dramatic introduction to Lagos, her first days would give her cause to think twice about her decision to take up this new appointment. It consisted of interesting introductory information from the Lebanese that the house she would live in was just round the corner from the spot where the Head of State had been assassinated a few weeks before. Also, with the rest of us, she was advised that the local and popular Bar Beach should be avoided that Thursday because on that site the public executions of the condemned plotters would be taking place. Makram was pleased to inform us that in any case, if we wished to see it, the event would be televised.

I had already considered the age-old problem confronting a manager having a relationship with a member of the staff, of not being seen to favour the partner over others in his team but it was a policy the owners themselves seemed to ignore. From the start it was apparent that Liz, not having been selected by the Atribs themselves, did not really have the same status as Sonia and Beverly. It would also unfortunately become apparent to me, that although she could well have changed that, by making herself more amenable and personable, she chose not to, or perhaps failed to see the need.

We did our best to avoid the barbaric events taking place a Bar Beach but the TV newspapers and news-carriers such as Makram, replayed the scenes continuously including detailed description of the public executions by firing squad and the almost festive reactions of the sizable audience.

In effect, after the executions, things did appear to settle down, if that is a term that could ever realistically be applied to Lagos. People seemed to refocus on the daily problems of earning a living, coping with shortages, the malfunctioning services and a chaotic traffic system. At the casino we returned to fully operational status and customers returned to enjoy a diversion from the trauma of the past month. I could now return to my task of evaluating facilities at my disposal, existing business, potential business, policy and procedures and the capability of our personnel and management team. It did not take very long to establish that of those items the only ones that could be said to give any cause for optimism was the existing turnover and indications that there were even bigger players out there. Every evening in the casino I would await the arrival of at least one of the Atribs and hope that I would get sufficient time alone with him to discuss the most urgent matters. This was by no means easy given that on entry they would, by tradition, go directly to their table at the far end of the gaming floor in full view of the numerous potential solicitants in the casino, be they friends, fellow countrymen, acquaintances, prospective business partners or simply favour-seekers. Jeff had first alerted me to the nightly ritual which he called the 'Parade'. One or both of the Atribs would enter followed in single file by Karouze, Robert Shahara a giant Lebanese Assistant and Mr Thomas a Nigerian who had been given an unofficial position as personnel Manager. If I was not actually involved in something at the time, on first sight of their arrival, I would contrive to meet them at the table to initiate my discussion before the procession of solicitants lined up; even then, depending on the person's importance to the Atribs, we could still be interrupted. I'd already accepted that corporate decision making, policy implementation and management autonomy were not only foreign words to my bosses, they were also alien concepts. Whether I liked it or not I would have to accept that they were what they were and would not change, so if I was to continue I would have to find more subtle ways to get my messages through to them.

I quickly established that they had no intention of spending any great amount on redesigning and redecorating the casino, as they considered, that in general, the local populace did not put a high value on style and décor and gamblers in expatriate community also accepted this was Nigeria. However, the brothers did assure me, that money would always be made available for the essential promotional tool of offering credit to chosen gamblers. From the start I felt it necessary to give them my opinion that the standard of dealing of the African staff was poor, that this needed to be improved as did the casino security procedures and to do all this would normally require a much stronger group of senior expatriate staff than we had at Federal Palace. Each time I made this or a similar assertion I would receive 'the shrug' occasionally followed by an understanding nod and 'Yes, understood…but you must do the best you can…'

Although it would normally be more productive to sit facing the person with whom you were having a discussion, as both Atribs logically chose to sit on the large gaming table facing out to the salon I would endeavour to position myself by their side to also have a clear and broad view of the activity in the salon. Of course I had learned from my first years in management in the casino business that it is always better when seated on the perimeter of the gaming floor to be able to see what is happening but here in Lagos it was even more important. I could see who was about to interrupt our discussion and usually determine the importance of the person and/or their message or request. I could also anticipate questions or comments I might receive about the activity taking place in front of us; sometimes used as a diversion from the sensitive subject I had previously raised. It also gave me the opportunity to quickly act on anything happening out on the gaming floor which I believed required my intervention; this, before it was either seen by Joseph or Mike or reported to them by a factotum such as Karouze to be conveyed to me somewhat disapprovingly. Of course in one major issue the presence and the participation of the two owners was essential, that of deciding who should be given credit. The fact that the Atribs had other very successful businesses in Nigeria signified connections and access to knowledge of just about everyone in the region and as a result they could determine who could be risked with credit and to what limit. Although these loans were unofficial, the Atrib family's status in the Capital also reduced the likelihood that anyone would consciously seek to renege on payment.

Of course, although this was an essential factor in the success of the casino I was managing, it was yet another area over which I, the supposed chief executive, had no effective control. They decided what amounts and to whom the credit would be given and, being entirely unofficial, the figures did not show on the daily accounts; furthermore, they made their own arrangements about collection. In fact the only indication that the money was being paid was the continuation of the player's right, on subsequent visits, to access further amounts. I was having difficulty to reconcile myself to the fact that so many aspects of the job I had taken on had been removed from my control i.e. casino design and decor, staff recruitment, financial management. When discussing this with Liz, she would say that as long as they were prepared to pay me for less responsibility, than a manager would normally have, I should accept it thankfully. Jeff, on the other hand, railed constantly against their ludicrous methods and pressed me to intervene each time he witnessed a deviation from London casino industry norms. I could not accept either position in its entirety. Although money had been, and continued to be, an important factor, I could not have it as my sole motivation and the Lebanese brothers' methods were undoubtedly questionable but they could not be entirely replaced by U.K. or any other country's regulation or business methods; we were, as Joseph himself would say, in Nigeria. I resolved to continue my campaign to introduce proper operating procedures on the games and improve the dealing and inspection of the tables. By improving security, increasing efficiency and hence productivity I hoped to gain more influence with the Atribs and perhaps more authority.

I had always been aware of the importance of a satisfactory social life and where this is essential wherever you may be it is even more necessary in a difficult environment such as Lagos. The presence of Liz had filled a crucial and uncovered area of my life because that city was certainly not a place for a young professional man to be without a romantic partner. I could well imagine myself on a night off, and after a stress relieving drinking session, eventually falling into dangerous company and territory. By day, she and I, would often visit the Ikoyi Club where, if an opponent could be found, I would play tennis then later join her and other expat staff for drink and snacks in Western style surroundings. A period of relative calm on the political front permitted us to concentrate on business, which meant turnover increased and hence gross profitability; the net company result I would never be able to determine. I was already learning that the owners of businesses, and most certainly gaming businesses, in third world countries always had the hidden costs of retaining their licence and avoiding interference from State organisations and others. As previously mentioned, there was also the doubt as to how much of the credit debt had been collected; here again I would find out that discounts were given to certain VIP's. The positive results were, as I had hoped, giving me a certain amount of authority to enforce my policies on the governance of the gaming floor. This message was getting through to those who might naturally resist any change that we cause them additional work or require them to be more diligent. I suspected it might also be seeping through to others who had more insidious reasons for retaining the defective system they had been working with until recently. All in all I had made myself unpopular with quite a number of people.

I had asked the owners several times why there were no females amongst the Nigerian staff employed in the casino. 'It's just the way it's always been here…' was the unsatisfactory reply. It was of course curious that the Lebanese, so keen to employ young attractive Western women, did not contemplate the possibility of Nigerian females. One theory was that the Nigerian girls would come under too much pressure from local gangsters to collaborate in illegal acts on the gaming tables. From what I was learning about the conditions in the Lagos ghettos and villages, where many of our staff came from, this was probably true but I feared it would be no less true of young male Nigerians. Because of the events that disrupted the first month of my employment and the subsequent period spent familiarising myself with my senior team and the owners' position on policy I had little contact with the African employees of our company. To manage any business in a foreign land it is of course essential to understand the culture, attitude and motivation of the local people; not only those who would be your customers but also those who work for you. So far, of those Nigerians who worked at Federal Palace, I had most contact with Mr Thomas. The fact that he himself only wished to be known as Mister was believed to be because it inferred status, the Thomas he was thought to have substituted for a family name which he believed would be unpronounceable for expatriates. Acceptability, particularly to foreigners, seemed to be a major motivation for Thomas who invariably dressed in a tight-fit business suit, starched collar and tie, with the cuffs of his shirts protruding inches below his jacket sleeves. The obsequious greeting he performed when meeting the Atribs he had extended to me, repeating it nauseatingly each time I had cause to address him during a shift. Unfortunately, I was beginning to think, the subservient attitude he displayed in front of his bosses was not entirely discarded when addressing some of his 'boys' as he called the staff supposedly under his supervision. While questioning other appointments I had asked Joseph what motivated them to employ Mr Thomas in the position of Personnel Manager and what were his actual duties. His answer confirmed more or less what I thought, that they needed a to have a local in a senior position but he didn't actually manage anyone, he conveyed instructions and information to the African staff that we had fed to him and he 'hopefully' informed us of anything we should know about their reactions, attitudes and behaviour. Atrib's use of the word hopefully was perhaps the most significant part of his reply. Not surprisingly the other Nigerian with whom I had had most contact in those early days was a Head Cashier called Enoch who had never really understood why we Brits sometimes called him Powell. Through no fault of his own the cash desk system was by Western standards somewhat chaotic due to undocumented withdrawals and repayments of credit and the Atrib's tendency, when the petty cash in their office safe was depleted, to avail themselves of quantities of Naira to meet some previously unforeseen expense such as a 'Dash'; perhaps the most important word in the Nigerian vocabulary, sometimes used as a term for gift or tip but more commonly recognised as the word for - bribe – be it to elicit a favour or evade some official inconvenience or sanction. In spite of Jeff's warning of irregularities in the Lebanese view of account management I had not anticipated just how complicated cash desk balances could be in this part of the world and in my first days I insisted on a series of procedural changes. The Nigerian cashier to his credit did attempt to apply them, in part by requesting documentation from the owners messengers such as Karouze, but in doing so met with criticism from them and in turn the Atribs themselves. I had then to intervene on behalf of the beleaguered Enoch, explain the policy and attempt to have the Lebanese comply; something to which they eventually agreed but did not always follow.

    I now attempted, and also encouraged the expat supervisors, to have more communication with the African dealing staff primarily during sessions of re-training and introduction of new table procedures. I hoped this would break down barriers and permit us to have more insight into what problems they encountered and how I might deal with them. Not altogether surprisingly, it soon became apparent that there were quite clear divisions between groups and nationalities in that some of the dealers were in fact not Nigerians and even those who were, came from diverse communities. Jeff, Nino and the girls, presumably because they were more approachable, started to get from some of the younger dealers and particularly the other Africans, some tentative suggestions that there was a hierarchy within the staff-room headed of course by the Nigerian Inspector Abdul. It was also implied that the new changes to the dealing procedures, and other security measures I had introduced, had not been well received. This was confirmed to me disingenuously by Mr Thomas when he offered the opinion that the some of the 'boys' were a little concerned and confused with all the changes that were taking place. Looking back now on this entire period it is difficult to imagine from where I found the resilience to carry on, I think it was probably a combination of reasons; personal and professional pride - I did not like to admit defeat; economic - tax free salary and bonuses higher than I could earn elsewhere ; obligation - to my friend Peter Byrne who had recommended me as the best man for the job.

The months went by, the problems were continuous but the profits were increasing, and by the end of that first year the owners having given me an extra bonus thankfully also agreed that both Liz and I could take a holiday back in UK.

CHAPTER 29

Our holiday was an opportunity to catch up with old friends and family, relax and enjoy some time together away from the daily pressure and stress of Lagos and Federal Palace Casino. However, although it was undoubtedly more relaxing, and for me comforting to see both my parents in good health again, by the time we were flying back to Nigeria, I did begin to suspect that my relationship with Liz was not entirely working. Ironically, when the pressures of Lagos were removed and the supportive roles were not quite so essential our general compatibility seemed to diminish leaving the physical attraction as the only real connection. My entry into the casino, where I was engulfed in the wave of internal discord, temporarily distracted me from consideration of private matters. Although I had implored the Atribs to support Jeff my deputy, and ensure others respected his authority during my absence, I was not entirely surprised to hear from him of multiple instances when his instructions were ignored or contravened. I was also to receive complaints from senior staff and the owners that he had failed to carry out certain duties and misinterpreted their actions. I had little doubt that Karouse, knowing of Jeff's reduced standing with his bosses would've ignored any gaming or cash desk procedure that proved to be inconvenient to him. Even others within the senior gaming staff, such as Makram and Salvatorri, would have paid only lip service to Jeff's directives and been quick to point out any of his perceived failings to the Atribs, via Karouze. Had not Beverly his wife, been one of Joseph's 'chosen' his position would have been completely untenable. As it was, even with my return and his removal from the direct firing line I couldn't see him staying for very much longer.

Among those few, which included the two girls, Nino stood out as one who had complied with procedures and abstained from internal politics. Perhaps because of that stance he did not seem to be greatly appreciated by the owners and did not seem himself to be too eager for promotion otherwise I would have considered him as a potential assistant. I'm not sure if my return inspired stricter application of the security procedures and hence more desperate measures by dishonest staff but within a few days we apprehended, in separate incidents, two dealers in acts of illegal stupidity. The first Nigerian boy had attempted unsuccessfully, when leaving the roulette table, to secrete a gaming chip of high value in what today has come to be known as an Afro haircut. Unfortunately for him his hair was not quite as thick as his head and the token was incriminatingly visible. The second attempt only two days later, by a young man who originated from the neighbouring Republic of Chad, surpassed the first, not only in the amount of three high value chips, but in misguided optimism. As he was about to be substituted by another roulette dealer, feigning uncharacteristic politeness he covered his mouth while coughing and inserted the chips; then in compliance with security procedure made an exaggerated display of showing clean hands before leaving the table. Nino, who had been inspecting, delayed the suspect's exit from the floor and then signalled me to attend his interrogation. The accused's tight-lipped response to Nino's questions amounted to several shrugs and a shake of his head until a pretended sharp prod to the stomach caused him to throw-up the jackpot. At first sight the actions of the two youths seemed particularly stupid, not just in the incompetent methods adopted, but in the fact that for a relatively small amount of money they had lost a position of which most people from similar underprivileged background could only dream. But I imagined it was more complicated. Foolish as they had been I could not believe they had not considered how the value chips would be converted into cash and this involved collaboration; so with whom were they collaborating? From the first incident the Atribs were convinced that the dealer was simply a fall guy, that he had been forced to carry out the action by the instigator/s. Because of this, they engaged a friend, who was a senior Police Officer to use the fear of further punishment to induce the boy to reveal who had been the instigator. After several days during which the second attempted theft had taken place I was told that the first boy had declared that the youth from Chad had forced him to do it and then when he failed had tried it himself. Even if this could be believed it left further questions unanswered, but I could only wait to hear what further investigation revealed while I directed my attention to other things.

One of those items was how, in common with all the other drivers, I would cope with the new Government edict designed to alleviate the Lagos traffic problem. I'm sure I was not the only one to suspect that the Minister who dreamt up this scheme had a financial interest in the manufacture or sales of cars. The new law said that car registrations starting with an odd number could be on the road only on Mondays, Wednesdays and Fridays while car registrations starting with even numbers 2, 4, 6 and 8 could drive on Lagos streets only Tuesday and Thursdays. Apart from the obvious immediate inconvenience to hundreds of thousands of business motorists there were other anomalies; there were always going to be more cars on the roads on the 'odd-number' days, because there are more odd than even digits - no registration numbers in Nigeria start with zero. Wednesdays seemed to be the day when many people and many odd-numbered vehicles were on the move. But the Atribs policy highlighted a tendency that would arouse the suspicion of a financial agenda, they provided two cars one odd and one even registration for all their people including myself. As the time moved on, traffic in Lagos would be as chaotic as ever but many more cars would be sold.

Results in the casino continued to improve driven mainly by losses from an ethnically diverse group of high rollers, all of whom availed themselves of our owners' credit facility. Several were, like the Atribs themselves, of Lebanese or Middle Eastern origin; one heavy gambler on American Roulette was a middle aged Spanish man who ran a successful fishing fleet. There were also Indian nationals who had been doing business throughout Africa and of course the Nigerian contingent some of whom carried the title of Chief. In all casinos players of this status are prized and must be handled with care, in this environment there were so many other factors to complicate the relations between manager and VIP client. For a start, some of them had cultural ties and/or a business relationship with our owners , then there was the question of the unofficial credit, and the fact that one or the other of the Atribs or their unofficial spokesman would be around most evenings. I could live with the fact that I would be by-passed by clients when they wished to discuss additional credit, what was difficult to accept was my bosses listening to, and attempting to address the petty complaints of some players instead of referring them to management. I had tried to avoid letting these conditions get on top of me and end up as disillusioned as Jeff. Having perhaps a more resolute approach, and the advantage of greater recognition by the Lebanese of my position, I had made some inroads but a series of incidents threatened to diminish my enthusiasm for the task. Two disputes in particular brought me to the point where I began to consider my position. The first was a typical reaction from a player who is losing when closing time arrives. At the appointed hour of closure a duty manager will signal his inspectors to announce the last shoe on card tables and the last three spins on roulettes. The timing and the number of spins can not be negotiable otherwise the whole procedure becomes a farce. However on this particular night a Lebanese customer and friend of the Atribs who was losing a considerable amount decided that he could not accept the casino closure while he was still in arrears and mounted a sustained vociferous protest. As he became verbally abusive toward the staff I intervened to receive an even more offensive reaction, before he stormed off to confront Joseph Atrib at his habitual position. It is understandable that you would not want to lose a good customer, and a friend, but there are things in the business that are not really negotiable; one, because to concede the point gives carte blanche to the individual to contest everything; two, it encourages others to do the same; three, it weakens the authority of the management not only in the eyes of the customer but also the staff. Joseph, instead of explaining that this was unfortunately a procedure that could not be changed and attempting to appease his friend by other means, accompanied the player back to the table and instructed the staff to allow him to play a few more spins. My emphatic criticism of this a little while later brought Joseph's apologetic shrug and the oft repeated phrase 'Jim...things are different here.'. A few moments later when Karouze came to inform us that the player had finished up by losing almost the same amount, their open palm-ed gesture said to me '...you see?' I did see, I could see they would never understand why a manager to do the job properly had to have authority and autonomy.

Annoyingly, at home or anywhere out of the work environment, where I might have expected some sympathetic understanding of my frustrations, from Liz I sensed only indifference. This was to be again evident just a short time later when I was confronted with another delicate political situation. On this occasion the tantrum was thrown not by a client but by a member of staff. Gordon Berry had been marked down as an unsatisfactory employee by my senior colleague Peter Byrne back in the Playboy days and his employment by the Atribs was due entirely to Joseph Atrib's desire to employ his wife Sonia. His ability in general would have ruled him out of my list of desirable candidates, but even more so, his infantile behavior. So it was not surprising when having been criticised for a series of mistakes he stormed off the floor and left me with no option but to suspend him from duty until further notice. Later in the evening when the appearance of the procession announced the immanent arrival of Joseph Atrib I made sure I reached the Lebanese first before someone else could present their view of the matter. Disappointingly, although not surprisingly, his concern was not that a senior expatriate had behaved unacceptably, but that the outcome might cause Berry, and hence his wife Sonia, to resign. This time I refused to move from my position that this man, at the very least, had to receive an official warning that any future misdemeanor would be his last.

'Let me talk to my brother'. Was another one of his stock responses that I'd become tired of hearing. The matter trailed on for several days during which my live-in partner once again gave me the impression that she did not entirely agree with my stance. When the Atribs finally accepted that a warning should be given to Berry that he could not repeat this behavior this he accepted without any of his usual petulant comments or gestures making me suspect that some consultations had taken place behind the scenes.

It could be said that for a while things were running smoothly, or perhaps that's an exaggeration because although the casino win was high and there were no major internal disputes there were of course the customary irritations. However, to prevent me from getting too complacent, my home life had become a succession of battles to the extent that Liz and I were in effect living separately within the same apartment.

At this moment Joseph Atrib, who had wanted to add her to his group of former Playboy girls, brought Simone to Lagos to visit her friend and former colleague Sonia, look at conditions at the Casino, Ikoyi and Victoria Island, and make a decision on their offer of employment. Ironically, in view of what was to happen in the future, this was another potential point of conflict, because once again I had not been consulted; possibly because Atrib knew that she would not have been my choice to bolster the expat team. After a few nights being feted and paraded around the casino and local clubs with her former Bunny colleague, Joseph then invited us all to a dinner at a fashionable restaurant. Not all took up the offer but I decided it was time for me to avail myself of his generous hospitality, loosen up, have some drinks and for entertainment have a few verbal jousts with the feisty Simone. By the end of the night we had done all that and surprisingly I found myself next door to my Ikoyi apartment in Sonia and Gordon Berry's spare bedroom with Simone; a fleeting surrender to temptation, assisted by alcohol, a fling, we both knew it wouldn't lead to anything.

Simone left a couple of days later with the understanding that she would review her present situation both at work and at home, consider the Atrib's offer, and come back to them with her decision within one month. Naturally, after a re-appraisal of her qualities, my position had changed with regard to her being employed at the Federal Palace. The term 'the calm before the storm' surely originated in Lagos. In any case we were now going through one of those periods of relative tranquility when results were being recorded without tantrums from the players or misbehavior from the staff. In the hotel they also had entered into what appeared to be a transition where services improved and a conscious effort was being made to attract visitors. I even felt relaxed enough to accept Joseph's invite to join them upstairs in the night club where, a prominent entertainer of that period on British television, Dianna Darvey was appearing. Having succeeded in passing an enjoyable few hours without any emergency calls from the casino I decided to go down for the closing period and see what had been happening during my absence.

On my arrival on the floor Jeff met me with a head waving so-so gesture. 'We're doing okay, Chidiac and Farcha lost some earlier, but Daboh's now winning a bit on French.' The winning player he referred to Godwin Daboh, was a Nigerian well known for his part in the overthrow of the Gowan regime and subsequent questionable tactics and financial dealings. As Jeff spoke we approached that table which was by far the busiest game in the casino at that fairly late hour. Daboh, who recognized me from his previous visits to the casino, looked up and gave me a nod of recognition and continued placing bets. At that point Salvatorri, who was in charge of the table, attracted my attention to point out some minor problem with equipment and comment on some earlier incident, both of which could have waited. This conversation, interrupted by the Italian's need to give instructions on the table, and a subsequent follow-up chat with Jeff, meant that I was present during several spins during which Daboh, betting heavily, apparently lost a considerable amount of the money he had been winning. The connection between my sudden appearance at the table and his dramatic reversal of fortune was all too clear to the insightful Nigerian.

'He make Juju on me!' or words to that effect, he roared angrily across the floor several times while pointing at me. He continued on this line for some time until Joseph Atrib sent Karouze to advise me to meet him in the office. As he was still on the floor himself this was a diplomatic way of telling me to withdraw from the scene. Having been accused of practicing Black Magic, which was unfortunately untrue, I would have been more inclined to remain to fight this false accusation but decided, as requested, to disappear to the office.

Joseph joined me a little later shaking his head. 'I am sorry Jim, this man is a craze, you know he has always been dangerous person… but o.k. he is now gone.'

He continued to offer words of encouragement but I found it difficult to respond. If I had been hoping to enjoy the tranquility of home I was to be disappointed here as well. My recent relationship with Liz had been largely uncommunicative but now she had seemly decided to vent her disapproval of my every action, eventually provoking from me a similar response which in turn threw her into a fury and a session of character assassination which almost ended in violence. I was puzzled by this development because it was in contrast to her earlier apparent disinterest; I began to think that she had heard of my brief affair with Simone and this had inexplicably caused a bout of jealousy. After a brief cessation of hostilities she erupted again and this time with the resistance crushing announcement that she was pregnant! She allowed me to agonize over this declaration for some time, refusing even to discuss it or state if her condition had been medically confirmed. I then learnt, from the Atribs, that Liz had officially resigned and would leave within weeks. They were no doubt aware of my strained relationship with her, otherwise they might well have been more concerned about my reaction. Joseph was in fact happy to announce that the vacancy she would create would be filled by Simone who had just agreed to accept their offer. During what remained of Liz's notice period I attempted several times to address the subject of her condition and future plans but became more and more convinced that she had invented the pregnancy as a tactic to annoy me. Possibly, because she had heard of my brief fling with Simone and the likelihood of her return to Lagos. When she had gone no further word was heard of her supposed pregnancy although Beverly, and other friends with whom she had been close, were informed of the many other ways I had failed her; most of which eventually reached me via gossip mongers. I felt I could now concentrate on all the other points of conflict at work, without the distraction of domestic problems, but curiously even at the casino I seemed be enjoying a peaceful hiatus marked by a series of excellent results gained without disputes either with clients or personnel. I also received a surprise when on the return of Mike Atrib from a foreign trip I was summonsed to the Office by his brother to be presented with an Omega watch as a token of their appreciation of my continued service in spite of a succession of difficulties. The watch was indeed appreciated, but not as much as the gesture itself. Another pleasurable event arrived a few days later when after much fiddling with the radio controls I succeeded in tuning in to the live commentary of the England v Scotland match at Wembley to enjoy listening to a 2-1 defeat of the 'Auld Enemy'. The next day I would be reunited with my 'New Friend'.

Simone arrived and initially lodged with Sonia in the apartment next door but in recognizing that we did indeed have the basis for a relationship she moved in with me in June of 1977. The physical aspect of our relationship I certainly found satisfactory, it remained to be seen if two people so dissimilar in terms of origin, upbringing, outlook and interests could form a lasting partnership; but we had made a good start.

The trouble free period at the casino had come to an end when we detected a series of attempted scams on French Roulette. Almost from our first days both myself and Jeff had stated doubts about the retention of this table, because the manner in which the play is conducted makes it less productive percentage-wise and considerably more vulnerable, in terms of security, than the American form of the game. In effect, it required a high level of expertise, supervision and surveillance which was not available, and would always be difficult to obtain, in Lagos. After revealing the details of this latest attempt, the individuals involved and historical statistics, it still involved a great deal of discussion before I finally achieved another small victory when the owners agreed to remove the game.

We had just dismissed a number of casino staff for dishonesty and as if to highlight the extent of corruption in Nigeria only a few days later I had also to remove our houseboy for blatantly stealing products from the kitchen. On discussing with Joseph Atrib the constant difficulty of refilling positions he nodded agreement and gave a reply that summed up the problem in Lagos. 'It sometimes better…if you think one of your staff is stealing, not to sack him…just change his name!'

Simone was beginning to realize the adjustments even she, a Western person with resources, had to make to live comfortably in Lagos. It brought us to realize just how resilient the vast majority of Nigerians had to be, just to survive. On one particular day, after continuous torrential rain throughout the previous 24 hours, Simone and I rose with the intention of driving to the supermarket only to find that the area surrounding our property was under water, so deep that we could not reach our car parked on higher ground out on the street. Our new houseboy Agustin, came to the rescue with an imaginative bridge consisting of large stones, bricks and pieces of wood. We then able to drive off through the flooded streets but a few moments later the car stalled. As I continuously revved the engine a Nigerian, navigating slightly higher ground, on a motorcycle later to be known as an Okada, smiled smugly and gave a derisive hand gesture as he passed me, mere car driver. His arrogance was to last only a few seconds as bike and rider suddenly plunged into a water-concealed ditch. As he resurfaced spitting water and attempted to drag his vehicle out of the mire the colourful woolen cap he'd worn floated off down the street. To complete this total reversal of fortunes our car engine then burst into life and we took off trying in vain not to look too smug.

Even without floods the management of our domestic life in Lagos was no easy task. There was the permanent difficulty of getting through the 'Go Slow' just to get to the shops, where we would often find a scarcity of basic products and, with the constant threat of power cuts, the few perishable items we had bought, could in one night be rendered inedible. However, even those tasks had become less tiresome in the company of my new partner who had a more durable and adventurist outlook than the previous.

A more satisfying and stable environment at home in our apartment enabled me to concentrate on the ever-present difficulties at the Federal Palace Casino. Of the two Bosses, I preferred to deal with Joseph. Both had their peculiarities but Michael, although the younger of the two, was in terms of authority the senior partner. Because of this he was invariably involved with the administration of their principal businesses, and therefore left much of the time-consuming duties of monitoring the casino, to his brother. Unfortunately, on the occasions when Joseph was also absent, he would delegate many of those responsibilities to 'factotums' such as Karouze or the newly appointed, Rudolph; both ill equipped to be involved in corporate decision making, the latter dangerously self deluded about his abilities. My relationship with Rudolph and, as a consequence, with the Atribs was to be put to the test when Joseph embarked on an extended trip to Europe. This Lebanese cultural tendency to deploy 'trusted' individuals to transmit their information, questions, requests and orders to a business manager such as myself, form the start I'd found enormously irritating. I had however managed to work around most of the annoying traits of Karouze and other less used individuals. But I was now to find, and have it confirmed by his countryman Makram, that Rudolph, having been personally appointed by Michael, considered himself a senior executive.

I could never be entirely sure that all information or suggestions, given to me by him, had in fact come from an Atrib and if later I seriously questioned a policy suggestion with Michael or Joseph, it would invariably lead to a discussion between the Lebanese in their own language. If I was firm in my opposition, and particularly if events had proven me right, the likely response from them would be that there had been some misunderstanding by me as to what their position was, or alternatively, Rudolph had not quite understood what policy I preferred. Maddening, time consuming, and often costly, as this process was, I was aware that any accommodation they had eventually reached with me was as much as I was likely to achieve without risking a situation where if I continued to protest they would be forced to assert their authority for fear of losing face with their own people.

A dispute involving Berry and Abdul was now to emphasize once again the differences between the corporate procedures which I had been accustomed to apply and the third world politic which prevailed in the Atribs' business dealings. In this particular occasion Gordon Berry while contesting a table procedure with the Nigerian had completely lost his temper and resorted to infantile name calling. Although it was well known to the Atribs that I had serious doubts about the attitude and integrity of the Nigerian on this occasion I was certain that Berry had committed the error and then conducted himself inappropriately. However, on reporting to Joseph the intention to censure my fellow Brit he suggested that for the moment I take no action. Believing that in some way he considered Abdul to have been the guilty party I explained the circumstances in more detail only to eventually realize that his call for 'no action' was based only on his assessment of the possible consequences. He did not want to have a problem with the only Nigerian inspector but he also did not want to provoke the departure of Berry and more importantly has wife Sonia. His suggestion was that Mr Thomas could inform Abdul that we were not happy about Berry's outburst and, he Joseph could speak to Sonia and ask her to calm her husband down. This solution did not sit well with me at all. At a time when I was trying to impose more discipline throughout the operation I could not be seen to ignore unacceptable conduct from an expat; it would give justification to a person such as Abdul to claim prejudicial policy if in the future should I have cause to bring action against him or any other African staff member. Circumstances were to come to my assistance only 48 hours later when Sonia informed Simone that she was pregnant and therefore they would some time soon be returning to England. However, before they had even set that date Jeff and Beverly also announced their long anticipated intention to leave. We would now have to recruit new senior staff.

At an earlier date the departure of Sonia might well have prompted Simone to also leave Lagos but by now it seemed events would not so easily come between us, except temporarily, as was to be proved one afternoon when we were making our way home after a shopping expedition. Approaching a junction at Victoria Island where, in the absence of a functioning traffic light system, a member of the Militia served as a traffic policeman, I slowed the car and inched forward trying to interpret the innovative hand signals employed by the uniformed official. The signals amounted to a waving hand, clenched fist, an open palm and a gesticulation we might make to demonstrate somebody chattering; all done in quick succession. As there were no traffic impeding my progress and no other obvious reason to stop I interpreted his sign to mean I should continue, which I did slowly, only to find him then make an obvious signal with both hands that I should immediately stop. He hurried to the side of my car having picked up a customary swagger-stick which he used to gesture that I exit from the car.

'Why you don go when I make stop?' He demanded. Or words to that effect.

I tried to explain that I didn't understand his signals which led him to make a hand gesture yet again and ask me what colour it was. When I didn't answer he signaled to a Militia car, parked off the road on the other side, which I had not previously noticed. We were immediately joined by two other officers while Simone with considerable concern exited our car to ask what was going on. Having asked me for documentation I gave them my passport and attempted to explain to them who I was and where and for whom I worked. After a confusing confab between themselves to my, and Simone's, horror they commanded me to accompany them in their vehicle to the police station. They would not clarify why I should be detained but did concede that Simone would not need to accompany me to the local Ikoyi Station and would have the right to take our car; she quickly agreed with me that she'd make directly for the Atrib's house to seek their assistance.

Knowing the way things usually worked in Nigeria, while on my way with my captors, I asked if there was a standard fine for my offence but was disappointed and somewhat worried to receive no response. Once at the Station I was led to a windowless room with three chairs and a small desk and locked in, without being read my rights or receiving procedural information. I wasn't sure how long I had been there, but the longer the better I rationalized, as it gave Simone time to find the Atribs and for them to take action on my behalf. But the door was then opened and the two militiamen re-entered this time accompanied by a third, who comfortingly carried a folder rather than any instrument of torture. While one stood guard by the door, in case the notorious traffic violator made a break for it, the other two sat opposite me at the small desk. The folder bearer proceeded to ask for my personal details and then informed me that I had been detained for the serious violation of refusing to stop when ordered to do so by a Government officer and failing to cooperate when I was detained and questioned about my action.

It wasn't easy to reply to such a ludicrous accusation but when I did attempt to respond I could see they had no interest in my statement. I then began to insist on legal representation but a sudden and hurried knock on the door saw another official enter to beckon my accusers to exit. It could only have been fifteen nervous and confusing minutes later when yet another officer entered and informed me that I should follow him out to the front desk, where to my enormous relief I found the imposing figure of the Atrib's man, Robert Shahara.

Traumatic as this event may have been to Simone and myself, to my Lebanese bosses it was just another irritation in the daily life of a Lagos resident. The reason for my detention was never fully clarified but it would seem that on being stopped I should not have indicated that I was a senior manager in the Federal Palace casino as it presented the prospect of a far greater reward than the customary 'dash' given by individuals to avoid inconvenience. Curiously I was to see variations of the so called hand signals being used, with just a little more clarity, by other military traffic police. They had been introduced as a substitute for the eternally non-functioning traffic lights; the hand signal I mistook for a chattering gesture was apparently designed to imitate the flickering of the amber light.

The replacements for Jeff, Beverly, Sonia and Gordon Berry had been under discussion, and even before they left we had all agreed that with the level of business we were getting we in fact were already short so in actual fact we needed to recruit six senior staff. However, what I had at first viewed as an opportunity to build my own team now turned into another situation in which I would have to arrive at an accommodation. Apparently it was becoming more difficult to obtain permits for expatriate workers. There was, for the Atribs however, the convenient possibility that several expats working for our competitor in Apapa Casino might be persuaded to transfer allegiance. This, I was told, would have the additional attraction of punishing the Lebanese owner of that operation who was suspected of having acted against the Atribs in dealings with authorities. Hence, the recruitment soon after of three Brits, one of whom Tony Rodgers, I had briefly worked with in London. As with Jeff at an earlier date, he was nominated by default rather than choice, to be my second in command being the only one with Western senior management experience. Maggie Packer and Alan Howard would be Inspectors as would another former colleague from Scotland Jimmy Brown and Shaheen a relative of Makram. More worryingly it was suggested by the owners that it would be politically advisable to fill the remaining Inspector vacancy by promoting another one of the Nigerian staff.

Joseph was no doubt concerned that the recent run-in with the Militia, my continued unease with staffing policies and the departure of my partner Simone's friend Sonia would cause us to reconsider our future in Lagos. I'm sure my general demeanor did not disabuse him of that thought that I'd be the next Brit to hand in my notice. Perhaps this was why, following a heated dispute with Rudolph, he finally intervened forcefully on my behalf, convincing his brother to do the same. Their factotem's continued interference in the management of the casino reached a point where he began to intervene in disputes between customers and staff ; this finally forced me to abandon my diplomatic approach to his presence and conduct. The manner of my instruction to him sent him scurrying off to his bosses but they would learn that this time I was not moving my position. To my surprise he was instructed that he should only make observations or suggestions directly to me. I had made some progress but perhaps an even more embittered opponent.

Home life continued to be satisfying, there may have been periodic power cuts but in my relations with Simone there was no lack of energy. The rest of the time at home we read and listened to music and when reception was favourable we tuned into the BBC World service. One day in particular I fiddled constantly with the controls to no avail and was just about to turn it off when through the hiss and crackle I caught the newsreader's voice '….announce the death of Elvis Presley…' then the connection was gone; as was a great boyhood favourite.

CHAPTER 30

I had delayed my trip home for some time but quite apart from needing a break away from Nigeria I wanted to see my parents. With the introduction of new expatriate staff it perhaps wasn't the best time to be absent from the casino but I doubted if there was ever a good time. At least with the arrival of Tony Rodgers, who unlike Jeff had actually been employed in the position of Assistant Manager by the Atribs, I would hopefully be leaving someone who had knowledge and experience and would be supported by the Lebanese. Unfortunately Simone, having not originally come as my partner, had a holiday plan that did not fully coincide with mine. She would therefore arrive in UK two weeks after me, spend a week with me and then remain for a few days more before rejoining me in Lagos. The first phase of my holiday was a return to London where I was invited by Peter Byrne to dinner at my former place of work the Playboy Club where we had both first met the Atribs. He was intrigued, and perhaps relieved he hadn't taken up the position, to listen to my experiences so far of Lagos and the job I had taken on. As with many others there who knew us from our time at Playboy he was also surprised at how well Simone and I had got on together. My next part of my holiday was back in Glasgow where I was happy to find my parents in good health and keen to hear of my time in 'Darkest Africa'. While also looking in at some of my old haunts I ran into my former girlfriend Janette and, in the light of my current contented relationship, was happy to feel not the slightest regret that we had not stayed together.

All was going well, until a few nights later when having gone out with some old buddies I was to suffer a similar, and in some ways more alarming, experience to that which I had recently suffered in Lagos. When the last bell announced the closure of a favourite pub we had visited I bade my mates goodnight and made for my rented car to go back to the hotel where I was lodged near my parents' house. I'm not entirely sure if it was a random check or I had been targeted because I was a young man driving home just after pub closing time. In any case, they stopped me just after I had taken off, breathalysed me and then instructed me to accompany them to the station. Deja-vu – only the faces and their colour had changed. I was then informed that I would then have a blood sample taken and while waiting for the result I would be held in custody. Unlike the Lagos experience, where I waited alone, here I had the delightful company of a person who didn't require any test to verify that his reeling and rambling was due to excessive consumption of alcohol. Another, who was apparently accused of carrying an offensive weapon and who most certainly had an offensive attitude. We were about to be joined by a third, who looked like he had been resisting arrest, when I was led out to be informed that the sample had shown an insufficient amount of alcohol to justify prosecution. As I had resisted alcohol for most of the night this came as no surprise but my inclination to complain was defeated by my desire to get out of that unpleasant environment as soon as possible.

Two days later Simone joined me for her first visit to Glasgow, a brief meeting with my parents followed by a trip to Liverpool before returning to London where we were invited to dinner at Playboy by our former manager Bernie Mulherne. The expansion of the brand, in its casino form, to Bahamas and other parts of the world seems certain and Bernie was sounding me out as a possible candidate for a management position in one of the new ventures. Without completely ruling myself out I couldn't honestly commit myself to a company whose policies I had opposed when I had last worked for them. I now returned to Lagos while Simone remained for a few days more to catch up with family and friends. In my discussions with my new Assistant Tony Rogers and other members of the senior staff, old and new, there seemed if anything to be even greater potential for conflict between them than there had been with the original team. Rogers I had already noted was extremely critical of the owners' policies including the financial terms that he had readily accepted only a month before, including the travel costs of his soon to arrive wife and two children. In spite of his negative views on their payment and policies in their presence he almost reached Mr. Thomas's level of fawning subservience. At this stage it was difficult to categorize the voluble Alan Howard, though Makram had already made his diagnosis which to me he was happy to impart. 'Zis man ees a crazee'.

Jimmy Brown fulfilled his duties in the casino but there was always the danger that his drinking habits outside of work would lead to problems. At this stage it seemed, of the new arrivals, the least problematic would be Maggie Packer. To add to any concern I might have of the new expatriates there were already indications that Nelson, the newly promoted Nigerian, had formed an allegiance to his countryman Abdul and was already showing some of the same annoying traits. One thing was clear, I was never going to become complacent in my position as Manager of Federal Palace Casino.

I did have something to lift my spirits, Simone was flying back in to Lagos and I was there to pick her up at Murtalla Mohammed Airport; re-named to honour the recently assassinated leader. I had left early with one of Atribs' drivers to make sure I was there on time, only to learn, that the flight was arriving late. As we waited in the car just outside the terminal it could be seen that 'my friends' the Militia were imposing themselves upon anyone who, unlike the Atribs' people, had not acquired, by dash, the right to park on that stretch. One car pulled up just in front of us and the driver, who must have reckoned that on seeing no official near enough at that moment to cause him a problem, he could quickly dash into the terminal, presumably to check on a flight time. But he had calculated wrongly; no sooner had he got through the entrance than a uniform appeared from nowhere to check if this was 'dash' authorised parking or the car should be detained. The Militiaman was moving to carry out Lagos car detention procedure, which amounted to removing the cap to deflate a tyre. When the driver, having seen him, raced out, shouting something and swiftly entered his car, the officer hurried to carry out his procedure. The driver gunned his ignition and the car jolted forward throwing the Militiaman off balance. However, any expectation the driver had that he'd escaped his parking sanction ended when another armed officer stepped out from between the cars in front and pointed his weapon at the windscreen. Unlike my own experience this could not be interpreted by the driver as anything other than a signal to stop! He fearfully exited from his car to find his earlier failure to respond correctly to an official procedure merited an immediate penalty; a teeth crunching blow to his face with the butt of the Militiaman's weapon. As I turned away shaking my head in disbelief at this bloody spectacle I noted my driver remained impassive. At the re-appointed time for Simone's flight to arrive I moved inside the terminal hopeful that the Atrib's contracted airport official would have ensured her swift passageway through the chaotic passport and document checkpoints. To my great relief and excited expectation I caught sight of her as she was waved through to Customs, - the final stage. There now seemed to be some hold-up and even from where I stood I could see from her body language that something had upset her. My nervousness dissipated slightly when I saw her munching, what looked like, an apple. I waited somewhat puzzled as to what was happening and what if anything I could do about it while Simone appeared to be eating more apples. After a few minutes she deposited her last bag on the trolley and made her way through to my waiting arms.

'What was all that about?' I asked as we hugged.

'Oh! I had some apples with me, you can't get good ones here, but they wouldn't let me pass …said it's illegal to bring them in. Can you believe such nonsense?' She said.

'They made you eat them?' I asked flippantly.

'Of course not…I just wasn't going to let them take them!' It was great to have her back and with a night off we could catch up on what we had missed.

After a brief romantic break we were both back in the political minefield that was Federal Palace Casino. My Assistant Rogers continued with his suggestion that we were not being rewarded sufficiently for the difficult job we were doing and now Howard seemed to have taken up the same theme. Because of the tone of Rogers's comments and his duplicitous attitude in general I was suspicious of his motives. At some times it sounded like an obscure invitation for me to propose some sort of illegal collusion that would extract compensation for us being exploited. But I wasn't sure if he actually looking to participate in such a scheme or was tempting me into leaving myself exposed by proposing it. He could then have me removed and replace me as casino director. To anyone reading this now it might sound as if I had a neurotic obsession but they were plotting against each other continuously so there was absolutely no reason to suppose that I wouldn't be a target.

Rudolph, who's authority was supposedly diminished following our dispute when the Atribs supported my position, now appeared to have become a target of his countryman Makram; or was it another duplicitous tactic? His throwaway comment implied that Rudolph had too much access to the money that was moved between the cash desk, the office safe and the Atribs' safes at their office and home. His suggestion was that I might want to request that the owners give me more control over these movements. In keeping with my response to the other suggestions from Rogers I would nod my head to acknowledge the intake of the information and suggestions but make no other response or commitment. Rudolph himself was now to approach me with some sensitive material; it seems he was disgusted to witness the recently arrived Alan Howard and Maggie touching each other erotically in the rest room. I again nodded acknowledgement of this essential information. Curiously, the only member who refrained from the tittle-tattle and campaigning was Nino Pertile who to my great advantage busied himself with unpaid additional duties such as helping me to re-cover the tables and finally find a way to re-position the table lights.

Simone and I would exchange gossip on our way home each night as of course she, during her breaks in the restroom, would also be exposed to other ridiculous stories and rumours from work colleagues. There was little doubt that without her I would have been unlikely to continue in that environment although being the boyfriend of one of the most shapely and attractive females in the city, and most certainly in the Federal Palace, presented other problems. Many of the affluent customers, particularly of the Lebanese and expatriate community had ambitions to win her attention. Some, unaware of my relationship with her, even asking me what their chances might be with the lovely English girl. One rich Arab was overheard to ask why this girl would be going with the manager when she could have so much more. Another, a friend of the Atribs, would make regular announcements when she passed. 'Oooh! The way she walks…!'
Not all my contact with customers proved embarrassing, there were times when I would meet interesting people as was the case when, on hearing me mention something about football, a Yugoslav visitor struck up a conversation with me. To my surprise he turned out to be the chief coach of the Nigerian international football team Jelisavcich Tihomir or Tiko as he was known in the football world. He was not a serious gambler and had come to the Federal Palace hotel for dinner and then for amusement had entered the casino. After an interesting and amusing discussion about our diverse careers and the difficulties of working and living in Lagos I was delighted when he asked me to be his guest on a visit to the National Stadium, followed by dinner.

Tiko's reputation had been greatly enhanced by his handling of the Nigerian team whose players, like many of their people in other professions, had shown great talent but little discipline, but he had gradually moulded them into a more formidable unit. They would now play Tunisia in Lagos in what would be a deciding match in the qualifying rounds that, if won, would take them to the World Cup Finals in Argentine. Just over two weeks later, accompanied by Nino, I returned to the Stadium with tickets given to us by Tiko. It was to be a disappointing night all round.

As with everything else in Nigeria they have a way of creating difficulty when there should be none. There was about half an hour to go before kick off when we arrived outside the ground but it seemed that the vast majority of spectators were still outside and with very poor signage I could see it was difficult to determine your individual gate number; not surprisingly there were no stewards in attendance. This was causing the kind of chaos we had seen at other major events, and of course at the airport. There also seemed to be a number of disputes going on and the Militia present intervened to invariably cause even more disturbance. Several times the crowds rushed towards one area to be driven back. I had just checked my ticket entrance number yet again to ensure we were moving towards the correct gate. Suddenly a fresh surge of people barged into us knocking me over. When I got back to my feet and recovered my breath to my horror the ticket, which I had naively placed in the top pocket of my short sleeved shirt, had disappeared. Nino hopefully scanned the immediate area but I had no doubt that the ticket very soon would be available for purchase on the other side of the stadium. There was of course no point in reporting to the Police and although we made our way to the Stadium reception I had little hope that anything could be done. For once my pessimism was to be proved wrong. At the entrance, where I had started my visit only two weeks before, I managed to persuade the guards that we were invited guests of the National Coach. I think being expatriates may have assisted us in this approach. We were taken the desk where by amazing good fortune a male reception manager remembered me from my previous visit and on hearing my tale seemed suitably shocked that an invited guest of the famed Tiko should have been subjected to such treatment. He bade us wait and moved off quickly through a passageway. At this point I was unsure what could be done and with the kick off time only about five minutes away I felt Nino should make his way to his seat perhaps to sit next to the new owner of my ticket. I had just about persuaded him to do this when the Nigerian came back waving two new tickets authorized by an assistant of the coach, '…who, you will understand at this moment is very busy!'

It was an outcome I couldn't possibly have predicted. We hurried through to our newly allocated seats to witness a result that I also could not have predicted, nor wanted to, for Tiko's sake. A late own-goal was to cost Nigeria the game and a place in the final stages of the World Cup. This outcome was sadly to bring about the departure of my new friend, from his position as Chief Coach but the continued improvement of Nigeria in the football world was later, by many, to be attributed to the groundwork done by Jelisavcich Tihomir.

After the drama of the World Cup I was soon back to the daily dramatics performed by casino personnel. Rudolph, chastened by the outcome of his last dispute with me, had been relatively quiet but apparently felt he had cause to comment on the general conduct of Alan Howard. Had he made a discreet observation to one of the owners or to me, it might well have been dealt with quietly but instead, on entering the restroom when several others were present , he chose to inform Howard directly that the latter was at times too loud and his behavior erratic. To confirm his assertion the Englishmen launched into a strident and irrational response that he continued after they both entered the gaming area causing me to intervene. In actual fact Rudolph's observation, however untimely, for once equaled my own view. The recently arrived Howard was most definitely a person who at times showed capricious tendencies. However, after my talk he appeared to calm himself, until a few days later when after another spat with Rudolph, this time initiated by himself, he informed me he intended to resign. I did not respond, except to inform Joseph Atrib of the possibility, and was not altogether surprised to learn a few days later that he had decided for the time being to remain.

He may have decided to remain but Simone and I, now accepting the likelihood that we would continue as a couple, were already discussing what we might do in the not too distant future when we decided to leave; a new plan at that time envisaged us running a B&B in Brighton. Yet another incident in Lagos was to make that plan look all the more inviting.

Early in the day I took our blue Honda and drove us down to Marina where on one side, on the dockside of Lagos Harbour, large merchant ships were moored and on the other, a line of public buildings guarded by Military personnel, who ensured that no unauthorized vehicle stopped on that stretch of the road. Having passed that area we parked on the marina parking area to make our way to Savannah Bank. Although there was a queue at every desk, the arrangement set up by the Atribs, whereby a member of the staff was 'dashed' to ensure efficient service, functioned perfectly and we were hastened into a back office to effect our transaction which involved the withdrawal of Niara. That part done we would now stop off at Folomo Centre for some shopping before returning home. As I pulled the car out of the parking area and back on to the Marina highway I could feel a slight juddering so I changed gear and accelerated a little more. The misfiring continued as we moved up the Marina, the engine finally surrendering and bringing the car to a halt in, of all places, the no-parking zone. I sat there gunning the engine for a few minutes without success then, expecting the arrival of the Militia at any moment, I opened the bonnet to signal a breakdown and we both climbed out.

The car make problem?' a passing motorcyclist stopped to ask. 'I mechanic …I look, no? I shrugged and nodded assent. 'Must do quick, Officers will come.'

Of that of course we were well aware of and in fact could see one in the distance look down towards us, as the Nigerian took a tool bag from his motorcycle and stuck his head in the bonnet. After a few moments he asked me for the car key, tried the engine once, which seemed to start but then stopped.

'I think go work.' he said getting out to look at the back exhaust then the engine again before offering me the key. 'I sure, do quick… before Officers come…'

They were indeed making their way down toward us, so Simone and I both climbed in, I gunned the engine and to our immense relief it started. Winding down the window I offered him a substantial reward which he accepted with exaggerated gratitude before taking off on his moto. Knowing the complications that can arise from being in the hands of the Militia I drove off as quickly as I could and we were both happy when a I had passed the prohibited area, but that happiness quickly dissipated when Simone opened the car's glove compartment to find the money we had taken from the bank was missing.

Only after relating our misfortune to some of our more experienced colleagues, and Joseph Atrib, did we realise the extent of our naivety. The 'a blockage inserted in the exhaust' was known to be means of causing breakdown in inconvenient locations, where emergency services can be offered to stressed occupants, particularly expatriates, who often leave articles of value in the car. Whether or not our 'mechanic' had targeted us earlier and observed our bank visit or had been extraordinarily lucky to meet a complete suckers and be doubly rewarded will never be known. Our disenchantment with life in Lagos must have been all too apparent, the Atribs insisted on reimbursing us for our loss.

The business at Federal Palace casino continued to grow and profits increased in spite of a lack of management and staff cohesion. This had much to do with the Atrib's connections and reputation and greatly to do with the location. I was irritated to think just how successful it could be with a proper recruitment policy, more comprehensive training, better security procedures and technology and an extensive marketing programme. I endeavored to put those points across whenever I could and had the feeling that although my Assistant Rogers voiced agreement with me in private, he did not seem to make any great effort to implement changes I introduced or bolster the argument for further changes with the Lebanese owners. I had learnt to take Makram's comments with a pinch of salt but something that he had said earlier about Rogers ingratiating himself with Rudolph and the Atribs in order to get my position was also being hinted at by others. Nino had said, that on my nights off Rogers spent a lot of time with one or the other of the Lebanese bosses.

In spite of the atmosphere at work I was normally able to put it all to the back of my mind when at home, mostly of course because of my amorous partner, but also because of a fortunate ability to switch off, listen to music, read a book or dabble with my writing. When not disturbed by heat due to Nepa power-cuts disabling the air conditioning I, unlike Simone who had occasional insomnia, could also sleep well. But in Lagos they can always come up with something different to test your resolve. One morning we were both jolted awake with a deafening sound that we could not immediately identify, nor determine its source. Then I began to vaguely recognise it as music and realise it was coming from the property behind our house. I rose first, pulled on a dressing gown and slippers and shuffled out to the hallway and through to the door to our rear balcony. The noise even before the door was open was almost earsplitting and the music that had disturbed me seemed to have been chosen with a degree of irony; Heilan' Laddie being a Scots folk tune made into a Scottish Regimental March. The sight in front of me when I opened the door, to be joined by Simone a few minutes later, could not have been more entertaining. The property to the rear of our, and other buildings on the street, had been taken over by the Lagos Fire department as a training centre and they had apparently set up, what amounted to, a simulated emergency site. On reception of an alarm call, the trainee teams were required arrive at the scene of the emergency, get into position quickly, setting up the necessary apparatus then rapidly climb frames and other obstacles with the equipment, such as hosepipes, to bring the situation under their control; all this within a determined time and to the accompaniment of the selected music. I don't know if it was the futile attempt to keep time to the curious choice of music or a simple lack of agility and coordination, but the scene resembled a music-hall comedy with uniformed recruits falling and colliding with each other, causing equipment to be broken and uniforms to be ripped. One thing had been made very clear, at Federal Palace Casino it would be very important to have an effective fire prevention policy.

Being in Nigeria is difficult at any time but having taken our holiday earlier we now had the unenviable task of spending Christmas and New Year in Lagos. The Atribs were, of course, not unaware of the sacrifice this required of an already disillusioned expat manager and gave a compensating Christmas bonus of $1,000., a sum that today is not inconsiderable, but in 1977 was remarkably rewarding. Had my campaigning Assistant known about it, he would have choked on his Christmas pudding. The other great compensation was of course that Simone and I would spend our first full festive season together and she would help me get through what was always a difficult emotional moment, that of being away from home when the bells heralded a New Year and no matter where you were they invariably played Auld Lang Syne.

The start of a new year in Nigeria means an opportunity to experience a new range of difficulties, the latest being a series of import restrictions covering coffee, tea, milk, mineral water, beer, rice and sugar. The Military Government of course blamed Western policies for these latest inconveniences. Apart from the irritation of frequent power cuts, shortage of foodstuffs, traffic congestion and then internal politics at the Casino I now had a new challenge; after a few weeks of intermittent headaches, fever and general fatigue, a doctor recommended to me by Joseph, diagnosed 'possible' malaria. It was true that I had probably not taken all the drugs and precautions previously advised and after a short period of taking the new treatment I seemed to improve enough to postpone, once again, our intention to get out of Nigeria. I had not taken much time off during my malarial bout but the few days I had been absent gave great scope for the expat contingent to fight with each other, to the extent that Alan Howard and Shaheen now refused to talk to Tony Rogers. Maggie had also begun to confirm, what some of us had felt for some time, that her boyfriend Howard was showing disturbing signs of stress. On the administrative side, the Atrib's political P.R. policy of permitting local Nigerian chiefs to sign unenforceable I.O.U.'s was becoming, in effect, a costly give-away, as hardly any of them honoured the documents they had signed. Fortunately the cash they did play and the amounts lost by all our other, mostly foreign players, still gave us a healthy result. Suspecting that some of the security procedures I had introduced were not always being enforced, a suspicion reinforced by comments from Makram and more definite statements from Nino, I re-launched this campaign. When I had discussed the security policy implementation with my Assistant Rogers he was as usual evasive, citing a number of reasons why it was not always possible to apply all regulations. I therefore decided that for a period I would dedicate less time to administrative duties and meetings and more time directly supervising the gaming activities. I had pursued this policy for a couple of weeks when Nino informed me that a young croupier from Togo, Issadore, who had previously made a reluctant and discreet complaint to us about his mistreatment by Nigerian colleagues, had once again cautiously informed him that he was being pressurised into committing illegal acts. I finally arranged out-of-work meetings with this young man to listen to his concerns and evaluate the veracity of his accusations. From those conversations it did appear that the increased emphasis on security had created a problem for those who previously had regularly filched additional earnings from the tables and had planned even bigger scams. It seemed the perpetrators of those acts, now in fear of being exposed, were exerting pressure on the few vulnerable non Nigerian Africans we employed, to carry out the cheat moves and share the results, confident that the outsiders if detected would be too fearful of retribution to reveal the originators of the plan. This to some extent was apparent in Issadore's initial reluctance to identify the conspirators and only after being assured by me that any action we took would never indicate that he had given us information, did he disclose several names, which not surprisingly included Nelson and Abdul.

In keeping with my promise I did not take any action against the named individuals nor did I reveal my discussions to Tony Rogers nor any other member of the staff save Nino with whom the boy had first confided and who also could be trusted to keep mum. At this stage I also delayed discussing the matter with the Atribs and instead initiated tighter controls including a revision of our system of allocating staff to the tables; in effect ensuring that no one had prior knowledge of what table they would be assigned to nor with whom they would work. Just over a week later Nino informed me that Issadore had heard other dealers say that someone had promised to make JuJu for me; a worrying attitude but an indication that the controls were having some effect.

Had Simone or myself believed that it was possible for someone to cast an evil spell on me, an incident shortly afterwards might well have been attributed to that malevolent power. We had decided to spend an afternoon of sun, sea and sand at the local Bar Beach. As I had little or no recent exercise and a tiring work regime I felt I should refresh and energise myself, and so leaving Simone stretched out on the beach, I trudged down the sand and plunged into the cool sea. Thrashing my way out through the waves switching from breaststroke to crawl, and even a pathetic attempt at butterfly, I took myself out a considerable distance from the shoreline. As I began my surge back to the shoreline the significant effect of the rip current forced me into even greater exertion and the first pangs of leg cramp gave me a frightening warning. The strength needed to withstand the undercurrent had now to come almost totally from my arms, as the muscles on both legs had painfully contracted. I was still some way from having land beneath my feet when another sudden counter flow washed me further back. Exhausted and fearing that not for long would I be able to keep my head above the surface I screamed for assistance while flailing my arms desperately. When all seemed lost a tidal wave, this time, swept me inshore towards two bathers who had heard my cry and now assisted me to cover the last few yards to the safety of the beach.

Meanwhile a Nigerian woman who had seen us arrive together rushed across to Simone. 'Why you lie about reading book when husband is drowning?' She chastised my completely unaware partner who, shocked by this announcement, scrambled down the considerable distance from our chosen beach position to the water's edge where I now lay, recovering from my narrow escape.

Having survived my day-off I now returned to the trials of managing the Federal Palace casino. Play on the tables was if anything increasing with considerable sums being risked by a number of players who had secured a credit facility from my bosses. Naturally, from time to time, one of the high rollers would hit a winning streak and this, because of their level of play, could amount to a sizable loss for the house and of course they, unlike the casino that had to wait for credit to be paid, wanted to collect winnings immediately leaving us with a temporary problem of cash flow. One Nigerian Chief recorded high wins on consecutive nights prompting an inquest which took place at the baccarat/meeting table attended by myself, both Michael and Joseph Atrib, Tony Rogers and the additional unhelpful presence of Rudolph. In actual fact none of their input was particularly helpful, being confident that the win had been legitimate and the game had been conducted as efficiently as possible, I was certain that providing the player continued to play we would return to an acceptable result. What I emphasised, in reply to the owners' question, was that no one could estimate exactly how long it would take to recover. As usual, Rogers did not give me much assistance in getting the message across that the only real concern was that the amount of money being played would continue at least on the same level and, if so, by maintaining our efficiency results would eventually return to a predictable level. At this stage Rudolph sought to enlighten everyone by revealing that this particular player was known to have a high degree of luck and at least one of the dealers we had used was known to have very bad history of spinning unlucky numbers. Perhaps the most worrying thing about the response to this revelation was that I was the only one who laughed. Fortunately, the player did continue gambling and very soon we returned to a positive result from his play; unfortunately the final recovery was made on a night when the dealer tagged as 'unlucky' happened to be off, salvaging the analytic reputation of one Lebanese factotum, or so he thought.

My insistence on strict table procedures and that senior staff be more vigilant was to pay off handsomely when Maggie Packer detected a scam being carried out by the recently promoted Nelson Dippo, who by all accounts had become an acolyte of the long suspected Abdul. Much as we would have liked to incriminate the latter, the condemned Nelson under interrogation, was probably too scared to implicate his gangmaster. Nevertheless the Atribs, now encouraged by our success, supported my campaign for stricter measures and behind the scenes conveyed, through people such as Mr Thomas, that our investigations would continue. Less than a week later we hit the jackpot when the disempowered Abdul, realizing his additional source of illegal income had come to an end, did what was almost unheard of by an indigenous worker in Nigeria, he resigned. If I had thought that we would now enter a period of tranquility at Federal Palace I was to be quickly disabused of that ridiculous optimism. The behavior of Alan Howard, always somewhat eccentric, seemed to have hit a new level of irrationality. His announcement of regret at the unfortunate departure of the 'noble Abdul' being indicative of his unpredictability, given that he was almost constantly in dispute with his expat colleagues. There was little doubt in my mind that the strain, on an already fragile temperament, of adjusting to stress of everyday life in Lagos was a major factor in his conduct and as it deteriorated I suggested to Atribs that he should be dismissed and encouraged to go home. After another series of misdemeanors this was finally agreed. A few days later both Atribs arrived at the casino to announce their acute embarrassment at the situation that had developed. Apparently it was a tendency of local Nigerians, when sacked, to camp on the street outside their former employer's residence and beg forgiveness, mercy or alms; it was certainly not expected of a white European former employee but Alan, as said before, was to say the least unpredictable.

At my suggestion the British consulate was contacted and advised that Howard, a British Subject, who had been on a temporary contract to work at the Federal Palace Hotel Casino, had been advised to return to U.K. after several incidents which seemed to indicate he was suffering from stress, an assessment that was now supported by his current behavior. It was emphasized that his employers the Atribs could arrange transportation to the airport, had provided a flight ticket to London and had paid salary he was due. The request was, that the consulate intervene and if necessary appoint a medical officer to supervise his departure.

All this was eventually put in place, much to the amusement of some former colleagues; but not me, as I had been increasingly concerned that had he remained in Lagos he would do himself some serious harm.

I was fortunate to meet him quite a number of years later and pleased to converse with a rational individual, which perhaps he had been, before he entered the chaotically demanding environment that was Lagos, Nigeria in the 1970's.

It wasn't too difficult to understand that any person with a sensitive or fragile disposition accustomed to the regulated and controlled environment of a European democracy might well find the living and working conditions in Lagos unbearably stressful. It was certainly true that had Simone and I not been so intensely interested in our new relationship and had we not enjoyed the company and support of each other, we would certainly have much earlier than we did. Each day seemed to present a challenge of some sort. For instance: Simone had a particular distaste for insects such as cockroaches, of which there was no shortage.

I myself had a revulsion to rodents, of which there was also no scarcity. By necessity we had to be continuously active at home to prevent infestations, particularly as Agustine our houseboy, like most other Nigerians, was unconcerned by their presence. Even in the casino office someone opened a desk drawer and I froze in shock as an enormous rat pounced out and bolted between my legs. But in spite of our hygiene and sanitary measures at home, I was to wake one day to meet with a new adversary. As Simone and I entered the lounge we caught sight of something dark moving on a hanging lightshade I moved across the room to see what it was when it, a bat, suddenly took off and swooped dangerously close to my face. Quite apart from the imminent danger of being bitten and contracting one of the potentially fatal viruses they were said to carry, their droppings or guano was also said to be a health hazard.

My initial plan, as I bade Simone leave the room and called I the houseboy from the kitchen, was simply to open the terrace door and the windows, thereby providing it with a means of escape, but it made no move from its position. I then attempted to prompt its departure with a rolled newspaper but instead put myself in its frenzied flight path. Now concerned that by opening doors and windows I was in fact inviting in all the other pests including mosquitoes, I therefore instructed Agustine to close all outlets and decided it was time to get aggressive, my weapon of choice being a tennis racquet. After frantic attempts with my serve, volley and backhand strokes, to my relief, an overhead smash finally sent it crashing to the wall and to be certain I had our boy quickly rap it in a duster and remove it.

As said before, it seemed Western expatriates were unduly conscious of the risk from vermin, parasites and reptiles than other nationals perhaps more accustomed to their presence. This made any potential exposure to them all the more disturbing and it was fortunate, given Simone's particular sensitivity to them, that most of the close encounters with non-human pests, as well as the human, were handled by me. But after a extended period when I had heard of the danger from snakes at the Ikoyi club, had the rat intrusion at the casino office and the bat attack at home I suppose I was on a physical red-alert. As I left hurriedly to go to a meeting at the casino, leaving Simone to relax at home, I strode over the high flood barrier of a doorstep and suddenly and alarmingly felt something slither up my fashionably wide trouser-leg. I instinctively clutched at my leg with both hands just above the knee and fortunately felt I had in some way impeded the invader's upward movement.

Shaking with nerves and beginning to drip with sweat I remained in a crouched position not daring to release my grip and praying I would not suddenly feel an incision from the creature's teeth or fangs. Trying to be a little rational I now considered what my next move had to be, I certainly could not release it to climb up to even more vulnerable parts of my anatomy. Of my two hands I calculated that the right was the one that held it secure. Slowly I relaxed my left hand's grip behind the knee and established this was the case. I could now smash the body of the intruder with the free hand but decided that might be even more dangerous, instead I decided to undo the top of my trousers and let them descend to where I held the creature. Heart still racing I unbuttoned, unzipped and slid them down to reveal the nodding spotted head of a harmless gecko that instantly extracted itself from its disposable tail and hopped off to safety as its sweat-soaked human adversary slumped with exhausted relief on the doorstep with a discarded tail as souvenir. After a few minutes recovery time I rose, trousers still at my ankles, but before I could pull them up the Indian woman who lived next door passed by giving me a questioning glance before disapprovingly turning her head as she increased her pace towards her home. I re-entered our home and on arrival in the front lounge my matted hair, sweat saturated clothes and dog tired expression had Simone, for once, lost for words.

Not all of my time was spent battling with wildlife, there was still time to handle the maneuverings of people like Rudolph, Rogers and Makram whose political activities would have really stepped up had they known that Simone and I were now seriously studying a life together back in England. Some of the plans envisaged a future outside of casinos, such as operating a small hotel, in somewhere like Brighton. But first we would confirm the permanence of our relationship by marriage which we now planned to take place in Britain during our next vacation; the preparation for that journey was to take us through another Lagos-style experience. A trip across the bridge to buy a couple of return tickets to London sounds, to those unaccustomed to Lagos, like an everyday task, instead of an all day traumatic ordeal.

Our short drive, in terms of distance, was in duration more than one hour, because of the 'go slow'. When I finally got near to our destination the place where I had intended to park, and the surrounding area, was full, so I had finally to leave the car in an area previously unknown to me. The Nigerian airlines booking office, adhering religiously to the national guidelines on customer service, was chaotic. Nevertheless, we eventually got to the service desk, purchased the flight tickets and made our way back to the car, which was parked near to what was in fact a depressed slum area with ramshackle huts. When still some way off, we were confronted with the first shock of seeing deflated tyres and, as we neared the vehicle, the alarming realisation that they had most likely been slashed by members of the group of locals standing menacingly nearby. Not quite knowing what to do and unsure of the exact motive for their action we quickly climbed into the car 'Will the car drive?' Simone asked, as I gunned the engine and shunted forward. 'Let's just drive and ignore them, see how far we get.' She said defiantly, as they moved closer threateningly, shouting and jeering.

I accelerated and the car moved off shuddering noisily, but at least clear of the immediate threat. I continued, knowing the tyres would soon be completely shredded but confident that soon we would be in a safe position to stop, abandon the car and hail a taxi.

Less than an hour later I had dropped my stoic partner off at our apartment and continued with the taxi to the Atribs' house to report our experience and arrange for the retrieval of the company car. Michael Atrib was demonstrably upset to hear of our misfortune and arranged two of his trusted minders to retrieve the car. When I insisted that I accompany them to make the location of the car easier, he agreed, advising me also to show them where the violation had taken place.

When I did show them where the car had originally been parked and the slum area where I believed these young men had come from, and they nodded knowingly, I thought, at least others would be warned to steer clear of that location. But a few days later, just prior to our departure for the airport, I was to hear with shocked disbelief that, it having been confirmed that the perpetrators had come from that locale, friends of the Atribs, as a corrective measure had torched the area to teach the denizens a lesson. We left to go back to U.K. now, more than ever, convinced that while there, we should make plans for a future outside of Nigeria.

CHAPTER 31

It had more or less been decided that we would have a quiet wedding at a registry office in Glasgow attended by my parents, and my cousin Jean and her husband David would act as witnesses. This would be followed by a celebratory dinner before Simone and I took off for a brief honeymoon trip around the North of Scotland before returning to London. By prior agreement when we arrived in London from Lagos, Simone remained there, at the home of her friend Gaye, while I continued to Glasgow to make the modest arrangements.

The absence of anyone from Simone's family or friends in the wedding plan was in part related to the suddenness of our decision and the fact that it would be in Glasgow. There were also some familial complications; her parents were separated and housed with Simone's mother was a son Gregg, from a previous non marital relationship. In all, the distance between the two families, not only in mileage, but also in lifestyle and philosophy would have made a coming together quite difficult. I myself would not meet Simone's mother and son Gregg until we returned to London as a married couple. So, many of the traditional customs may have been missing from the ceremony, but it has been said, that a grand and impressive wedding is less important than a lasting and successful marriage; this we hoped to confirm.

The formalities we went through without complication, undoubtedly my mother would have preferred a church wedding but that would of course have been hypocritical on our part. The enjoyment of our honeymoon trip had fortunately not been reliant on Scottish weather and we were soon back in London to meet the other half of the family and start the important task of planning our future together.

At this point I was once again to have the fortunate intervention of my friend Peter Byrne who had previously proposed me for the Lagos job and now offered me an escape to what seemed like an exciting project, that of being his number two when they opened one of Spain's first casinos in Cadiz, the Andalucian region of the country. The project would not start for some months so it would give me time to return and work an extended notice period at the Federal Palace where, it had to be said, that in spite of the difficulties I had encountered, I had been financially compensated by the Atribs at a higher level than initially contracted, and they had invariably endeavored to solve the problems both personal and professional that an expat manager meets in Lagos. Before leaving London, Simone and I took the fortuitous decision to buy our first home using some of the money we had earned in Nigeria. Already showing a keen interest in real estate Simone sourced the property, a basement apartment with one bedroom, lounge, kitchen and a small back garden, situated in Challoner Court, off North End Road, in West Kensington. The price we paid of £ 17,000. seems, by today's values, to be almost loose change. So, I returned to Lagos with a new wife, new job and new home while in my absence the owners, management and staff had continued with the same old politics and problems.

A reunion of former colleagues setting up for the future

The Atribs, expressed disappointment on learning of our planned departure at the end of November, but they could not have been entirely surprised. However they seemed to appreciate the five month period of notice which allowed time to restructure the management team; or as Simone and I privately joked, time for schemes, plots and maneuverings by those who would remain. Alhough prior to informing the owners we had diplomatically not announced our plan to any of the staff, however, within a few hours it was already common knowledge. Of those who would remain only Nino showed any real regret and indeed confided to us that he and his partner Francesca would probably also consider leaving.

Curiously, during this final period in Lagos I was to be approached by two investors, who as guests of Federal Palace casino had known me for some time, and as such thought I would be suitable for the position of Director of their new casino project in Lagos. My participation was of course impossible, not only because Simone and I had planned to leave Nigeria but also because I would never have considered any move that would put me in competition with the Atribs. However, after a second meeting with them, out of curiosity, I agreed to look over the proposed site, give my opinion on it's viability and advise them on a possible expat candidate for the position of Casino Director.

The location, the Mainland Hotel, as the name suggested was across the bridge on the mainland where there was certainly a high population density but whether the wealthier clientele, used to the more tranquil and upmarket surroundings of Victoria Island, would be prepared to play there, was for me one of the first considerations. I did pass on some suggestions on the layout of the casino and the facilities they would need but did not go into any great detail. On the recruitment of their Gaming Director I sounded out various contacts and in the end based on his C.V., work record and information from former colleagues, recommended they accept the application of Ian Payne. At this point I informed them that I would take no further part in their plans other than to meet Ian, introduce him to the difficulties of living and working in Lagos, especially for a Western expatriate, and advise him on how best to adapt to those conditions. In actual fact, as I emphasized to them, without the strong support of local shareholders, such as the Atribs, I myself could not have achieved anything.

I was sure, and it was confirmed, that the Atribs were aware of the new project. To avoid any unpleasant reaction, should the news reach them through others, I had informed Joseph of the Mainland offer and my refusal, suggesting that perhaps the new operators had heard from someone that I had intended to leave Federal Palace. He seemed unconcerned by the prospect of a casino opening on this site.

When Ian Payne did arrive I found him to be an extremely agreeable and enthusiastic individual. In fact in those early days I began to doubt if his approach would be suitable for the rigours of Lagos. On one of his first days I had invited him to Federal Palace to lunch at the hotel where I also thought to introduce him to Joseph Atrib, - a back-up plan in case some day he required outside assistance. After lunch he informed me that before joining me downstairs on the casino floor he "was just going to make a quick trip to down to the Savannah bank to open an account and would be straight back." I laughed, and asked him if he had been there before, which of course he had not. I began to explain to him the difficulties, not least the traffic problems, and more importantly that in dealings with the banks a prior 'arrangement' had to be made i.e someone had to be dashed. I offered to accompany him and introduce him to my 'man'. Ian would not entertain this idea as he was of the belief that we shouldn't encourage that sort of behavior; rather than argue, I permitted him to find out for himself. Several hours later he returned, soaked with sweat to admit that he had been unable to even reach the front desk. He somewhat reluctantly agreed to accompany me the following day, where with the aid of 'my contact' at the bank we completed the task. This episode compounded my initial fear that his idealistic and friendly approach might be seen, in that environment, as a weakness; thereby exposing him to even more pressure than we had faced. I had not counted on his quiet resilience and determination to get things done. The operation for which he had been recruited as General Manager, the Mainland Hotel Casino was to be a success. However at a later period, after I had left Nigeria, Ian's integrity was to clash with the unprincipled approach of the existing Military establishment. Having refused credit to one of their officers he was then obliged to have him removed when his behaviour became disruptive. The officer returned a little later in a military vehicle with armed support to arrest Ian. Fortunately he was eventually released, shaken but unharmed. At a later date, unconnected with this incident, all casinos were closed by the Military Government prior to the elections in 1979. By the time they were permitted to re-open, Ian had moved on.

To return to that initiation period of Ian Payne; at that point I felt confident to say to the Mainland shareholders that I would take no further part as they now had a knowledgeable, professional Manager of the utmost integrity but, that he would need support from them, as the Atribs had supported me, in matters which were peculiar to Nigeria and which lay outside the normal duties of a Western manager. They agreed, thanked me for my assistance and, unsolicited by me, demonstrated their gratitude with a payment of $ 10,000. U.S. An unbelievable amount in those days, particularly as I had given only basic advice and assistance.

Simone and I were now winding down at Federal and here we were also being generously treated having had all monies which we had saved in the local currency exchanged by the Atribs into dollars and transferred from Nigeria to my western account on top of that they added a bonus. I may have had a difficult time in Lagos and a troublesome task to lead the management of the Federal Palace Casino but at least it could be said to have been financially rewarding and given us a solid base from which to start our married life. There was however to be a final reminder from a section of the local populace of just how risky life can be in Lagos.

On one of our last evenings Nino and his wife-to-be Francesca invited us to join them at the National Theatre which was showing Doctor Zhivago, the film starring Omar Sharif and Julie Christie. Rather than take both vehicles we accepted Nino's offer to go in his Land Rover. The film was most enjoyable and when the final scene closed and the credits began to roll we rose to take our leave quickly to avoid any congestion exiting the carpark. As we made our way out some unrecognisable music was being played which we assumed to be incidental. It became noticeable however that the Nigerians were lingering and we only became aware why, when insults began to be thrown at us for disrespecting the National Anthem. In actual fact, unbeknown to us, the Anthem " Arise, O Compatriots" had only recently been adopted and not having attended any ceremony in which it had been played we had not recognised the piece. We paused and attempted to explain but the intimidating reaction from a group of Nigerians prompted us to make a more hurried exit. They now followed, threatening violent punishment for our disgraceful national insult. As they came threateningly close two other Nigerians intervened to hold back the tide and allow us to move rapidly to Nino's vehicle to make our escape.

The following evening when I spotted our rescuers entering the casino I commented to Nino who remembered that in thanking them he had mentioned we worked in the casino, which of course explained their presence. Well, it was one of the few occasions when we could say that people seeking 'Dash' actually merited the award.

The moment now arrived to take our leave of Lagos, Nigeria having said our goodbyes and received the best wishes from the Atribs and our colleagues at Federal Palace; of the latter group not all were unhappy to witness my departure. Although Nigeria had been a taxing experience, both Simone and myself would always look upon it as being a rewarding period in our life, in more ways than one. It was the place where our relationship blossomed and we created a financial base for our future life together, but also we both had experienced another world, of vastly different lifestyles and cultures, that although often demanding and at times frightening, was above all intriguing.

A night out as a newly wedded couple

www.ingramcontent.com/pod-product-compliance
Lightning Source LLC
LaVergne TN
LVHW091534060526
838200LV00036B/604